W9-DFW-835

BRITISH AND AMERICAN PLAYWRIGHTS

1750–1920

General editors: Martin Banham and Peter Thomson

Samuel Foote and Arthur Murphy

OTHER VOLUMES IN THIS SERIES

Plays by
Samuel Foote and Arthur Murphy

THE MINOR
THE NABOB
THE CITIZEN
THREE WEEKS AFTER MARRIAGE
KNOW YOUR OWN MIND

Edited with an introduction and notes by
George Taylor

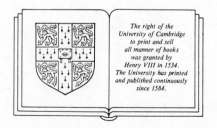

The right of the
University of Cambridge
to print and sell
all manner of books
was granted by
Henry VIII in 1534.
The University has printed
and published continuously
since 1584.

CAMBRIDGE UNIVERSITY PRESS
CAMBRIDGE
LONDON NEW YORK NEW ROCHELLE
MELBOURNE SYDNEY

Published by the Press Syndicate of the University of Cambridge
The Pitt Building, Trumpington Street, Cambridge CB2 1RP
32 East 57th Street, New York, NY 10022, USA
296 Beaconsfield Parade, Middle Park, Melbourne 3206, Australia

First published 1984

Printed in Great Britain at the University Press, Cambridge

Library of Congress catalogue card number: 83–18930

British Library cataloguing in publication data
Foote, Samuel
Plays by Samuel Foote and Arthur Murphy. – (British
and American playwrights, 1750–1920)
1. English drama – 18th Century
I. Title   II. Murphy, Arthur   III. Taylor, George
IV. Series
822'.6'08   PR1269

ISBN 0 521 24132 4 hard covers
ISBN 0 521 28467 8 paperback

WD

GENERAL EDITORS' PREFACE

It is the primary aim of this series to make available to the British and American theatre plays which were effective in their own time, and which are good enough to be effective still.

Each volume assembles a number of plays, normally by a single author, occasionally by two, scrupulously edited but sparingly annotated. Textual variations are recorded where individual editors have found them either essential or interesting. Introductions give an account of the theatrical context, and locate playwrights and plays within it. Biographical and chronological tables, brief bibliographies, and the complete listing of known plays provide information useful in itself, and which also offers guidance and incentive to further exploration.

Many of the plays published in this series have appeared in modern anthologies. Such representation is scarcely distinguishable from anonymity. We have relished the tendency of individual editors to make claims for the dramatists of whom they write. These are not plays best forgotten. They are plays best remembered. If the series is a contribution to theatre history, that is well and good. If it is a contribution to the continuing life of the theatre, that is well and better.

We have been lucky. The Cambridge University Press has supported the venture beyond our legitimate expectations. Acknowledgement is not, in this case, perfunctory. Sarah Stanton's contribution to the series has been substantial, and it has enhanced our work.

Martin Banham
Peter Thomson

CONTENTS

ILLUSTRATIONS

ACKNOWLEDGEMENTS

I would like to thank the general editors of this series, and in particular Peter Thomson, who not only suggested this edition but invited me to give my first ever university lecture on Arthur Murphy as part of his own eighteenth-century theatre course. I must acknowledge the assistance of Professor Kenneth Richards and my colleagues in the Drama Department, Manchester University, for the study leave in which I was enabled to consult the Huntington Library manuscripts, and the British Council for the research grant that financed the visit to America. I have received great help from the librarians and curators of the Henry E. Huntington Library, San Marino, California, the John Rylands Library, Manchester, and the British Theatre Museum, also from the staff of the Cambridge University Press, particularly Sarah Stanton in preparing the edition for publication.

GWT

INTRODUCTION

It was long a common misconception that comic drama in the eighteenth century, and particularly in the forty years following the 1737 Licensing Act, lapsed into a state of lachrymose gentility known as Sentimentality. This myth originated in the criticism and controversy surrounding the plays of those most successful eighteenth-century comic writers, Goldsmith and Sheridan. It is undeniable that Sentimental Comedy was a theatrically fashionable genre in the 1760s and 70s and was prevalent enough to inspire Goldsmith's essay 'On the Theatre', which was published in the *Westminster Magazine* of January 1773, where he described the style as one 'in which the virtues of Private Life are exhibited, rather than the vices exposed; and the Distresses, rather than the Faults of Mankind, make our interest in the piece'. However this was written as a puff for *She Stoops to Conquer*, partly to anticipate some of the critics' objections, but also to exaggerate the author's own originality in order to stimulate public anticipation of the new play. Because of the success of *She Stoops to Conquer*, shortly to be followed by the plays of Sheridan also in the 'laughing tradition', and because of the very plausibility of Goldsmith's critical argument, the myth of sentimental domination passed into the commentaries of the nineteenth-century literary historians. It was only in the scholarly reassessments of the twentieth century that the sentimental vogue was recognised for what it had been, a theatrical fashion that accounted for a smallish number of plays in some essential way 'different' from the more numerous conservative comedies, which continued to provide the staple diet of the Georgian theatre.

It is of course true that the brittle cynicism and brilliant wit of the great Restoration comedies failed to survive into the eighteenth century. Farquhar, Cibber and Steele all contributed elements of geniality, respectability and pathos, but the didactic, exemplary moralising and the self-indulgent emotion, which Goldsmith had distinguished as specifically sentimental, was a major feature of only a minority of plays. When Allardyce Nicoll began to catalogue the drama of the period in his *History of English Drama* (1927), he was surprised that, 'when we look at the typical dramatic fare of the period, we may be inclined to wonder whether, after all, it was not sentimentalism which was the fashion insecurely planted in the theatre'.[1] Since then, H.W. Pedicord's *The Theatrical Public in the Time of Garrick* (1954), R.W. Bevis's *The Laughing Tradition* (1980), and, above all, the statistics of *The London Stage* (part 4, ed. G.W. Stone Jnr, 1962), have confirmed that (depending on the author's precise definition of Sentimental Comedy) there were something like eight to ten performances of traditional comedies to every one performance of a sentimental full-length piece. The proportion of sentimental afterpieces was conderably less, as it was into the two-act afterpiece that the broader and bawdier traditions of satire and farce were channelled.[2]

Nevertheless, although these statistics of performances are a conclusive indication of the audiences' general taste in comedy, the authors themselves were turning out a higher proportion of sentimental new plays – Bevis suggests possibly half the mainpieces between 1740 and 1780.[3] Many of these were quite unsuited to the stage, and, if performed, survived for only a night or two. The majority were aimed at a reading public rather than a theatre audience. It is clear, even from the traditionally comic pieces published in this collection, that writers tended to clean up and sentimentalise their stage pieces when they came out in published form. The Sentimental Movement had always been more apparent in novels than in the drama. Certainly most of Murphy's revisions for his *Collected Works* make his comedies seem rather more sententious and pathetic than they appear in their original manuscript form. Both he and Foote were champions of the traditional comedy of humour or of manners, in which laughter is provoked by the ridiculous excesses of folly and affectation, or by the misunderstandings and cross-purposes of the comic situation. They, together with Colman the Elder and David Garrick, maintained the 'laughing tradition' with considerable ability well before the supposed revival of comical comedy by Goldsmith and Sheridan; and, even if certain elements in the plays of Murphy, Garrick and Colman can be categorised as sentimental, the same can be said of their more famous successors.

If to us many of these mid-eighteenth-century plays seem rather unremarkable in comparison with the novels or poetry of the period, it is probably because the writers of the time considered writing for the theatre as a commercial rather than an artistic venture. Under the Restoration, and indeed back to Tudor times, playwrights were aiming to please the most sophisticated, well-educated section of society, the aristocrats and courtiers. Since the 1688 Revolution, which ushered in the political and social preeminence of the mercantile and gentry classes, the theatre found that it was playing to an audience that was drawn from the City, and even the suburbs, as well as the purlieus of St James. Some writers, like Cibber and Steele, in their different ways, felt they had to write down to these new audiences, and one senses in their work a certain patronising condescension. Others, like Farquhar, Fielding, Lillo and Gay tended to write from a more bourgeois point of view of their own. Their work may have been less polished than that of the Restoration wits, but it demonstrated those middle-class, Georgian virtues of good sense, good humour and that pugnacious quality they called 'bottom'. The 1720s and 30s had seen the emergence of several new types of drama, the ballad opera, the bourgeois tragedy, the satirical burlesque, not to mention those non-literary entertainments the pantomime and the Italian opera. As places of entertainment, the theatres had gained a commercial independence from the traditional patronage of the court. In political terms this was recognised by the Licensing Act, whereby legal prohibitions replaced influence and self-interest as the regulating factors;[4] in business terms the adjustment can be traced through the risks and failures catalogued in Cibber's *Apology*, to the financial stability of the long managerships of Rich and Garrick; and in artistic terms the change was encapsulated in Dr Johnson's famous couplet:

> The drama's laws the drama's patrons give,
> For we who live to please, must please to live.

The age of Foote and Murphy was one of consolidation rather than of innovation. They exhibited no great originality in form, but by a gradual evolution in response to the tastes of the town, which rowdy audiences were not slow in communicating, their plays gained a workmanlike efficiency that can be compared with the consistently competent standards of television comedy writing in England today. Drury Lane, like the BBC, had a reputation for excellence in presenting the classics; under Garrick the standard of acting was generally high and production was efficient, but new plays, though thoroughly entertaining, tended to be often predictable and seldom thought-provoking. Covent Garden, like the stereotyped image of commercial television, specialised in the more spectacular variety of shows: music, scenery and speciality acts seeming to have more drawing power than the literary quality of the plays. But just as today, when the occasional production by independent television displays an originality above the generally predictable standard, it was at Covent Garden that the original talents of Gay, Cumberland and Goldsmith first made their appearance. Of course this comparison should not be stretched too far, but I think the similarity of a dual monopoly created a pressure to respond to the box office just as the television channels have to maintain respectable ratings, and this tended to cause a similar stereotyping of comic techniques and the repetition of successful formulae. The plays of Foote, Murphy, Garrick and Colman all tend towards situation comedy; the same set of family relations, the same type of social conflicts are worked through time and again. The attitudes, and most of the characters, remain the same, only the intrigues, the tricks and the 'affecting scenes' of reconciliation, recognition and reformation are changed or rearranged to give a spurious impression of originality.

To an extent this has always been the case with comic drama, from Plautus to Molière, and the charge of plagiarism can so easily be made against all eighteenth-century comic playwrights that it is hardly worth making. It is only when one gets immersed in the drama of the time, or becomes addicted to various situation-comedy series on television today, that the new slant on a threadbare theme assumes the status of an original stroke of genius. It was Sheridan's good fortune to be the last exponent of a tradition of which Murphy was arguably an equal master; it was Foote's misfortune that he failed to realise that his original satirical slant to the situation-comedy formula was not enough to establish his work as a genre of its own; or to put it another way, in more classical terms, he compromised the Aristophanic qualities, which he had inherited from Fielding, with the tired old plots of New Comedy, which were expected of him by the critics, the audiences and the Lord Chamberlain's Examiner of Plays.

Foote

If Foote was not original enough to have earned himself a place on the lower slopes of Parnassus with Fielding and Gay, never mind a lofty seat with Jonson and Molière, he was the maverick of the mid-eighteenth-century theatre, and his achievements both as writer and manager were to have a significant influence on the development of the London stage. Born in 1720 into a landowning family of Cornish gentry, Foote came to London in 1740, after being expelled from Oxford, to enroll at the Inner Temple, where the sons of provincial JPs were normally expected to gather a smattering of law, and a smear of urban sophistication during their time off from study. Foote, like many Templars, took the time off more seriously than any lessons he may have attended or law books he may have read. His tastes were fashionable and inevitably expensive, and, although he probably joined Macklin's acting classes in 1743 for a bit of a jape, appearing as 'a young gentleman never before on any stage' as Othello to Macklin's Iago at the Haymarket on 6 February 1744, he was obviously talented enough to repeat the experiment at Drury Lane on 10 March. That autumn he enrolled as an actor with Thomas Sheridan, the manager of the Smock Alley Theatre, Dublin, and so began his theatrical career. However, Foote was too extravagant a personality to settle for repeating other writers' lines; he was a stand-up comic rather than a straight actor, and he soon began to exhibit a talent for comic impersonations and mimicry. In April 1747 he hired the Haymarket Theatre, where he had made his amateur debut, and where, ten years before, the last of Fielding's political burlesques had been banned by the Licensing Act. Under the Act only Drury Lane and Covent Garden were allowed to present regular drama, and Foote decided to circumvent the law by using the 'Concert Formula', which had been employed by such varied entertainers as Fielding himself, Colley Cibber's eccentric daughter Charlotte Charke, and Charles Macklin. Since 1740, Henry Giffard had presented plays at Goodman's Fields under the pretence of giving concerts or amateur 'diversions', and it had been there that Garrick had first appeared in 1741. Foote advertised his entertainment as follows:

> At the Theatre in the Hay-market, this Day will be perform'd a Concert of Musick. With which will be given Gratis a New Entertainment, call'd 'The Diversions of the Morning'. The principal Parts to be perform'd by Mr Foote, Mr Shuter, Mr Cushing, Mr Castallo, Mrs Hallam, Mr Lee, Mr Burton, Mr Hallam, and Miss Moreau.

> To which will be added a Farce taken from 'The Old Batchelor',
> call'd 'The Credulous Husband'. Fondlewife by Mr Foote; Bellmour,
> Mr Lee, Laetitia by Mrs Hallam.
> With an Epilogue to be spoken by the B-d-d Coffee House.
> Tickets to be had at Mr Waller's, Bookseller in Fleet-Street. To
> begin at Seven o'Clock.

Perhaps because he was performing in the evening, or because he was
including a cut version of a regular comedy, or because his company were all
established professionals, Lacy, the manager of Drury Lane, invoked the Act
and on 23 April the performance was banned. But Foote displayed the
ingenuity that was to mark his career as an alternative impresario by changing
the Concert into an invitation at midday on 25 April 'to drink a Dish of Chocolate with him, and 'tis hoped there will be a great deal of good Company and
some Joyous Spirits; he will endeavour to make the *Morning as Diverting* as
possible'.[5]

The Diversions of the Morning was perhaps Foote's most original contribution to the development of the London theatre. It was not a proper play at
all, but a sort of revue, in which sketches were strung together by the most
flimsy of plots, and in which Foote himself took a number of parts in order to
take off various well-known characters. *The Diversions* underwent several
transformations of both title and content, being known as a *Dish of Chocolate*,
Dish of Tea, *Auction of Portraits*, *The Virtuoso* and, eventually, *Taste*, in which
it gained its most regular dramatic form and was published in 1752. Typical of
the characters Foote took off were a quack doctor, the Chevalier Taylor; a
popular educationalist, Orator Henley; an auctioneer, Christopher Cock; a
magistrate, Thomas de Veil; and a follower of fashion the original of which has
not been traced, but whom Foote called Lady Pentweazle. Most were of
ephemeral interest, as they were indeed charlatans worthy of ridicule, but in
his early performances Foote, often with the aid of Harry Woodward, also
made a feature of taking off leading actors from the patent houses.

Two acts from *The Diversions* have survived which were vehicles for the
parody of actors. 'Tragedy à la Mode', which resembled Fielding's *Tom
Thumb*, was printed in Tate Wilkinson's *Wandering Patentee* (vol. I, pp. 285–
98), and a rehearsal scene, in which Foote took off his old instructor Charles
Macklin directing Spranger Barry in a scene from *Othello*, was printed in the
John Bee edition of *The Works of Samuel Foote*.[6] The second of these is particularly interesting as it indicates something of the new 'naturalistic' style of
acting associated with Macklin. He tells his Othello to 'grind' rather than
declaim his words, while considering

> the mode of the mind – that a man's soul is lost, and tost, and crost,
> and his entrails broiling on a grid iron – bring it from the bottom of your
> stomach, sir, with a grind, as 'Tor-r-r-ture me!' . . . Now throw me
> from you, and I'll yield; very well! – keep that attitude – your eye fixed

> – there's a figure! – there's a contrast! His majestic rage – and my
> timorous droop.

However the mimicry of fellow actors proved a two-edged policy. Foote could only get authority to present his irregular entertainments at the Haymarket over the summer, and during the winter season he had to take his *Diversions* to the patent houses or to Dublin, where the burlesque of the regular company was unwelcome to the management, if not to the audiences. It was self-interest and an instinct for professional survival that led Foote to the principle he propounded in the Introduction to *The Minor*, that he would spare the actors, 'because, by rendering them ridiculous in their profession, you, at the same time, injure their pocket'. It was because actor–managers like Garrick, Thomas Sheridan and even Macklin had the power to injure Foote's own pocket that he eventually let them alone.

Foote's other early plays, although they still provided characters taken from life for him to mimic, fell more properly into the conventional form of the two-act afterpiece. His impersonated eccentrics tended to be cast in the role of parents or guardians, who, as in Molière, frustrate the love matches of the younger generation. In *The Author* (1758) he used the two-act form to explore for the first time a specific theme with some social implication: the plight of the penurious hack and the power of the philistine patron. However, despite some pertinent comment on the practices of publishers and booksellers, it was, as usual, the individual portraits of Cadwallader and his wife Becky that captured the audiences' attention. The part was based on a certain Mr Apreece, a foolish Welsh gentleman, who, it was said, had encouraged Foote to impersonate him on stage. When the play actually came out, Apreece regretted the joke, withdrew his permission and got the Lord Chamberlain to ban the play's performance. The next piece that Foote wrote is the first one represented in this volume, *The Minor*.

So far Foote's work had been merely entertaining, and, although the influence of Fielding's dramatic satire is apparent in the style of his plays, they had none of Fielding's serious content. It is arguable that Foote was never really seriously committed in criticising the aberrations of society, but from 1760 onwards he did tend to write plays around potentially serious topics, and in several cases a genuine concern is discernible behind the surface mockery and theatrical fun. *The Minor* was to involve him in such controversy that he had to think seriously about his intentions and define his position, but as early as 1747, in his essay *The Roman and English Comedy Considered and Compared*, he had presented the historical justification for personal satire, and so won for himself the title of the English Aristophanes. In his dedication to *Taste* (1752) he had repudiated the obligatory plot structure of a love intrigue in favour of 'confining the eye to the single object of Satire', and proclaimed that 'the follies and absurdities of men are the sole objects of comedy'. In fact most of his plays did utilise a love intrigue, but often it is so unimportant to the main drift of the satire and so crudely introduced that its function is patently obvious, which is to provide a neat marriage and a dance to end the play. In *The Minor*, however, the love interest, though introduced late in the action, does have a significant role in the development of Foote's general theme.

The Minor

The Minor is the best known of Foote's plays and kept the stage into the nineteenth century. Its reputation was won partly on its own merits. It is a neat three-act comedy which combines a traditional intrigue, a smattering of social satire, a scene of sentiment, and a handful of caricatures more satisfactorily integrated into the plot than was the case in some of Foote's other farces. However, *The Minor*'s chief claim to fame was that one of the main subjects of its satire was the influence of the Methodists, and in particular the extravagantly emotional appeal of George Whitefield's revivalist preaching, or 'field oratory', at his tabernacle on the Tottenham Court Road. The Methodists, under the leadership of John Wesley, had broken from the Church of England in 1739, chiefly because they felt that the established Church had settled into a state of self-satisfied apathy and was doing nothing to minister to the poorer classes of society, whose need for both material and spiritual aid was of the greatest. To an extent the split had been an administrative necessity when Wesley failed to find a bishop prepared to ordain priests of his persuasion, who would work among the submerged classes outside the parish system, but it also had a spiritual content, whereby salvation was equated less with good works than with the desire for regeneration into a state of grace. God's grace is more readily granted to those who blindly believe and seek salvation from the depths of their suffering, than to those who are complacent, comfortably off, and more prepared to indulge in intellectual speculation than in irrational faith. It was precisely this element of 'enthusiasm' that Foote, and most sophisticated theatregoers, distrusted: 'Enthusiasm in divinity is a kind of religious phrensy [*sic*], that mistakes the dictates of an inflamed imagination, the vapours of a troubled brain, for the operation of a divine possession'.[7] His was the distrust of fanaticism, and suspicion of the irregular methods used to finance the new movement, which we can see today in the establishment reaction to some of the more eccentric religious sects that emerged in the 1960s and 1970s on the West Coast of America or on the fringes of traditional Buddhism, and which are often accused of exploiting the spiritual starvation of the unhappy and the underprivileged.

To a modern audience, used to a more blatantly didactic theatre, Foote's criticisms may seem rather unsatisfactory, a mere side swipe not fully integrated into the action of the play, and presented as the 'humour' of the hypocritical Mrs Cole, and in the rather tasteless epilogue, which relied for its effect not on a genuine exposé of Whitefield's methods, or message, but on Foote's ability to take off his bathetic style of preaching and his unfortunate squint. His answer to criticism of this last point was classic but unconvincing: 'If men with these infirmities will attempt things, which those very infirmities have rendered them incapable of properly executing, it is their own fault if the source that should acquire them compassion degenerates into a fountain of ridicule'.[8] It was a principle that should have put pay to his own career once he lost his leg in 1766; an actor with a wooden leg is considerably more incapable than a preacher with a squint.

However, the controversy over *The Minor* did cause Foote to define and defend his position as the leading theatrical satirist of the day, both in the introductory scene of the play and in his 'Letter to the Reverend Author of the Remarks Critical and Christian on the Minor'. He rejoiced in the sobriquet of the English Aristophanes and proclaimed himself firmly in the tradition of classical comedy: he pointed out that Shakespeare, Jonson and Molière had all caricatured individuals in their plays, and claimed that comedy had always had a utilitarian purpose over and above mere entertainment. He rejected the description of his play as a farce, which he defined as,

> a kind of theatrical, not dramatic, entertainment, always exhibited at fairs, and too frequently produced at playhouses; a sort of hodge-podge, dressed by a Gothic cook, where the mangled limbs of probability, common sense, and decency, are served up to gratify the voracious cravings of the most depraved appetites: this I call farce. Comedy, on the other hand, I define to be an exact representation of the peculiar manners of that people among whom it happens to be performed; a faithful imitation of singular absurdities, particular follies, which are openly produced, as criminals are publicly punished, for the correction of individuals, and as an example to the whole community.[9]

More succinctly, in the introductory scene of *The Minor*, he pointed out that in the case of a religious charlatan, 'Ridicule is the only antidote against this pernicious poison. This is a madness that argument can never cure, and, should a little wholesome severity be applied, "persecution" would be the immediate cry.'

In fact it was *The Minor* itself that ran the risk of persecution. Under the Licensing Act, once Foote had a general authority to perform at the Haymarket, he was not required to submit plays to the Examiner for detailed censorship, and it was in recognition of this general authority to perform that Foote dedicated the play to the Lord Chamberlain himself, the duke of Devonshire: 'Your Grace has thrown open (for those who are denied admittance into the palaces of *Parnassus*) a cottage on its borders, where the unhappy migrants may be, if not magnificently, at least, hospitably entertained.' It was only when he wished to present *The Minor* in one of the palaces of Parnassus, Drury Lane, in the autumn of 1760, that a copy had to be officially submitted to the

Lord Chamberlain's office. It was actually the third printed edition, already headed 'as performed at the New Theatre in the Haymarket', that the managers, Garrick and Lacy, put in the hands of the Examiner of Plays. The Lord Chamberlain was then approached, not only by Lady Huntingdon,[10] a patron of Whitefield's, but by the Archbishop of Canterbury, who was particularly concerned with the use of religious phrases in a stage play. Devonshire, however, was himself a close friend of David Garrick's, and wrote to him on 25 October 1760, granting permission to present the play:

> I had a long conversation with his Grace, who would have authorized me to have used his name to stop 'the Minor', but I got off from it, and concluded with sending a recommendation by Mr. Pelham to the author, to alter those passages that are liable to objection: His Grace would not point them out, so I think very little alteration may do.[11]

It was said that Archbishop Secker had refused to be specific because he realised that Foote was capable of publishing the censored version, 'Corrected and prepared for the press by his Grace the Archbishop of Canterbury.'[12] Nevertheless, although the play as a whole was passed, the copy in the Larpent Collection indicates that the Examiner did follow up the criticisms and cut most of the objectionable phrases, although the main satirical idea of the methodistical bawd remained. Details of the Examiner's excisions are listed in the Note on the Texts (p. 41 below), where it will be seen that the main loss was the Epilogue, where Foote, as Squintum, took off Whitefield's style of preaching.

When *The Minor* is looked at as a performing script, it soon becomes clear that the controversial issue of Methodism is hardly central to the structure of the play, indeed Mrs Cole, based on an actual Covent Garden bawd, Jennie Douglas, is not the only subject of Foote's mimicry. The card-sharp Loader was based on a certain Mr Lookup;[13] Smirk was the auctioneer Abraham Longford, and in performing the part Foote also took off Longford's predecessor Christopher Cock, whom he had already introduced into *The Diversions of the Morning* and Fielding had satirised in *The Historical Register*. Finally, the part of Shift was played as a caricature of either Weston or Tate Wilkinson.[14] The latter had pirated the play when it was first presented in two acts in Dublin, and was to perform it at Covent Garden from 24 November 1760, in direct competition with Foote's own performances at Drury Lane. In 1763 the two actors joined forces in a performance of the play, incongruously splitting the part of Shift between them, Wilkinson playing Shift himself, and Foote Smirk, who is Shift in disguise.

So far this pot-pourri of impersonation was typical of Foote, but the dramatic substance of the play was more fully worked out than usual. The rival systems of education propounded by Sir William and Richard Wealthy, Foote may have developed from Terence's *The Brothers*; the convention of the benevolent incognito testing the values of the younger generation was one he had already used in *The Author*, and it was to reappear in Cumberland's *West*

Indian, Goldsmith's *Good Natured Man* and Sheridan's *School for Scandal*; while much of the character of Mrs Cole had probably been stolen from Joseph Reed's *Register Office*. All these varied elements Foote brings together, and, although the result is hardly a seamless garment, it is not quite the rag-bag implied in the criticism of Richard Bevis, who claims that the play is 'over-plotted', and has

> enough story for a five-act comedy. In the melee Foote lost control of the tone. After asking us to laugh at sharpers and follies for two acts, secure in the knowledge that George's straits are artificial, he suddenly gives us a character, Lucy, who is in real trouble and requires immediate sympathy and assistance. The comic law of 'no consequences' is rudely violated. Ridicule and outrage are unexpectedly displaced by pathos, and the play becomes emotionally incoherent.[15]

Although, to an extent, one must agree with Bevis, and even with those critics who give the Lucy scene the pejorative label of sentimental, it does in fact give the satire that bite which Foote claimed to be missing from mere farce. Lucy's distressed situation was not untypical of the age, its causes are closely tied up with the 'pernicious poison' of Mrs Cole's hypocrisy, and George's response to her appeal is more like the traditional good nature of a Tom Jones than the self-conscious squeamishness of a Bevil Junior. The seriousness of Lucy's plight is also an essential ingredient of the main plot. It would have been absurd for Sir William's silly charade to have succeeded in regaining his prodigal son. It needed the shock of real hardship and injustice to make Young George's reformation even probable in terms of his character, or acceptable in terms of theatre. All these considerations give the scene a sobering seriousness and the play as a whole a cutting edge. The Aristophanic qualities of Foote's work are not just restricted to personal abuse, caricature situations and the quick-fire routines of a stand-up comic; he does show in this play, as in several others, including *The Nabob*, a genuine anger at the social abuses of his age, and, although the Whore's Progress is halted in the nick of time, it is wrong to see Lucy's emotional plight, and George's generous response to it, in the same light as the excessive delicacy and mawkish moralising of the truly Sentimental Drama.

It is true that the central plot of tricking and testing the extravagant Minor is not handled with particular skill or consistency, but, as in many purely popular entertainments, then as now, it was the telling scene and the comical situation, rather than the precise logic of plot or character that appealed to the audience. Argument and analysis would have proved merely boring. Foote's didacticism is that of immediate ridicule – and, in the case of Lucy, immediate sympathy – rather than a carefully argued case or a psychologically consistent character study. Bevis is right when he claims that most critics have unfairly condemned Foote for failing to achieve what he never set out to do, but even he asks for a more classically unified effect than Foote, as a popular entertainer, intended to create. Although *The Minor* is an important play in assessing Foote's reputation, the reaction it caused at the time was out of proportion to the content of its argument, and critics ever since have been disappointed that it lacks the polish of a Sheridan or the vehemence of a Jonson. What it does have, however, is what Foote set out to provide: enough of a plot to raise a few serious questions, provide a few scenes of comical misunderstanding, and a few opportunities for him to display his talents as a mimic. Maybe the issue of Methodism was being exploited rather than explored, and Foote was cashing in on a controversy, as has ever been the case with successful showmen, but there is enough genuine concern expressed in the Lucy scenes and enough cynicism in his portrayal of Mrs Cole, to have fired the original controversy and to indicate that Foote really did see danger in the irrational enthusiasm of the field orators. In *The Nabob* too we will see, perhaps even more clearly, that Foote did have a conscience and a sense of concern that his reputation as a rake and a wit tended to hide from his contemporaries.

Foote's accident and the Haymarket patent

Possibly as a result of his brush with the Lord Chamberlain over *The Minor*, Foote found, in the summer of 1761, that the licence under which he had normally performed at the Haymarket had been granted to 'a man who had a pack of dancing dogs',[16] and that he had to make alternative arrangements. These were to rent Drury Lane Theatre in partnership with Arthur Murphy, on the understanding that each would provide three new two- or three-act comedies. As we shall see, when discussing *The Citizen*, Murphy wrote all his three plays, but Foote produced nothing.

From 1762 to 1766 Foote made sure of the Haymarket licence during the summer, and, as his own manager, brought out a number of plays, which, following the example of *The Author* and *The Minor*, tended to concentrate on a single theme of satire rather than the indiscriminate sketches of *The Diversions*. *The Liar* (1762) was adapted from Corneille and is perhaps his least topical comedy. *The Orators*, *The Mayor of Garrett*, *The Patron* and *The Commissary* were all topical and each explored a particular aspect of social or political activity, although it is only in *The Commissary* (1765) that one gets an impression of Foote's being a moral satirist as well as a light entertainer. *The Commissary* has been published in R.W. Bevis's collection of *Eighteenth Century Afterpieces* (Oxford, 1970), and in his opinion, 'It gives in the compass of three acts a selection of the best Foote had to offer . . . an asset to the laughing tradition which challenges the idea that he never developed or matured.'[17]

In 1766, however, Foote's career took an unexpected turn and one that was to be of great importance for the subsequent development of the British stage. He had a serious accident while attempting to ride a mettlesome horse in the company of the Duke of York, George III's brother, at the home of Lord

Mexborough. Foote had to have his leg amputated, and, as some sort of compensation, the Duke of York arranged for Foote's occasional summer licence to be changed into a royal patent. Although this was intended to last only for his lifetime, the title of Theatre Royal remained attached to the Little Theatre in the Haymarket after his death, and, from when George Colman took over its management under annual licence in 1777 until the 1843 Theatre Regulating Act, the Little Theatre shared, for the period 15 May to 15 September, the same professional status as the two major houses. Much of the early 1800s was to be spent in trying to extend its summer season into a year-long management, but well into the nineteenth century the Haymarket was the recognised home of light legitimate comedy.

Foote's accident had an effect on all aspects of his career, manager, performer and writer. Now that his control over the Haymarket was secure – he bought the building itself once he knew he had the patent – he enlarged the auditorium, re-equipped the stage and extended the company of actors. Before 1766 he had normally worked with a small company of twelve, many of whom were inexperienced, but now he increased his company to twenty-one actors, ten actresses and four dancers (1769 season), most of whom were drawn from the established professionals of the winter houses. He was also entitled to present legitimate tragedy, and in 1769 he brought his old employer, Thomas Sheridan, from Dublin, to star in a number of Shakespeare plays, coinciding with Garrick's jubilee celebrations at Stratford. As a performer, who had often appeared in several parts in the same play, Foote had obviously lost some of his versatility, but fortunately some of his characters were already suitable for a lame actor; Mrs Cole complains of her 'rhumatise', and Peter Paragraph in *The Orators* was based on the one-legged Dublin printer, George Falkner. However, his wooden leg did cause Foote to reduce his own acting and rely on the support of the other established comedians that he had brought into the Haymarket company, such as Woodward, Palmer, Weston, Bannister, Shuter and his old sparring partner, Tate Wilkinson. Thus began the tradition of excellent comic ensemble acting for which the Haymarket was to remain famous for at least a century. As a writer, Foote showed his customary ingenuity by creating roles that specifically exploited his lameness. In 1768 he produced *The Devil upon Two Sticks*, in 1770 *The Lame Lover*, and in 1771 his part in *The Maid of Bath* was Sir Christopher Cripple. Eventually audiences got used to his disability and Foote reassumed many of his favourite roles and wrote new parts in which no attention needed to be drawn to his leg. The first of these was *The Nabob*, written in 1772.

The Nabob

Nevertheless, Sir Matthew Mite, the 'nabob', was a moral, even if not necessarily a physical grotesque. As an officer of the East India Company, he has

returned home prepared to deal with the English with as much ruthlessness as
he had the Indians, from whom he has extorted his fortune. It was one of the
better results of the increasingly fashionable humanitarianism of the British
upper classes that, although they might indulge themselves in sentimental
fiction, they did develop in fact a conscience about the exploitation of their
colonial dependants in the Third World – even if not in America or in the newly
industrialised cities of their own country. The prosecution of Warren Hastings
in the 1780s was the more famous example, but Lord Clive had been indicted
for the misgovernment of Bengal early in 1772, and a bill had been introduced
into Parliament 'for the better regulation of the affairs of the East India
Company'. Clive was acquitted of specific crimes, but his methods, and those
of other East India Company officers, were still considered unacceptable by
many who knew little of the actual conditions in India. Also, although he did
not make a particularly strong point about it, it is significant that Foote refers
to the important Somersett case of 1772, in which the owning of slaves was
finally declared illegal on British soil, for the whole anti-slave-trade agitation
that developed in the last decades of the century had its roots in the reaction of
shame at the exploits of the nabobs.

Mary Belden claims that Foote was not aiming specifically at Lord Clive in
his portrait of Sir Matthew Mite, but at either General Richard Smith, whose
being the son of a cheesemonger may have inspired the name Mite, or Sir
Matthew White, both of whom worked for the East India Company.[18] Both
men must have felt that they were possible candidates for the attack, for they
invited Foote to dine with them shortly after the play opened. It is a mark of
Foote's cool nerve, his wit and his disarming charm that he was able to convince
them that neither of them was intended, and that they were to be included in
the disclaimer he had put in the mouth of Thomas Oldham:

> But there are men from the Indies, and many too, with whom I have
> the honour to live, who dispense nobly and with hospitality here what
> they have acquired with honour and credit elsewhere; and, at the same
> time that they have increased the dominations and wealth, have added
> virtues, too, to their country.

However, it is clear that Foote's anger as well as contempt had been stirred
by the excesses of the nabobs as a class. Much of the satire in the play is aimed
at Sir Matthew's parvenu lack of polish, culture and tact, but he is no Monsieur
Jourdain, he is a bourgeois red in tooth and claw. Not only are his 'possessions
arising from plunder . . . treacherously and rapaciously gained', but his use of
money in England is just as irresponsible and vicious as it had been in India. In
order to improve his profits from the tea trade he advocates the burning of
cargoes; when he wants an estate in Berkshire he tells his agent to 'give the
fellow four times the value, and bid him turn out in a month'; and the 'treaty'
he offers the Oldham family is as heartless and as irresistible as any of his
dealings with the Indian rajahs. Even the venal Mayor of Bribe'em, who has

come to offer his borough's parliamentary seats for sale, considers Mite's behaviour to have been that of a Tartar – added to which his largess has caused inflation in 'the price of provisions for thirty miles round'. However, even in a portrait of almost melodramatic villainy, Foote, the stand-up comedian and impressionist, had to include a lighthearted sketch, which inevitably lessened the satirical bite of his more serious criticism. One subject of satire that has never lost its appeal is that of pedantry, and in act III Foote introduced a completely irrelevant burlesque of a meeting of the Society of Antiquarians, where Sir Matthew gives a lecture inspired by that of Dr Samuel Pegge, who in December 1771 'gave us next the History of Whittington, but could make nothing at all of his *cat*, though she is his constant companion in all statues and pictures: and I firmly believe, if not a rebus for some ship which made his fortune, she was the companion of his arm chair, like Montaigne's'.[19]

Another element of parody is better integrated into the fabric of *The Nabob*, and that is the exaggeratedly sentimental language of the worthy merchant, Thomas Oldham. In terms of the plot he is the hero, he stands up to Sir Matthew, he provided the money that saves his brother's family from disaster, and he continually points the moral, but as a character he is written as a blatant theatrical cliché. There is no real motive for his delay in paying off Sir Matthew's mortgage, and certainly none for distressing the young lovers for reasons which, according to his son, 'in tenderness he chose to conceal'. Sir Matthew himself has no time for Thomas's 'refinements' and in the end, although Mite has not won this time, he remains unrepentant and a dangerous threat to others sharing the traditionally decent standards of the Oldhams. Neither the aristocratic bluster of Lady Oldham nor the moralising of the London Merchant have any effect on him:

> MITE: Is this manoeuvre according to law? . . . Our practice is differ-
> ent in the Mayor's Court at Calcutta. – I shall now make my bow,
> and leave this family, whom I wished to make happy in spite of
> themselves, soon to regret the fatal loss sustained by their obsti-
> nate folly.
>
> THOMAS: Nor can it be long, before the wisdom of their choice will
> appear, as, by partaking of the spoil, they might have been
> involved in that vengeance, which, soon or late, cannot fail to fall
> on the head of the author; and, sir, notwithstanding your seem-
> ing security, perhaps the hour of retribution is near!
>
> MITE: You must, Master Oldham, give me leave to laugh at your
> prophetic effusion. This is not Sparta, nor are these the chaste
> times of the Roman republic. Now-a-days, riches possess, at
> least, one magical power, that, being rightly dispensed, they
> closely conceal the source from whence they proceeded. That
> wisdom, I hope never to want. – I am the obsequious servant of
> this respectable family! Adieu!

Such a contrast of unrepentant villainy and platitudinous morality was to become the stock in trade of Victorian melodrama. In Foote's play the effect is intentionally comic, as can be seen by his further parody of sentimental stage conventions in his next play, *Piety in Pattens, a Primitive Puppet Show*. At the same time his mockery of the hero increases the seriousness of his warning against the ruthless machinations of the villain. The Nabob has the last word in the argument and we are still left with the feeling that 'his contrivance and cunning has been an over-match for a plain English gentleman or an innocent Indian'.

Insofar as the two comedies published here are a fair example of Foote at his most serious, it is easy to see him as something of an anachronism in a period when 'humour' had lost the viciousness of Jonson for the geniality of Goldsmith. In Squintum, Mrs Cole and Sir Matthew Mite, Foote had characters as potentially grotesque as Tribulation Wholesome, Ursula the Pig Woman and Volpone, but, although he was quite capable of defending the principles of classical satire in theory, the taste of the time had become too genteel and too squeamish for full-blooded Jonsonian comedy, even if Foote had been talented enough to compose it. Despite his repudiation of farce as a 'sort of hodge-podge', that was often all that Foote had to offer his Haymarket audiences, although at least he never made a compromise with sentimentality, which is what one finds in Murphy, Goldsmith and Sheridan, all of whom claimed to be champions of laughing rather than weeping comedy. Foote's failing was one of dissipation. Rather than chastise one particular vicious humour, pursuing it to its root cause, or exploring its persuasive influence throughout society, he continually shifted his aim, let off squibs in all directions, and was always ready to settle for the merely amusing, even when he had found a subject fit for scorn, and one that genuinely offended his sense of fair play and social justice.

A performer who could overcome the loss of a leg, and a writer who could maintain almost single-handed a genre of theatre that was often lashed by the critics and occasionally brushed with the law, was clearly not the light-weight that some of his more sober contemporaries wished to consider him. When Boswell speculated that Foote's thoughts on religion were merely superficial and that he 'seized the first notions which occurred to his mind', Johnson agreed that 'he is like a dog, that snatches the piece next him'. But Foote was more genuinely in the tradition of the great satirical dramatists, Jonson, Wycherley, Gay and Fielding, than Johnson's dismissive criticism implies. When Boswell said that 'Foote had a great deal of humour', Johnson agreed again, but he rejected Boswell's final suggestion that 'he has a singular talent of exhibiting character': 'Sir, it is not a talent; it is a vice; it is what others abstain from. It is not comedy, which exhibits the character of a species, as that of a miser gathered from many misers; it is farce, which exhibits individuals.'[20]

Thus spoke a champion of neo-classicism, which always advocated the general rule rather than the particular example, but Foote traced his inspiration back to the genuinely classical model of Aristophanes, who also dealt with the particular and the topical. With the revival of the Aristophanic spirit in Monty Python and Dario Fo we can perhaps now appreciate the special place Foote has in the history of topical satire, and that his talents in this sphere deserve recognition, together with those of Fielding and W.S. Gilbert, both of whom are presently regaining a measure of critical respect as dramatists over and above their reputations as novelist and librettist.

On the other hand, Murphy was held in higher regard by Dr Johnson. His sense of comedy and satire conformed more nearly to the neo-classical norms of unity and consistency. However, it is significant that even his dramatic effectiveness was at its weakest when he followed most closely the formal rules of the five-act comedy. Murphy never claimed that his farces were really comedies, but in fact he gave his two-act afterpieces a respectability and seriousness that actually should have entitled them to the description of 'petites comédies'.

Murphy

Arthur Murphy was born in western Ireland in 1727. Before he was two years old his father, a Dublin merchant, was lost at sea when sailing to America. Mrs Murphy took Arthur and his elder brother James to London whence Arthur was sent to the Jesuit College of St Omer in France. Here he received a full classical education, which he must have felt somewhat wasted when in 1747 he was apprenticed to his uncle Jeffrey French, a merchant in Cork. In 1749 he refused to make a transatlantic journey similar to that on which his father had perished, and instead returned to London where he became bookkeeper to a company of bankers. However, unlike his brother James, Arthur was not content with the commercial life, and, like a number of Irish emigrants before him, he turned his hand to journalism as the start of a career as a man of letters.

In 1752, at the age of twenty-five, he was contributing a regular column, the 'Gray's Inn Journal', and other occasional pieces to Henry Fielding's *New Craftsman*. From the outset Murphy allied himself with the Tories, who, although supporters of traditional attitudes and conservative policies, had long had the support of the finest writers in London, from Swift and Pope to Fielding and Smollett. There was little chance at this stage of Murphy's gaining the valuable patronage of the court party, which, despite George II's personal animosity towards them, was led by Pitt the Elder and the Duke of Newcastle and was committed to a policy of imperialistic expansion at the expense of the French. By adopting an attitude of hostility to the government in his writing Murphy became attached to the faction of Henry Fox, and from the start of the Seven Years War in 1753 he wrote continuously in support of the peace party.

Maybe Murphy wanted his literary activities to develop into a political career, but in the eighteenth century politicians, without a private fortune to buy their way into Parliament, had to have the genius of an Edmund Burke to earn the complete patronage of a wealthy aristocrat, and Henry Fox, though friendly, was not yet convinced that Murphy deserved that kind of support. There was, of course, another lucrative means of advancing a career of literary talent, and that was in the theatre. Of the two friends who had walked from Lichfield to London in 1737 to make their fortunes, Dr Johnson may have been the greater genius – he certainly thought so himself – but it was David Garrick who had made his fortune the faster. In his essays for the *Gray's Inn Journal* Murphy had often praised Garrick highly and had written intelligently about all aspects of the theatre. He had inevitably made the acquaintance of Samuel Foote, who had encouraged him to write for the theatre and even to attempt acting. In 1753 Murphy submitted a two-act afterpiece, *The Young Apprentice*, to Drury Lane, but was appalled when Garrick casually offered to 'improve' it for him.[21] It was not accepted at Drury Lane until 1755 after Murphy himself had rewritten the piece, and it was presented as *The Apprentice* on 2 January 1756. Meanwhile Murphy had appeared on the stage at Covent Garden as Othello (the same inappropriate choice as Foote's debut) and had acquitted himself respectably enough to be taken on by Drury Lane in 1755. His presence in the company must have helped towards the acceptance of *The Apprentice*.

This first play was a great success, and is remarkable on two main counts. Firstly, in Dick, the besotted amateur actor, who tries to plan his own life like the plot of a popular drama and who spices his conversation with an inexhaustible supply of quotations, he provided the comedian Harry Woodward with a splendidly theatrical vehicle, and, secondly, the play made good use of Murphy's own personal experiences. Before joining the professional theatre he had frequented the amateur 'Spouting Clubs' and he introduced a scene for Dick's fellow spouters that is both extremely funny and suspiciously lifelike. Murphy himself admitted that the crotchety merchant Wingate was based on his uncle Jeffrey,[22] and the situations in the play must have borne some relationship to his own experience of apprenticeship. This quality of combining the theatrical with the truthful was to be a mark of all Murphy's best writing. In 1755 he had proposed writing a sequel to Foote's *The Englishman in Paris* (1753), but he was foolish enough to put the idea to Foote, who instantly wrote his own sequel, *The Englishman Return'd from Paris*. On 3 April 1756, a month after Foote's play at Covent Garden, Murphy's *Englishman from Paris* was presented at Drury Lane. His was the more thoughtful of the two pieces. As usual Foote had used his play to build up a broad caricature of a Frenchified fop, but Murphy drew on the experience of his French education and presented a more balanced satire of the affectations of both the French and British. In his next play, *The Spouter*, Murphy introduced a caricature of Foote, along with other Covent Garden actors, as Dapperwit, a plagiarist author: 'It is true, a

Gentleman told me the subject first; but in confidence, too! By way of consulting my Judgement . . . To consult me! A Blockhead!'[23] However, and no doubt for the same reasons that Foote's own parody of the actors in *The Diversions of the Morning* was unpopular with the theatre managers, *The Spouter* was never performed, and Murphy's next play to be presented was *The Upholsterer* in 1758. Here, once again, Murphy drew on personal experience, this time of his journalistic activities. Quidnunc, a coffee-house politician, in a fine Jonsonian humour, is addicted to reading the news and following the latest journalistic controversy.

By 1758 Murphy had given up acting – by all accounts he would have never have been more than a 'useful' performer – and, as well as concentrating again on journalism, contributing 'The Theatre' essays to the *London Chronicle* and in 1756–7 editing *The Test* in specific support of Henry Fox, he had applied in 1757 to the Inns of Court. His having been an actor was held against him, but Fox's influence eventually won him a place in Lincoln's Inn. When he was called to the bar in 1762 Murphy had at last found a stable and lucrative career, but, like many members of London's literary circle, he kept up his other interests in journalism and the theatre. His dramatic criticism in 'The Theatre' column was some of the earliest critical analysis to be found in a London newspaper, and has been described as emphasising

> precisely those values that characterize Murphy's own plays and express the taste and prejudices that mark his interests throughout his long connection with the stage. The criticism rests on the naturalness and decency that Murphy always demanded in drama. It calls for truthful characterization and the emergence of plot from character, the staples of Murphy's own plays. His distaste for sentimentalism, for the excesses of pantomime; his preference for classical unity rather than the hybrid forms of tragi-comedy – these were his views throughout his career, and they are the basis of the criticism in the *London Chronicle*.[24]

In 1759 he turned his hand to tragedy, translating Voltaire's *L'Orephelin de la Chine*, so as to provide an interesting part for Garrick as the trusty mentor of an exiled prince. Murphy also used the play as a lever in his continuing search for political patronage, when, on the advice of Henry Fox, he dedicated the play to the Earl of Bute, tutor to the young prince, who in 1760 was to succeed his grandfather as George III. The subject matter of the play was well suited to compliment Bute and in 1762 we find Murphy editing *The Auditor* in support of Bute's first ministry. From henceforth Murphy the journalist was to be a government man, which was a development, as we shall see, not necessarily to the benefit of his theatrical ventures.

In January 1760 his first full-length comedy *The Way to Keep Him* started its life as an afterpiece, to be expanded into a mainpiece of five acts on 10 January 1761. This study of married life is a classic situation comedy, with one couple

suffering because the wife has given in to the tedium of matrimony and forgotten how to charm her husband, and the other couple suffering because the
husband thinks it is unfashionable to love his wife and so insults her just to
impress his friends. This play was to hold the stage throughout Murphy's
lifetime and was, in terms of performance, one of the most consistently successful full-length repertory plays written in the 1760s, averaging a steady five or six
performances every year, and receiving no less than seven royal command
performances in its first ten years. It was at about this time that Murphy submitted *The Man Does Not Know His Own Mind* to Garrick, but in the first of
many altercations with the manager it was returned. It was eventually to
develop into Murphy's finest comedy, and his last, being performed in 1777. In
1761 Murphy made up his disagreement with Samuel Foote, and the two of
them joined forces to present a season of comedies over the summer at Drury
Lane. I have mentioned how Foote failed to produce his promised quota of
plays for this venture, but Murphy provided three, the full-length *All in the
Wrong*, which presented a complicated plot of intrigue, misunderstanding and
cross purposes, and two excellent short farces, *The Old Maid* and *The Citizen*,
which appeared together as a double bill on 2 July 1761.

The Citizen

The Citizen is the most obviously farcical of the short pieces in this collection.
Its plot is utterly contrived and its characterisation is of the broadest. The
characters are quintessential social types – the squire, the merchant, the rake
and the whore – added to which are George Philpot and Maria, two delightful
variations on traditional themes. George, a would-be man-about-town, is in
fact a brash merchant's apprentice, hardly more sophisticated than Dick in
Murphy's first play, but full of good humour although with very little sense.
Maria is a delectable pert miss, for whom Murphy wrote two excellent scenes
in which she makes a fool of her city suitor. In one she plays a country simpleton, and in the other a flirtatious blue-stocking. The part was specifically
written for Murphy's mistress, Ann Elliott, a comedienne of charm and ability,
and to whom he dedicated the play.

The funniest scene of the play has all the elements of traditional farce. The
son shows off to the courtesan while his father hides under the table, and when
he refuses to fight with his gentleman rival he gets beaten with the flat of his
sword. Slapstick, bawdy, cross-purposes and a comical recognition are all
involved in this splendid comic situation. Literary critics may not consider
these qualities to be of the highest kind, and J.P. Emery judges the play
'inferior to Murphy's other farces', and that 'the interest of the reader lessens
after the opening scene, in which the delightful Maria misleadingly creates the
expectation of an excellent play, and the plot of the farce,in spite of diverse
threads, lacks sufficient substance'.[25] Perhaps 'substance' is what the *reader*

requires, but the theatre audience is better pleased with swift action and a
sense of immediacy and fun. Immediacy is precisely the quality that Murphy's
dialogue provides for the actor. Not only is the jargon of the merchant and the
squire appropriate to their class, but the brisk colloquial conversation of the
younger characters has a theatrical effectiveness not immediately apparent to
the reader. In particular the device of uncontrollable laughter, provided for
both Wilding and Maria, seems very awkward on the page, but would prove
quite infectious when performed by skilled comedians. So too would the
Epilogue, split between Old and Young Philpot, where the apparently casual
style of expression, with incomplete sentences, shared phrases, expletives and
asides, is nicely counterpointed by the formality of the rhyming couplets.

It is in a farce of this kind, artificially contrived, but with vividly observed
characters, that the convention of the aside comes into its own. The actors can
take the audience into their confidence, indicating that they too find the characters they are playing somewhat absurd, and the situation in which they find
themselves embarrassing and comical. In a farce as broad as this we do not
expect the actor to lose himself within the fiction of the role, and it is a theatrical
delight when one character shares with the audience an awareness of the
artificiality of the scene at the expense of another character who is overcome
with passion or panic because he has surrendered to the fictitious situation. It
is even possible to share this sense of absurdity at one's *own* plight or
emotions, as in the case of Old Philpot under the table, and one has only to
imagine a master of this technique, such as Frankie Howerd or Zero Mostell,
playing the scene to appreciate the scope Murphy has allowed his actors to play
with, as well as *for*, their audience. Indeed, as with the best comic creations of
this kind, the personality of the comedian does achieve a certain identification
with the role, or rather the role becomes identified with the comedian. Ann
Elliott became associated with Maria, in the way Woodward had become
identified with Dick in *The Apprentice*. In fact Woodward took over the part
of George Philpot from Foote, when the play became a regular Covent Garden
afterpiece. In 1789 George became a vehicle for John Bannister, and it was his
performance in the play that led Leigh Hunt to acclaim *The Citizen* as 'the first
farce in the English Language'.[26]

Hunt's description of Bannister also indicates the effectiveness in performance of the 'set-piece', which to the reader often seems too contrived. Murphy
was adept at providing these descriptive speeches, and a performer like
Bannister could make good use of them:

> If any thing can excel the grave moniedness he affects in order to cheat
> his father, it is his description of the garret-author, of that miserable
> pamphleteer who, holding one baby on his knee and rocking another
> in the cradle with his foot, is writing a political essay with his right hand
> while he occasionally twirls round a scrag of roast pork with his left:
> during this description the mirth of the audience becomes impatient to

express itself, till the admirable mimic having wound up to his climax
by a picture of the author's wife washing clothes in a corner to the song
of *Sweet Passion of Love*, it bursts into a tempestuous approbation.
As is usual with Hunt's criticism, he points out some of the details of the actor's
contribution to the success of such a speech. He indicates that the secret was
for the actor to discard for the moment the personality of the character he is
playing, and adopt that of the subject of his description. After a similar setpiece
in *Three Weeks After Marriage* Sir Charles says that Lady Racket 'would make
a most excellent actress'. Thus, according to Hunt,

> Bannister puts himself in the situation of the belaboured pamphleteer,
> he dandles his child, then writes a line, then rocks the other child, then
> writes another line, then gives the griskin a twist; his handkerchief is
> taken out and he becomes the author's wife, accompanies the dabs and
> scrubbings of the washing tub with *Sweet Passion of Love*, and as it's
> ardour grows more vehement screams out the tender love-song to the
> furious wringing of her small linen.[27]

Other comic performers who succeeded in *The Citizen* included Edward
Shuter and Charles Mathews the Elder as Old Philpot, and Jane Pope,
Elizabeth Farren and Dorothea Jordan as Maria. The play was still in the
repertoire in 1820 when Oxberry remarked in his edition for *The New English
Drama* that 'the characters . . . are set forth with a masterly hand. So fresh,
indeed, are the colours, so true to life in their general rather than individual
form, that they might very well pass for portraits of the present day' (vol. XI,
p. ii). In other words, Murphy followed Dr Johnson's prescription for comedy,
'to exhibit the character of a species', unlike Foote, who exhibited the individual, and, although the species may no longer exist today, Murphy's farce is
still more suitable for revival than either *The Minor* or *The Nabob*.

In the short term, however, *The Citizen* fell victim to a dispute between
Murphy and the managers of Drury Lane. He had understood that all his new
plays were to enter the general repertoire with the usual number of author's
benefit performances. However, Garrick did not want to act in *All in the
Wrong* himself, and apparently did not want to produce *The Citizen* at all.
Perhaps Murphy had insisted that Ann Elliott be taken along with the play and
Garrick did not want her in his company; or perhaps Garrick was already in
negotiation with George Colman, whose *The Jealous Wife* had been the hit of
the previous season, to replace Murphy as the virtual resident dramatist at
Drury Lane. In December 1761 Garrick wrote to Colman that:

> Mr Murphy has at last declar'd off with me, & in a letter to O'brien
> [*sic*] says, that he has been so great a loser by ye Managers of Drury
> Lane that he can never have any dealings with us – wish me joy my dear
> friend, but keep this to yourself for Many Weighty Reasons.[28]

Whatever the internal politics of the disagreement were, the result was that
Murphy deserted Drury Lane, and *The Citizen* was not performed again until

the following summer, when Miss Elliott rejoined Foote's Haymarket company. In November 1762 she and the play were presented at Covent Garden under the management of John Beard, and it was at that theatre that Murphy's next few plays were produced.

Three Weeks After Marriage

Unwisely for his career as a dramatist, Murphy became considerably involved in a journalistic controversy before his next important plays *No One's Enemy But His Own* and *What We Must All Come To* were presented at Covent Garden on 9 January 1764. Part of this paper war was purely theatrical, Murphy having been attacked in Charles Churchill's satire on actors, *The Rosciad*, which had appeared in March 1761 and in which Murphy's writing was castigated as feeble plagiarism and his acting as appalling:

> Still in extremes he knows no happy mean,
> Or raving mad or stupidly serene.
> In cold-wrought scenes the lifeless actor flags
> In passion, tears the passion into rags.[29]

Murphy answered the piece with a particularly unsavoury attack in *An Ode on the Naiads of the Fleet Ditch*. Churchill was in turn supported by Robert Lloyd in *Genius, Envy and Time* and in *An Epistle to Charles Churchill*. The whole controversy was satirised in *The Murphiad*, an anonymous poem, probably by William Shirley, and *The Meretriciad* by Edward Thompson. The final blow in this particular battle was struck by Murphy in the *Examiner*, which appeared in November 1761. Throughout this pamphlet war George Colman had been part of a triumvirate with Churchill and Lloyd who were set against Murphy and who had championed the acting of Garrick in *The Rosciad*, and perhaps the battle did much to sour the relations between Murphy and Garrick and so contributed to his replacement by Colman as the leading Drury Lane dramatist.

However, Murphy did not restrict his journalism to theatrical issues, and in June 1762 he re-entered the arena of politics as editor of *The Auditor* in defence of Lord Bute's government, which was being brilliantly attacked in the famous *North Briton* edited by John Wilkes and Murphy's old enemy, Charles Churchill. At about the same time Murphy was called to the bar and because of this, as well as his writing, it is not surprising that he did not produce any more plays until 1764. On 9 January of that year the new five-act comedy, *No One's Enemy But His Own*, accompanied by the afterpiece *What We Must All Come To*, later to be known as *Three Weeks After Marriage*, was presented at Covent Garden. Both met with a hostile audience. That it was Murphy's political opposition to the immensely popular Wilkes that caused their failure can be judged from the fact that when *All in the Wrong* had been played at Drury Lane on 15 December 1763 for a royal command performance, 'the galleries clapped and cried out "Let *us* be all in the right! Wilkes and Liberty!" '[30] On 9 January *No One's Enemy But His Own* was hissed and *What We Must All Come To* was jeered. The management did all they could to save the mainpiece, but the afterpiece was dropped. *No One's Enemy But His Own* was kept on for three nights, with *The Upholsterer* and *The Citizen* replacing the farce, so that Murphy got his first benefit on the 11th. On the 12th the king commanded *The Way To Keep Him* at Drury Lane, and on the 19th the final performance of *No One's Enemy But His Own* at Covent Garden. But even the king's support did not help, indeed it only drew more attention to Murphy's position as a government hack, and so this was the last performance of any Murphy play that season, at either theatre, before the period of the actors' benefits. For their benefits at Covent Garden Woodward and Shuter revived the afterpieces *The Citizen* and *The Upholsterer*, and O'Brien, who had been an ally of Murphy in his argument with Garrick, put on *The Way To Keep Him* at Drury Lane, although, according to the prompter, he was not well suited to the Garrick role of Lovemore.[31] Finally, Mrs Yates revived *The Orphan of China*, which was a risky venture as it had long been out of the repertoire and was generally recognised as a pro-Bute political play. Murphy seems always to have kept the friendship of several actors despite his differences with managements, and it was in recognition of Mrs Yates's loyalty that his next play, *The Choices*, was specially written for her benefit in 1765, although it had to be presented anonymously.

In 1766 Murphy attempted the same method to get a performance of *The School for Guardians*, which he had originally written in 1763 and submitted to Garrick. It had been rejected at that time, but when the manager heard that Murphy intended to give it to Ann Elliott for her benefit at Covent Garden he tried to forestall the play, which was based on Wycherley's *The Country Wife* and Molière's *Ecole des Femmes*, with an adaptation of his own, *The Country Girl*. Murphy was justifiably furious, not only that Garrick was repeating the trick that Foote had played on him over *The Englishman from Paris*, but that:

> [the play] has been lately given up to Miss Elliott . . . Luckily, you cannot wound me; but I leave it to yourself to judge whether it becomes Mr Garrick to contend with a girl! . . . I vow to God I have no interest in this piece, and if it was not for her I would burn it. It consists of three plays by Molière moulded into one. I want neither profit nor reputation from it. But I own I am stung to the very heart at this attempt to hurt her.[32]

Murphy had specially adapted the part of Margery Pinchwife into that of Mary Ann, and it is clear from her success as Maria in *The Citizen* that Ann Elliott would have been well suited to the role. However, Garrick's *Country Girl* came out first, on 25 October 1766, and, despite its hurried composition, was more successful than *The School for Guardians*, which appeared on 17 January 1767 and received only seven performances.

Late in 1767 Murphy tried once again to use a benefit performance to regain a place in the theatre for his condemned farce *What We Must All Come To*, when Frances Abington presented it in a musical version entitled *Marriage à la Mode, or Conjugal Douceurs*, to follow her performance in *The Way to Keep Him*. However, it was presented only once and it was not until 1776, when William Lewis persuaded Murphy to change the name finally to *Three Weeks After Marriage*, that it eventually achieved its deserved success. It was performed at Covent Garden on 30 March 1776, Lewis playing Sir Charles and Mrs Mattocks Lady Racket. Ann Elliott for whom the part had been written had died in 1769. The play remained in the Covent Garden repertoire for the rest of the eighteenth century, and was successfully performed well into the nineteenth. Mrs Abington left Drury Lane in 1782, and in 1783 she played Lady Racket, eighteen years after she had presented the musical version. Mrs Jordan was another actress who found much to relish in the part.

As with *The Citizen*, it is a play that rewards its performers with some extremely effective dialogue. Unlike so many self-consciously witty plays of the period, *Three Weeks After Marriage* gives the actors lines that are apparently spontaneous as well as amusing, and allows the comedy to proceed, not so much from the repartee, as from the situations and the characteristic responses of those involved. Although it is more of a domestic comedy than *The Citizen*, all taking place over one evening at Mr Drugget's house in the suburbs, we are once again presented with a conflict between a middle-class merchant family and upper-class intruders. In this case, however, it is the sophisticated aristocrats who are satirised more harshly. The retired merchant Drugget is nowhere near as unpleasant as Old Philpot, he merely suffers from a vulgar taste in landscape gardening, and his wife's snobbery is silly rather than vicious. Their humours are those of Goldsmith rather than Jonson, and in the end they are seen to be fundamentally concerned for their daughters' happiness. It is the men of fashion who prove to be the more destructive. Even so, Sir Charles Racket is not a bad man, he is just foolish and pettyminded, as is Lady Racket; in fact they are not an unattractive couple.

Murphy does not present us with grotesque characters in this play, whom we can despise as well as laugh at, but rather with some basically ordinary people, whose conflicts arise out of misunderstandings and a rather trivial scale of values. The whole thing is a storm in a teacup, and the result of boredom rather than fundamental character defects. One might argue that a marriage being destroyed over a card-table squabble is a condemnation of the superficial lifestyle of a parasitic aristocracy, but I do not think it is a satirical portrait that Murphy is holding up to his audience. The implication behind all the various titles given to the play is that such folly is universal, and it is the inevitable pattern of petty bickering that is at fault, rather than any question of moral principle or class distinction. The Rackets do not really dislike each other, they do not really want to quarrel, they do not really care about cards – at which neither is an expert. Their quarrel is merely typical, and Murphy's skill is that he traces the development of the quarrel, its truces and its renewals, with an acute ear for the unthinkingly provocative remark, and a perceptive awareness of how easily a marriage can founder in the shallows of triviality.

In his Advertisement to *What We Must All Come To*, when it was first published in 1764, Murphy pointed out that it was the passions rather than the personalities that gave rise to the complications of the play:

> The violent differences between *Sir Charles* and *Lady Racket* about a trifle, and the renewal of those differences by venturing, after they had subsided, to resume the object in thorough good humour, are, it is conceived, founded in Nature, because similar incidents often occur in real life. To shew the passions thus frivolously agitated, and to point out the ridicule springing from their various turns and shiftings, was the main drift of the ensuing scenes.

This awareness of the psychology of emotion does, perhaps, place Murphy's play into the category of being sentimental, as opposed to being a comedy of humours or of manners, but it is sentimental only in so far as it is concerned with 'sentiments' or passions of the mind. Its moral is satirical, even cynical, rather than exemplary or dogmatic, which are the qualities usually implied by the term sentimental.

Even though the play is centred on the vagaries of emotional behaviour, Murphy does not ignore the characteristics of social status. Indeed he presents very accurately and amusingly the appalling lack of taste in Old Drugget's passion for topiary and garden gnomes. And if the distinction between the worthy Woodley and the foppish Lovelace is only superficially drawn, the amoral good humour of Dimity, and the bored arrogance of the Rackets is portrayed with considerable subtlety. However, when the play was printed in 1776, and revised for inclusion in *The Works*, Murphy removed several specific references, such as those that placed the Drugget's house in Fulham, and named the Racket's gaming house as Arthur's. These revisions seem to indicate the neo-classical, generalising tendency that was applied to plays as literature, and to suggest that Murphy himself wished to have his work remembered not as part of the city-comedy tradition, in which one can place Foote, but as comedies of manners, in which characters are defined by their interaction rather than their social function, and humour arises from the skirmishes of wit and folly rather than from class conflict or social satire. Certainly in his full-length comedies Murphy did not use the broader canvas that five acts furnished him to elaborate details of place and circumstance, but instead concentrated on the clash of wits and the interplay of characters, and in this his inspiration seems to have been more French than English.

Know Your Own Mind

It is clear that *Know Your Own Mind* owes much to the influence of French models. Its plot is based to a great extent on Philippe Destouches's *L'Irrésolu* (1713), and, although Murphy completely anglicised his version and made several alterations and improvements, the tone of the play, when compared with the more traditionally English style of Colman or Goldsmith, has a definite quality that may be described as neo-classical or French. The precise nuances of social class, the details of physical environment and the individuality of humours, which had typified much English comedy since Jonson, is less apparent in Murphy's full-length play than in his farces. If one wants to find a comparable style in English drama one must look to Congreve or Steele, rather than to Wycherley, Farquhar or Fielding. Of all the plays in this collection *Know Your Own Mind* is the one that most closely approaches Sentimental Comedy. However, a comparison of the Larpent Manuscript, which I have mainly followed, with the final version printed in *The Works*, shows that the more obviously sentimental passages, such as those including Miss Neville, were added or elaborated for the reader, and that the 'low' comedy of the servants was reduced after its performance in the theatre.

Know Your Own Mind had been some seventeen years in preparation. Murphy had first suggested it to Garrick in 1760 under the title *The Man Does Not Know His Own Mind*, but it was rejected, as it was again in 1764 after the fiasco of *No One's Enemy But His Own* and *What We Must All Come To*. In 1767 Isaac Bickerstaffe, the author of several musical comedies and ballad operas, negotiated a reconciliation between Murphy and Garrick, and it was agreed that *The Man Does Not Know His Own Mind* would be performed at Drury Lane with Murphy's tragedies *Alzuma* and *Zenobia*. *Zenobia* appeared on 27 February 1768, but it was followed by an argument over payment, and both *Alzuma* and the comedy were withdrawn. In 1771 further negotiations were opened for its performance, this time with Murphy's best tragedy *The Grecian Daughter*. This play was presented on 26 February 1772 with considerable success, providing an effectively pathetic role for Mrs Barry, which was revived by Sarah Siddons in 1782. However, once again the comedy fell foul of theatrical politics. Murphy wished Mrs Barry to play the part of Lady Bell, which he had originally intended for Ann Elliott; Garrick on the other hand seemed to support the claim of Mrs Abington, and, although they had reached rehearsal stage in December 1772, Murphy withdrew the play on the pretext that he objected to Garrick's casting of the parts.

This was the final rupture between Murphy and Garrick, and it marked the end of his playwriting career, in that the plays subsequently presented at Covent Garden had all been started before 1772. *Alzuma*, rejected in 1768, was performed on 23 February 1773; *Three Weeks After Marriage*, condemned in 1764, was performed on 30 March 1776; and, finally, *Know Your Own Mind*, started in 1760, was performed on 2 February 1777 with a prologue that clearly indicated that Murphy regarded it as his last dramatic composition. In the prologue Murphy lamented the passing of several performers of his generation; Garrick had retired the previous year, and Spranger Barry had died even more recently. Henry Woodward was suffering his final illness, and this was a particular loss to *Know Your Own Mind*, as Murphy had intended him to play Dashwould. Woodward had ensured the success of Murphy's first play as Dick in *The Apprentice*, and he would certainly have been a better casting than Charles Lee-Lewes who eventually played Dashwould. However, William Lewis was well suited to the part of Millamour. Leigh Hunt considered him 'the Mercutio of the age, in every sense of the word mercurial',[33] and in *The Records of a Stage Veteran* his greatest qualification was described as his animal spirits:

> No greyhound ever bounded, no kitten ever gambolled, no jay ever chattered (sing, neither the bird nor man in question ever could) with more apparent recklessness of mirth than Lewis acted. All was sunshine with him: he jumped over the stage properties as if his leap-frog days had just commenced; danced the hay with chairs, tables, and settees, and a shade never was upon his face, except that of the descending green curtain at the end of the comedy.[34]

Unfortunately the part of Lady Bell, perhaps the most delightful and important in the play, was entrusted to Mrs Mattocks, an actress that could hardly be compared with Ann Elliott, who had inspired the role, or even Mesdames Barry or Abington. Although an accomplished actress, Boaden considered her 'manner somewhat broad. She was the paragon representative of the radically *vulgar* woman, of any or no fashion, or whatever condition or age.'[35] She and Lewis may have been ideal as the Rackets in *Three Weeks After Marriage*, but vulgarity was the very last quality needed for Lady Bell.

This weakness in the original casting should be remembered when making the inevitable comparison with Sheridan's *School for Scandal*, which, when it opened three months after *Know Your Own Mind* at Drury Lane on 8 May 1777, cast a shadow over Murphy's play from which it has never subsequently emerged. Sheridan had of course brought together probably the best ensemble comedy company of the century, led by Tom King, Robert Palmer and William 'Gentleman' Smith, with Mrs Abington as Lady Teazle providing the charm that Mrs Mattocks had failed to bring to Lady Bell. It was not until Dorothea Jordan took up the role in the first Drury Lane performance in 1789, with John Bannister as Dashwould, that Murphy's play received the quality of performers it deserved. The question of whether the script itself measures up to Sheridan's masterpiece will be considered later, but it must be pointed out that once again Murphy's reputation as a dramatist was considerably damaged, as it had been throughout his career, by the unfavourable circumstances of his play's first performance. His political involvements had alienated many playgoers over the years, and, more importantly, the managers of Drury Lane. Garrick had been prepared to work with him, although he could not tolerate for long Murphy's continual arguing about casting and payment, but Sheridan, with political ambitions of his own as a friend of the radical Whig, Charles James Fox, son of Murphy's first patron, was in no way inclined to cooperate with the rival playwright. The actors too, with whom Murphy had made friends through Ann Elliott and in the early days when he himself had been a performer, were either dead or retired by 1777. Murphy had always cultivated other activities, his legal practice and his literary work, and so he seems to have taken leave of the theatre without much apparent regret.

Despite the fact that Millamour's incorrigible lack of decision can be seen as a kind of humour, *Know Your Own Mind* as a whole is definitely conceived in the style of a Restoration comedy of manners. It is no accident that Millamour's name echoes that of Millamant, nor that the poem that he gives to each of his three fiancées is a copy of a Congreve song. The whole play owes much to *The Way of the World*, even though its main plot came from the French. Malvil is as hypocritical a villain as Fainall, Harry Lizard (renamed Lovewit in the printed edition) is an obvious Witwou'd, and that name too is echoed in Dashwould's. Mrs Bromley is a rather pale reflection of Lady Wishfort, but above all Lady Bell can stand with credit beside the model of Millamant, full of wit and teasing, yet fundamentally sensible and warm-hearted. The plot too, although not quite as obfuscated as that of *The Way of the World*, is not the most important element of the drama. Millamour's changes of mind obviously lead to many situations of embarrassment and confusion, but the happy outcome is never in doubt, and it is only in the sub-plot of the flight of Miss Neville and the unmasking of Malvil that the play achieves any degree of suspense or surprise. Although there are rivalries of both love and wit within the play, they are there to provide occasions for repartee and good-natured skirmishes rather than major dramatic conflict. This means that the play lacks the theatrical excitement of, say, the screen scene in *The School for Scandal*, beside which the unmasking of Malvil is comparatively weak.

The comedy, therefore, as in *The Way of the World*, depends for its success on character and dialogue, and here Murphy provides a satisfying mixture of the familiar and the original. The two fathers we have met before, not only in *The Minor*, but in many eighteenth-century comedies. However, Bygrove is a nice variation on the disapproving authoritarian. That he is chasing the widow is no surprise, but that he condemns Dashwould's sarcastic wit with an equally witty sarcasm of his own seems psychologically sound as well as amusing. The well-intentioned and incompetent hero of the play, Millamour, is to an extent a dramatic contrivance, an artificial humour, whose indecision is necessary to create the crossed purposes of a situation comedy, but, as with the Rackets in *Three Weeks After Marriage*, Murphy illustrates the thought processes of misunderstanding with an insight and precision that is delightful in itself. Perhaps Millamour's reformation is not entirely convincing, but Lady Bell's final capitulation shows that she at least does not expect him to have changed completely. She still teases him, and we can be sure that she is well able to deal with any future fickleness on his part: 'I have promised him my hand – and so – (*Holds out both hands.*) which will you have? Puzzle about it, and know your own mind, if you can.' As has already been suggested it is Lady Bell who is the star of this particular play. She never seems to take anything too seriously, but at the same time we have no doubts of her genuine attachment to Millamour or her concern for the unfortunate Miss Neville. Her sentiments are admirable, but expressed with a vivacity that allows no hint of sentimentality. She can hold her own against the wit of Dashwould, the envy of her sister, the machinations of Malvil and the authority of her mother, without falling into either the cattiness of Lady Jane or the insipidity of Miss Neville. She has in fact the very qualities that make Millamant and Beatrice great comic roles – she too can tease and flirt and do so without seeming to lack decency or sincerity.

The original of Dashwould, the most interesting male character that Murphy introduced into the play, is not to be found in *L'Irrésolu*, and indeed, despite his busy intrigue, he is not essential to the development of the dramatic action. It is as a commentator on the protagonists, and as an amusing character in his own right, that Dashwould takes the centre of the stage. If Lady Bell is a guileless flirt then Dashwould is a generous gossip. It is in the basic goodness of these two characters that the main sentimental content of the play is to be found, but because their sense of humour and their style of dialogue is so ironical their moral perspective appears good-naturedly robust rather than mawkishly pious, as in genuine Sentimental Comedy. It was suggested that Samuel Foote was the model for Dashwould, indeed his final quip that he would not sacrifice a friend to a joke, 'except now and then, when the friend is the worse of the two', has been attributed to Foote in Samuel Rodger's *Samuel Foote's Table Talk*. However, unlike the portraits in Foote's own plays, there is no suggestion that the role was intended as a recognisable take-off of the satirist. Perhaps in the versions of 1760 and 1764 Murphy was tempted to subject his old friend to some of his own medicine, and had even considered Harry Woodward for the part because he was as capable a mimic as Foote, but by 1777, after the Lady Kingston affair, during which Murphy had acted as one of his legal advisors, Foote was a sick and broken man.[36] Moreover, Murphy's own theatrical taste would have made him realise that in this classically conceived comedy of manners a personal portrait would have been sadly out of place. No doubt there was much of Foote in Dashwould, but Murphy seems to have distilled this influence into a genuinely comic fictitious character.

Yet the concept of Dashwould as a character is perhaps better than the execution, for, although several of his descriptions of acquaintances and fashionable personalities are suitably satirical, there is a lack of the pointed epigrams that raise an immediate laugh at the scandalmongers of Sheridan's *School*. I think it is Murphy's inability to come up with enough one-liners that must make his comedy ultimately inferior to that of Sheridan. His dialogue is smooth and polished, it comes off the actor's tongue naturally and with ease, but it fails to sparkle and to surprise. Maybe it is because Murphy's Dashwould must in the end prove to be a decent fellow that his gossip is less outrageously funny than the vicious tales of Backbite, Crabtree, Candour and Sneerwell. Dashwould, Millamour and Lady Bell may exchange witty descriptions, and Sir Harry can chime in a chorus, but they are too nice to build up the climaxes of exaggerated vindictiveness one finds in Sheridan. Malvil, too, although obviously a model for Joseph Surface, has not quite the slimy tone of Joseph's sentimental innuendoes. Murphy gives him many hypocritical epithets, but he lifts them rather too accurately from the sentimental literature of the time, and somehow Malvil's drunkenness does not quite fulfil the dramatic potential of the scene. It is not funny enough in itself to compensate forgoing the absolute hypocrisy of Joseph Surface, who has persuaded himself that his villainy is still compatible with the high moral opinion he has of himself. Malvil is a simple dissembler, Joseph has deceived even himself.

It is in this straightforward villainy opposed to the basic decency of the main characters that I think the sentimental weakness of *Know Your Own Mind* lies, rather than where it is usually indicated as being, in the Miss Neville sub-plot. Although Miss Neville has a sentimental tendency to weep at her distress and moralise on the injustice of Mrs Bromley, there is an almost unconscious flaw in each of the women that makes them more interesting than a merely senti- mental interpretation of the sub-plot would warrant. Murphy increased the sententious nature of Neville's reflections in the printed version of the play, but it is clear from the manuscript, which I take to be the original acting text, that Miss Neville was not originally intended as a whinger. Her attitude is more one of anger at her humiliations than self-pity. Given that emphasis, Miss Neville emerges as rather unattractively self-righteous and unappreciative of Mrs Bromley's original kindness. Mrs Bromley herself is very skilfully written for what might seem at first a two-dimensional stock character. One can feel some sympathy for her resentment at the apparent lack of gratitude from Miss Neville, although hostility on both sides is perhaps the inevitable result of their relationship and is implicit in any state of dependence and patronage. Like Dashwould, Mrs Bromley is fundamentally well intentioned, even kind, and it is irritation and thoughtlessness that inspires most of her cruelty to her poor relation.

I think it was unfortunate that Murphy replaced Trinket's comments in act II, scene 1, that Neville is 'an ill-natured, proud, good-for-nothing puss', with an extension to Neville's soliloquy, which at the same time makes it more self-conscius and more self-justifying:

> Oh! State of dependence! For mere support, to be subject every hour
> to caprice and arrogance! – Is it pride that makes me feel with this
> sensibility? No, my heart can answer it is not. I can bow to the hand

that relieves me; but I cannot stoop to the servile office of pampering
vanity and ostentation, with low and fulsome flattery.

Perhaps Murphy thought that such reflections were necessary in a reading
version, but they would certainly prove mawkish on the stage. I am sure that
given an interpretation of Miss Neville that took for its starting point another
line that Murphy subsequently cut, that she was able 'to beat down the price'
of La Rouge's lace, one could create a character that is not merely sentimental,
but who, like Malvil in a different way, uses the jargon of sentimentality to
conceal a rather more vigorously critical attitude towards her situation than
might at first appear.

The other element that suffered in Murphy's adaptation of the play for his
reading public was the playing down of the comedy of the servants. He replaced
the opening scene's blustering on and off the stage with a simple description
from Millamour's servant Charles. Such a description could still be played as a
setpiece in which Charles imitated his master, but this would not compensate
for the theatrical effectiveness of everyone rushing in all directions. Perhaps my
own taste is for the farcical rather than the literary qualities of Murphy's comic
skill, but it does seem that, whatever its virtues, even his best full-length play
lacks something of the theatrical vigour, satirical bite and what eighteenth-
century critics would call the *vis comica* of his afterpieces.

A modern audience, I believe, would find *Know Your Own Mind* a little
insipid, although as I have argued it would be unfair to categorise it as sentimental. The problem is that we have lost the classical taste for unity and
decorum, which Murphy, as a classical scholar himself, felt he ought to aspire
to. As I suggested at the outset, the development of television comedy has led
us to prefer our entertainment to be concise as well as neat, and the fact that
most stage comedy as well as 'serious drama' in the twentieth century has been
predominantly concerned with social conflicts and distinctions means that we
are more likely to be drawn to the tradition of the city-comedy as exemplified
by the afterpieces published here, rather than to the more formally correct and
intricately wrought drama of the five-act comedy of manners and intrigue. I
believe that the popular entertainment of the eighteenth century, as represented by the farces of Foote and Murphy, could still prove entertaining to a
modern audience, so I recommend these plays not only for study from a historical or literary point of view, but for actual revival and performance on the
stage today.

NOTES

1   A. Nicoll, *A History of English Drama 1660–1900* (6 vols., Cambridge, 1923–
    59), vol. III, p. 171.
2   In his contribution to *The Stage and the Page*, ed. G.W. Stone Jnr (Berkeley,
    1981), pp. 3–29, Robert D. Hume argues persuasively for abandoning the
    terms 'sentimental' and 'laughing' comedy, as they have led critics into

exaggerating the generic differences between them. However, it is my opinion that the terms as coined by Goldsmith had a meaning for his readers and should therefore still be used – although with care.

3   R.W. Bevis, *The Laughing Tradition* (London, 1980), p. 61.
4   For details of the effect of the Licensing Act see Watson Nicholson, *The Struggle for a Free Stage in London* (New York, 1906), and *The London Stage*, part 3, introduction ed. A.H. Scouten (Illinois, 1962), pp. xlviii–lx.
5   *General Advertiser*, 22 and 25 April 1747, quoted in M.M. Belden, *The Dramatic Work of Samuel Foote* (New Haven, 1929), pp. 7–9.
6   *The Works of Samuel Foote*, ed. John Bee [John Badcock] (3 vols., London, 1830), vol. I, p. lvii.
7   'A letter to the Reverend Author of Remarks Critical and Christian on the Minor', reprinted in *The Works*, ed. Bee, vol. I, p. ciii.
8   *Ibid.*, vol. I, p. c.
9   *Ibid.*, vol. I, p. xciv.
10   See J.P. Gledstone, *George Whitefield, M.A., Field Preacher* (London, 1900).
11   *The Private Correspondence of David Garrick*, ed. J. Boaden (London, 1832), vol. I, p. 120.
12   *The Works*, ed. Bee, vol. I, p. cxii.
13   *Notes and Queries*, 10th series, VIII (1907), 141.
14   In *The Works*, Bee suggests Weston, vol. II, p. 5; Wilkinson considered himself to be Shift, *Memoires* (London 1790) vol. II, p. 240f. and *The Wandering Patentee* (York, 1795), vol. III, p. 37.
15   Bevis, *The Laughing Tradition*, p. 157.
16   A.Murphy, *The Life of Garrick* (London, 1801), vol. I, p. 360.
17   Bevis, *The Laughing Tradition*, pp. 160–4.
18   Belden, *Dramatic Works*, p. 147.
19   J. Nichols, *Literary Anecdotes* (London, 1816), vol. III, p. 578; quoted Belden, *Dramatic Works*, p. 152.
20   J. Boswell, *In Search of a Wife*, ed. F. Brady and F.A. Pottle (Yale, 1957), pp. 344–5.
21   *Garrick Correspondence*, ed. Boaden, vol. I, pp. 66–7.
22   H.H. Dunbar, *The Dramatic Career of Arthur Murphy* (New York, 1946), pp. 21–2.
23   *The Spouter* (London, 1756), p. 26.
24   R.D. Spector, *Arthur Murphy* (Boston, 1979), p. 30.
25   J.P. Emery, *Arthur Murphy* (Philadelphia, 1946), p. 74.
26   Leigh Hunt, *Critical Essays of the London Theatre* (London, 1807), p. 12.
27   *Ibid.*, pp. 68–9.
28   D. Garrick, *Letters*, ed. D.M. Little and G.M. Kahrl (Oxford, 1964), pp. 348–9.
29   C. Churchill, *The Rosciad* (London, 1761).
30   H. Walpole, *Letters*, ed. P. Toynbee (Oxford, 1903–5), vol. V, p. 421.
31   Hopkins diary, quoted in *The London Stage*, part 4, ed. G.W. Stone Jr (Illinois, 1968), vol. II, p. 1048.
32   *Garrick Correspondence*, ed. J. Boaden, vol. I, pp. 241–2.
33   Quoted by W. Clark Russell, *Representative Actors* (London, n.d. – c. 1872), p. 209.
34   *Ibid.*
35   *Ibid.*, p. 196.
36   See Biographical records, pp. 35–6, below.

BIOGRAPHICAL RECORDS

Samuel Foote

27 January 1720	Samuel Foote baptised at Truro, Cornwall. Son of Samuel Foote, MP for Tiverton, and Eleanor, daughter of Sir Edward Goodere.
1737	Left Worcester Grammar School for Worcester College, Oxford.
1740	Having lost his scholarship by misbehaviour, Foote came down without a degree. Enrolled at the Inner Temple, but does not seem to have pursued any legal studies.
January 1741	Published an account of the murder of Sir John Dinely Goodere by Captain Samuel Goodere. Foote was their nephew.
6 February 1744	Acted Othello, with Macklin as Iago, at the Theatre, Haymarket. He repeated Othello at Drury Lane on 10 March.
1744–5	Acted the winter season at Smock Alley Theatre, Dublin, under Thomas Sheridan.
1745–6	Acted at Drury Lane in several comic roles.
22 April 1747	Presented *The Diversions of the Morning* as a 'Concert with Entertainment' at the Haymarket. It was stopped on 23 April, but re-opened on 24 April as 'A Dish of Chocolate'.
18 April 1748	Presented *The Diversions* at the Haymarket as 'An Auction of Paintings', for a run of thirty-six performances.
3 April 1749	*The Knights* (two-act comedy) at the Haymarket.
1749–53	On the receipt of a large inheritance, Foote left for an extended continental tour, until he had exhausted the fortune.
11 January 1752	*Taste* (a reworking of *The Diversions* in two acts) presented at Drury Lane.
24 March 1753	*The Englishman in Paris* (two-act comedy) as Charles Macklin's benefit at Covent Garden.
30 October 1753	Foote returned to Drury Lane to act Buck in *The Englishman in Paris*.
December 1754	Waged a satirical campaign against Macklin's 'British

	Inquisition', a course of lectures and demonstrations at Macklin's coffee-house in Hart Street.
16 December 1754	Foote presented *A Writ of Inquiry on the Inquisitor General* at the Haymarket.
1755–6	Engaged to act at Covent Garden, and presented *The Englishman Returned from Paris* (two-act farce, 3 February 1756).
1756–7	Engaged at Drury Lane, and presented *The Author* (two-act comedy, 5 February 1757).
1758	Engaged at Smock Alley, Dublin. Tate Wilkinson acted with him for the first time.
1758–9	Engaged at Drury Lane, where he and Wilkinson first performed the 'Rehearsal' act II of *The Diversions*, as Puzzle and Bounce (17 October 1758).
18 December 1758	*The Author* banned by the Lord Chamberlain, at the request of Mr Apreece, who had been caricatured as Cadwallader.
9 November 1759	Before leaving for Dublin, Foote read part of *The Minor* at a 'Comic Lecture' at the Haymarket. In these 'Lectures' he caricatured most of the leading actors of the day.
28 January 1760	Presented *The Minor* (two-act version) at Crow Street Theatre, Dublin. Wilkinson pirated the play for Smock Alley.
28 July 1760	Expanded *The Minor* to three acts for the Haymarket; it ran for thirty-five performances.
25 October 1760	Acted in *The Minor* for Garrick at Drury Lane. Wilkinson acted it in rivalry at Covent Garden from 24 November 1760.
July–August 1761	Foote and Murphy hired Drury Lane for a summer season of comedies. Each were supposed to provide three new plays, Foote provided none.
1761–2	Engaged at Covent Garden, and presented *The Lyar* (three-act comedy, 12 January 1762).
1762–66	Foote presented a regular summer season at the Haymarket, taking winter engagements in Dublin. His new plays were *The Orators* (three-act entertainment, 1 May 1762) *The Mayor of Garrett* (two-act comedy, 20 June 1763), *The Patron* (three-act comedy, 13 June 1764) and *The Commissary* (three-act comedy, 10 June 1765).
January 1766	Leg amputated after a horse-riding accident at Methly, near Leeds, the home of Lord Mexborough. By 18 June

	he was back on stage acting in *The Minor* at the Hay-market.
5 July 1766	At the instigation of the Duke of York, who had been present at Foote's accident, he was granted a royal patent to present, during his lifetime, a summer season (15 May to 15 September) at the Haymarket. Foote now bought the theatre building and increased his company of actors (nineteen in 1765 to thirty-seven in 1767). He engaged such stars as Barry (1767), Thomas Sheridan (1769), Woodward (1771) and Bannister (1774), to perform in tragedy and regular comedy.
29 May 1767	*An Occasional Prologue, in Prose-Laconic* to open the refurbished Haymarket Theatre.
1767–76	Foote alternated his regular summer season with winter engagements in Dublin and Edinburgh, no longer appearing, even occasionally, at Drury Lane or Covent Garden.
30 May 1768	*The Devil upon Two Sticks* (three-act comedy).
21 June 1769	Contributed scenes to Isaac Bickerstaffe's *Dr Last in his Chariot*.
1769	Published *Wilkes, an Oratorio*. Not written for performance, but a literary satire against John Wilkes and the radical 'Patriots'.
22 June 1770	*The Lame Lover* (three-act comedy).
26 June 1771	*The Maid of Bath* (three-act comedy).
1772	The stage of the Haymarket Theatre was enlarged for the performance of pantomimes and other scenic entertainments. By 1772 the company numbered fifty-one and Foote presented fifty-six performances over the summer.
29 June 1772	*The Nabob* (three-act comedy).
21 June 1773	*The Bankrupt* (three-act comedy).
23 August 1773	*Piety in Pattens*, part of 'The Primitive Puppet Show', originally presented in February 1773.
15 July 1774	*The Cozeners* (three-act comedy).
August 1775	*A Trip to Calais* (three-act comedy) was banned by the Lord Chamberlain, at the request of the Duchess of Kingston, at this time on trial for bigamy, as she was to be 'taken off' as Lady Kitty Crocodile.
19 August 1776	*The Capuchin* (three-act comedy) 'altered from *A Trip to Calais*'. Foiled in his attack on Lady Kingston, Foote, in this play, caricatured her private secretary, Jackson, an Irish Priest, as Dr Viper. Jackson's own revenge was

to encourage Foote's dismissed coachman to bring a charge of homosexual assault against him.

With the legal aid of Arthur Murphy as his barrister and character references from 'persons of the very first respectability', including two royal dukes, several noblemen, Sir Joshua Reynolds and Edmund Burke, Foote was acquitted. However the case jeopardised his popularity and broke his health.

16 January 1777	Sold the Haymarket Theatre to George Colman, who continued the summer seasons under an annual licence from the Lord Chamberlain, Foote's patent rights being personal to himself.
May–July 1777	Foote made his final appearances at the Haymarket, his last being in *The Maid of Bath*, 30 July 1777.
21 October 1777	Died at the Ship Inn, Dover, on his way to France for convalescence after a stroke.

Buried in Westminster Abbey.

Arthur Murphy

27 December 1727	Arthur Murphy born in Roscommon, Western Ireland, son of Richard Murphy, a Dublin merchant, and Jane, daughter of Arthur French, landowner.
1729	Richard Murphy lost at sea, *en route* to Philadelphia.
1735	Jane Murphy, with her sons James and Arthur, moved to London.
1736–44	Arthur Murphy was a scholar at the English Jesuit College of St Omer, near Boulogne.
1747	Employed as a clerk by his uncle, Jeffrey French, a merchant of Cork.
1749	Having refused to sail to Jamaica for his uncle, Murphy returned to London as a bookkeeper for a company of bankers.
July 1752	Probably started contributions to Henry Fielding's *Covent Garden Journal*.
21 October 1752	Started his own column, the 'Gray's Inn Journal', in the *New Craftsman*.
29 September 1753–September 1754	Edited the *Gray's Inn Journal* as an independent periodical.
January 1754	Submitted his first play, *The Young Apprentice*, to Garrick for performance at Drury Lane. Although accepted for the 1754 season, it was not performed while Murphy was at Covent Garden. Contributed a prologue

	to Samuel Foote's *The Knights* (1 April 1754, Drury Lane).
October 1754– May 1755	Enrolled, on Foote's advice, as an actor at Covent Garden. He took over several of Spranger Barry's roles, including Othello, and Jaffier in *Venice Preserved*.
September 1755– May 1756	Enrolled as an actor at Drury Lane, playing fewer leading roles.
2 January 1756	*The Apprentice* (two-act farce) performed at Drury Lane. Also in January he published *The Spouter, or the Triple Revenge* (two-act farce), which included caricatures of Garrick, Rich, Foote and Theophilus Cibber. It was not performed.
3 April 1756	Performed *Englishman from Paris* (two-act farce) for his benefit at Drury Lane. It was designed as a sequel to Foote's *The Englishman in Paris*, but Foote produced his own sequel, *The Englishman Return'd from Paris* (24 March 1756, Covent Garden). Murphy's play was never published.
November 1756– July 1757	Gave up acting and returned to journalism. He edited *The Test*, a political weekly in support of Henry Fox and against the war policy of William Pitt the Elder.
1757–8	'The Theatre' contributions to the *London Chronicle* set a new standard in journalistic dramatic criticism.
June 1757	Finally decided on a legal career, refused by the Middle Temple and Gray's Inn on the grounds of his being an actor, but the influence of Henry Fox gained him admittance to Lincoln's Inn.
30 March 1758	*The Upholsterer* (two-act farce) performed at Drury Lane.
21 April 1759	*The Orphan of China* (five-act tragedy, after Voltaire) performed at Drury Lane. Published with a dedication to Lord Bute, tutor to the Prince of Wales, who became King George III in 1760. Bute became Prime Minister in 1762.
24 January 1760	*The Desert Island* (three-act poetical tragi-comedy) performed with *The Way to Keep Him* (three-act afterpiece), at Drury Lane. At about this time his five-act comedy *The Man Does Not Know His Own Mind* was submitted to Garrick, but refused.
10 January 1761	*The Way to Keep Him* expanded to five acts and performed at Drury Lane.
June–August 1761	With Foote, who had been refused his usual Haymarket summer licence, Murphy rented Drury Lane to present

a season of comedies. These included his *All In The Wrong* (five-act comedy) 15 June 1761, *The Citizen* (three-act farce) and *The Old Maid* (two-act farce), both on 2 July 1761.

1761   Murphy and Garrick argued over the terms on which the summer plays would be incorporated into the regular Drury Lane repertoire, and by December Garrick had opened negotiations with George Colman, whose *The Jealous Wife* had met with great success that season, and from 1761 Colman replaced Murphy as the chief Drury Lane dramatist.

11 June 1761   Published a satirical *Ode to the Naiads of the Fleet Ditch* in answer to Charles Churchill's *The Rosciad*, which had included a harsh attack on Murphy's acting. The pamphlet war continued with the anonymous *Murphiad* and Murphy's poem *The Examiner* (November 1761).

1762   Prepared an edition of *The Works of Henry Fielding, with a Life of the Author*.

10 June 1762   Renewed political journalism with *The Auditor* in defence of the government under Lord Bute against the attacks of John Wilkes and Charles Churchill in the *North Briton*.

21 June 1762   Called to the bar, and from 1763 worked regularly as a barrister, particularly on the Norfolk circuit.

9 January 1764   A double bill of *No One's Enemy But His Own* (three-act comedy) and *What We Must All Come To* (two-act farce) was presented at Covent Garden but, coinciding with the prosecution of John Wilkes and *North Briton*, no. 45, Murphy's political reputation worked against him with the public, both plays were damned. With the support of a Royal Command Performance *No One's Enemy But His Own* lingered for a few performances, but *What We Must All Come To* was withdrawn, to appear some years later as *Three Weeks After Marriage*.

23 March 1765   *The Choices* (two-act farce) performed for the benefit of Mrs Yates at Covent Garden.

October 1766   *The School for Guardians* (five-act comedy) based on Wycherley's *The Country Wife* and Molière's *L'Ecole des Femmes* was written for the benefit of Murphy's mistress, Ann Elliott, an actress at Covent Garden. It was not presented until January 1767 as Garrick forestalled the play with his own play, *The Country Girl* (25 October 1766, Drury Lane).

November 1767	Isaac Bickerstaffe negotiated a reconciliation between Murphy and Garrick with the understanding that Murphy's two tragedies *Alzuma* and *Zenobia*, and his comedy *The Man Does Not Know His Own Mind* would be performed at Drury Lane.
27 February 1768	*Zenobia* (five-act tragedy) performed at Drury Lane, with Spranger Barry and Mrs Dancer in the leading roles. There was further altercation between Murphy and Garrick and the other plays were put aside, while Murphy concentrated on his legal career.
1770	A new plan to stage *Alzuma* was dropped by Garrick after Hugh Kelly's *A Word To The Wise* was damned because of the author's political writing against John Wilkes, who was now in the midst of the Middlesex election affair. Garrick feared that Murphy's Tory politics would be held against him.
26 February 1772	*The Grecian Daughter* (five-act tragedy) performed at Drury Lane. This was Murphy's most successful tragedy.
23 February 1773	*Alzuma* finally presented at Covent Garden.
1774	Amongst his legal duties Murphy appeared before a House of Commons Committee concerned with a new copyright bill. It failed to become law.
1776	Murphy represented Foote in his sensational trial for indecent assault. They achieved an acquittal.
30 March 1776	*Three Weeks After Marriage* was presented at Covent Garden. This was *What We Must All Come To*, which had been damned in 1764, under a new title. This time it was extremely successful.
2 February 1777	*Know Your Own Mind* (five-act comedy) performed at Covent Garden. Garrick, who had refused the original version in 1761, and again in 1764 and 1772, provided an epilogue. This was the last important play by Murphy and it was overshadowed by Sheridan's *School for Scandal* (8 May 1777, Drury Lane), which 'improved' on several elements in Murphy's play.
1783	Wrote *The Rival Sisters* for Sarah Siddons, but it was not performed at this time.
1787	Having failed to be appointed a King's Counsel, despite his past government support and his being the senior barrister on the Norfolk circuit since 1783, Murphy quitted the bar and left his Lincoln's Inn chambers. This was perhaps linked with an intention of returning to the

	theatre as a dramatist for John Palmer's ill-fated Royalty Theatre venture.
20 June 1787	The Royalty opened with *As You Like It* and Garrick's *Miss in her Teens*. It was forced to close immediately for infringing the patent houses' monopoly of legitimate drama. It reopened on 3 July as a burletta theatre. Murphy wrote an opening address, two prologues and a poetical satire, *A Tale from Baker's Chronicle*, for Palmer.
10 September 1787	*Almirina*, a burlesque tragedy, was presented at The Royalty and ran for thirty-three performances. It has been attributed to Murphy, but the script has not survived.
15 April 1788	The House of Commons rejected Palmer's petition against the patent house monopoly. It had been drawn up by Murphy and signed by 'several thousands'.
1792	Published a new edition of Johnson's works with an *Essay on the Life and Genius of Samuel Johnson*.
1793	Edited Charles Macklin's plays, to be sold by subscription for the benefit of the now aged actor.
16 November 1793	*The Rival Sisters* (five-act tragedy) written in 1783, was finally performed at Drury Lane for Sarah Siddons's benefit.
1794	Published a translation of *The Works of Tacitus*, on which he had been working for several years.
1795	Lord Chancellor Loughborough reappointed Murphy to the commissionership of bankruptcies, which he had resigned in 1787. This was a virtual sinecure and was generally considered to be a reward for Murphy's political journalism over the years on behalf of the Tories.
1798	Published a five-act 'closet tragedy' *Arminius*, which was a polemic attack on the French Revolutionary Jacobins.
1801	Published his *Life of David Garrick*.
18 January 1805	Died at his home in Knightsbridge, and was buried at St Paul's, Hammersmith.
1811	Dr Jesse Foot, who had attended Murphy in his later years, published his *Life of Arthur Murphy*, which included a brief autobiographical sketch, completed by Murphy shortly before his death.

NOTE ON THE TEXTS

In collating the texts for this edition I have not followed the strict scholarly practice of reproducing either the earliest or the latest versions of the plays. My guiding principle has been to provide the most stageworthy version, always bearing in mind that it is easier for a director to cut than to dig out extra material from early and obscure editions. As a rule, therefore, I have tried to include as much text as possible, ignoring the cuts of later editions, whilst including their added dialogue. However, a comparison of versions does seem to indicate that in details of phraseology and punctuation, it is the earlier versions, particularly the manuscripts as submitted to the Licenser (now in the Henry E. Huntington Library, San Marino, California), which are more actable than the versions which appeared in print. This is particularly true of the plays of Arthur Murphy, who, as an established literary author of essays, poems and classical translations, felt it necessary to tidy up his scripts for a reading public. As well as regularising the grammar of his plays, sometimes at the expense of their colloquial spontaneity, he also tended to polish up the sentiments and aphorisms he had given to his characters. As, in this respect, twentieth-century taste differs considerably from that of the reading public of the later eighteenth, I have usually stayed with his first thoughts, which, although the differences may be very slight indeed, do tend to demonstrate the conversational ease and liveliness for which Murphy was praised by his contemporary critics. Foote was obviously less jealous of his literary reputation, and there is so little pattern in the variations I have found between different editions, that I am tempted to conclude that he left matters of punctuation to the printer. In his case, therefore, I have adopted twentieth-century usage, using the full stop and the comma, where the eighteenth century tended to rely on the colon and the dash.

The Minor by Samuel Foote

The present text follows that of the 1760 third edition, in three acts, which was submitted by Garrick to the Examiner of Plays and endorsed by him 'As it is now acted at the New Theatre in the Haymarket' (Larpent manuscript no. 177). This text is virtually the same as that in Bee's edition of *The Works* (1830) and in Inchbald's *London Stage* (1808). However the Examiner's copy indicates that he demanded the deletion of certain words and sentences, sometimes suggesting acceptable alternatives, and it was presumably with these amendments that the play was performed at the patent houses. The reasons why these passages were considered objectionable is discussed in the Introduction, but listed here are the alterations demanded by the Examiner:

    1.   Delete six 'damns' from the Prologue.

2. Delete Loader's two references to the Baron as 'a son of a bitch'.
3. Delete examples of Methodist cant or jargon.
   (a) Delete, 'SIR GEORGE: No bad scheme, Dick. Thou hast a fine, sober, psalm-singing countenance, and, when thou hast been some time in their trammels, may'st make as able a teacher as the best of 'em.
   DICK: Lord, sir, I want learning.
   SIR GEORGE: Oh the spirit, the spirit will supply that, Dick, never fear' (p. 59).
   (b) Delete, 'MRS COLE: But for him I had been a lost sheep; never known the comforts of the new birth, no' (p. 61).
   (c) Delete, 'MRS COLE: Her time is not come. All shall have their call, as Mr Squintum says, sooner or later. Regeneration is not the work of a day, No, no, no.' Substitute, 'All will come to it sooner or later, as Mr Squintum says, Reformation is not the work of a day. No, no, no' (p. 62).
   (d) Delete, 'MRS COLE: The good gentleman piloted me into the harbour of grace'. Substitute, 'Piloted me into harbour' (p. 63).
   (e) Delete, 'MRS COLE: He was the precious instrument of my spiritual sprinkling' (p. 63).
   (f) Delete, 'MRS COLE: I was wished to Mr Squintum, who stept in with his saving grace, got me with the new birth, and I became, as you see, regenerate and another creature.' Substitute, 'I was wished to Mr Squintum, and I became, as you see, a new creature' (p. 63).
   (g) Delete, 'SIR GEORGE: With what ease she reconciles her new birth to her old calling' (p. 64).
4. Delete Lucy's phrase in act III, 'By all that's holy' (p. 73).
5. The most damaging cut of all, the deletion of Squintum's pathetic story of the mother and child from the Epilogue (eleven lines from 'With labour, toil . . . ' to 'Why Providence an't dead') and five lines from the end, beginning 'Think you to meet with side-boxes above?' These cuts rendered the whole Epilogue unperformable and Foote never delivered it at Drury Lane.

The Nabob by Samuel Foote

There is little difference between the original Larpent manuscript (no. 335) of 1772, the first printed edition of 1778, and the Bee edition of *The Works* (1830). However, there are some lines in the manuscript for Sir John and Lady Oldham which I have included as they seem to make the first act rather more lively by increasing both her arrogance and his complacency, whilst making it clearer than in the printed editions that Sir John was content to accept Sir Matthew Mite's 'treaty', as his understanding of their financial plight was better than his wife's. The only other differences are in the names of some of the minor characters, and here I have followed *The Works*.

The Citizen by Arthur Murphy

As *The Citizen* was first performed as part of the 1761 Murphy/Foote summer season, there is no Larpent manuscript to indicate its original form. Indeed the first printed edition was not of the three acts which were performed on 2 July at Drury Lane, but of the two-act afterpiece version which was played on the last night of the season, 8 August, following Murphy's *All in the Wrong*. The present text has been prepared by comparing the first edition of 1763, 'as it is performed at the Theatre Royal, Covent Garden', and Murphy's final version in *The Works* (7 vols., London, 1786). In fact the only differences are in punctuation, and, as explained above, I have tended to follow the earlier version, as being more theatrical.

Three Weeks After Marriage by Arthur Murphy

As this play started life as *What We Must All Come To* in 1764, when it was damned, and was not revived under its new title until 1776, the present text has proved rather problematic. It has been collated from the manuscript of *What We Must All Come To* (Larpent manuscript no. 231), the first printed edition of *Three Weeks After Marriage* (G. Kearsley, 1776), *The Works of Arthur Murphy* (7 vols., 1786) and the versions in the collections of Inchbald (1808) and Oxberry (1820), both of which are supposed to have been taken from the Theatre Royal prompt copies. There are considerable differences between them all, the extremes being the manuscript of *What We Must All Come To* and the version in *The Works*. Some phrases were introduced to echo the new title; more play was made of Drugget's gardening humour; and a few specific references were made more generalised, for instance 'Fulham Road' became 'The London Road'. Murphy also regularised the text for a reading public, so that certain phrases and sentiments were made more literary or decorous. As these might seem rather stilted in the mouth of an actor, I have tended to retain the more colloquial usage of the earlier versions. However, on the principle that a director can always cut, and also because of its intrinsic merit, I have included the new material that Murphy added to the play for *The Works*, even though, on the evidence of the Inchbald and Oxberry editions, it might never have been part of the acting script. These passages extend the most lively episodes of the play, the arguments between Sir Charles and Lady Racket. There is more abuse, a more complicated explanation of the card game – in the original the claims that each partner made were in fact inconsistent – and, above all, a new piece of business at the end of act I in which the couple exit and reappear using the opposite proscenium doors. This last is a nicely theatrical idea, whereas most of Murphy's alterations for *The Works* usually made the text more literary. It would seem, from the Oxberry acting edition, that Nancy's songs were normally cut in performance, but, although the convention does seem rather contrived, I have retained them in this edition.

Know Your Own Mind by Arthur Murphy

Although Murphy probably revised *Know Your OwnMind* considerably from the time he first submitted it to Garrick in 1764 and its performance thirteen years later, we can only consider the changes he made between the earliest extant text, which was that submitted to the Licenser in 1777 (Larpent manuscript no. 425), the first printed edition of 1778, and the version published in *The Works*. Although some changes have been adopted from the 1778 and 1786 editions, I have generally followed the Larpent manuscript, as it seems to be the most effective as an acting edition. The alterations Murphy made for *The Works* make the play more sentimental, particularly in the treatment of Miss Neville, who lost several bitter, even catty, remarks, and gained a few self-consciously sentimental reflections. The bustling opening scene of the servants was cut, so that the play started with the moral argument between Sir John and Mr Bygrove on the education of their sons. The character of Trinket disappeared, and with her the farcical scene in which Bygrove mistakes the servant for her mistress. Both these servant scenes were obviously more effective in performance than read on the page, and in each case I have followed the original version. Their excision may very well reflect the critical distaste for 'low' comedy, against which Goldsmith took particular exception, when *She Stoops To Conquer* was criticised in 1773 for being too 'low'.

However, there are some additions which Murphy made in the 1778 edition, which might have been added during the rehearsal period, and which ought to be incorporated into a definitive text. Firstly there were the new 'characters' of Sir Volatile Vainlove and Jack Spinbrain, whom Dashwould described in act II, without which Lady Bell would seem to eclipse Dashwould as the chief scandalmonger of the scene. Secondly, Murphy clarified the plot between Malvil and La Rouge, by including the scene in act II when Malvil reserves the *appartement* in La Rouge's lodgings, and by Malvil citing Dashwould, rather than Mrs Bromley, as the authority for Sir Harry's reputation as a womaniser.

A final difference is that Sir Harry Lizard was renamed Lovewit in 1778, a minor emendment, but one which contributes to the general impression that the reading version of the play was rather more genteel, even genial, than the original version as presented on the stage.

THE MINOR

A comedy

by SAMUEL FOOTE

Tantum Religio potuit suadere Malorum

First performed in a two-act version at Crow Street Theatre, Dublin, on 28 January 1760; first performed in a three-act version at the Haymarket Theatre, on 28 July 1760, with the following cast:

The introduction	
FOOTE	Mr Foote
SMART	Mr Smith
CANKER	Mr Misdale
PEARSE	Mr Pearse
The play	
SIR WILLIAM WEALTHY	Mr Baddeley
MR RICHARD WEALTHY	Mr Hyde
SIR GEORGE WEALTHY	Mr Shaw
SHIFT	Mr Foote
LOADER	Mr Davis
DICK	Mr Weston
TRANSFER	Mr Blakey
MRS COLE	Mr Foote
LUCY	Miss Burden

SCENE: At first the theatre; subsequently, the scene is laid at some coffee-house nearby.

Tantum Religio: 'Religion could persuade men to so much evil', Lucretius, Book I, 45.
Mr Shaw: for 28 July 1760 only, subsequent billing: 'Mr Smith'.

1 Foote as Mrs Cole in *The Minor* at the Haymarket, 1760

To his Grace
WILLIAM DUKE OF DEVONSHIRE,
Lord Chamberlain of his Majesty's Household

MY LORD,

The Minor, who is indebted for his appearance on *the stage* to your Grace's indulgence, begs leave to desire your further protection, at his entering into *the world*.

Though the allegiance due from the whole dramatic people to your Grace's station, might place this address in the light of a *natural tribute*; yet, my Lord, I should not have taken that liberty with the Duke of Devonshire, if I could not, at the same time, plead some little *utility* in the design of my piece; and add, that the public approbation has stamped a value on the execution.

The law, which threw the stage under the absolute government of a lord chamberlain, could not fail to fill the minds of all the objects of that power with very gloomy apprehensions; they found themselves (through their own licentiousness, it must be confessed) in a more precarious dependent state, than any other of his Majesty's subjects. But, when their direction was lodged in the hands of a nobleman, whose ancestors had so successfully struggled for national liberty, they ceased to fear for their own. It was not from a *patron of the liberal arts* they were to expect an oppressor; it was not from the friend of freedom, and of man, they were to dread partial monopolies or the establishment of petty tyrannies.

Their warmest wishes are accomplished; none of their rights have been invaded, except what, without the first poetic authority, I should not venture to call a right – the *jus nocendi*.

Your tenderness, my Lord, for all the followers of *the muses*, has been in no instance more conspicuous than in your late favour to me, the meanest of their train; your Grace has thrown open (for those who are denied admittance into the palaces of *Parnassus*) a cottage on its borders, where the unhappy migrants may be, if not magnificently, at least, hospitably entertained.

I shall detain your Grace no longer, than just to echo the public voice, that, for the honour, progress, and perfection of letters, your Grace may long continue their candid *censor*, who have always been their generous *protector*.

I have the honour, my Lord, to be, with the greatest respect and gratitude,

> Your Grace's must dutiful,
>> most obliged
>>> and obedient servant,
>>> SAMUEL FOOTE

Ellestre, July 8, 1760

---

jus nocendi: the right to harm.

INTRODUCTION

Enter CANKER *and* SMART.

SMART: But are you sure he has leave?

CANKER: Certain.

SMART: I am damned glad on't. For now we shall have a laugh either with him, or at him. It does not signify which.

CANKER: Not a farthing.

SMART: Do you know his scheme?

CANKER: Not I. But is not the door of the Little Theatre open?

SMART: Yes. Who is that fellow that seems to stand sentry there?

CANKER: By his tattered garb and meagre visage, he must be one of the troop.

SMART: I'll call him. Hello, mister – (*Enter* PEARSE.) What, is there anything going on over the way?

PEARSE: A rehearsal.

SMART: Of what?

PEARSE: A new piece.

SMART: Foote's?

PEARSE: Yes.

CANKER: Is he there?

PEARSE: He is.

SMART: 'Zounds, let's go and see what he is about.

CANKER: With all my heart.

SMART: Come along, then. (*Exeunt.*)

        (*Enter* FOOTE *and an* ACTOR.)

FOOTE: Sir, this will never do! You must get rid of your high notes and country cant. Oh, 'tis the true strolling . . .

        (*Enter* SMART *and* CANKER.)

SMART: Ha, ha, ha! What, hard at it, my boy! – Here's your old friend Canker and I come for a peep. Well, and hey, what is your plan?

FOOTE: Plan?

SMART: Ay, what are your characters? Give us your group. How is your cloth filled?

FOOTE: Characters?

SMART: Ay – Come, come, communicate. Why, man, we will lend thee a lift. I have a damned fine original for thee; an aunt of my own, just come from the North, with the true Newcastle burr in her throat; and a nose and a chin! – I am afraid she is not well enough known, but I have a remedy for that. I'll bring her the first night of your piece, place her in a conspicuous station, and whisper the secret to the whole house. That will be damned fine, won't it?

FOOTE: Oh, delicious!

SMART: But don't name me. For, if she smokes me for the author, I shall be dashed out of her codicil in a hurry.

FOOTE: Oh, never fear me. But I should think your uncle Tom a better character.

---

the Little Theatre: the Haymarket.

SMART: What, the politician?

FOOTE: Ay; he that every day, after dinner, as soon as the cloth is removed, fights the battle of Minden, batters the French with cherry-stones, and pursues 'em to the banks of the Rhine in a stream of spilt port.

SMART: Oh, damn it, he'll *do*.

FOOTE: Or, what do you say to your father-in-law, Sir Timothy, who, though as broken-winded as a Hounslow post-horse, is eternally chanting Venetian ballads? *Kata tora cara highlia.*

SMART: Admirable! By heavens! – Have you got 'em?

FOOTE: No.

SMART: Then in with 'em my boy.

FOOTE: Not one.

SMART: Prithee why not?

FOOTE: Why, lookee, Smart; though you are, in the language of the world, my friend, yet there is one thing you, I am sure, love better than anybody.

SMART: What's that?

FOOTE: Mischief.

SMART: No, prithee –

FOOTE: How, now, I am sure that you, who so readily give up your relations, may not have some design upon *me*?

SMART: I don't understand you.

FOOTE: Why, as soon as my characters begin to circulate a little successfully, my mouth is stopped in a minute, by the clamour of your relations: 'Oh, damme – 'tis a shame – it should not be – people of distinction brought upon the stage!' And so, out of compliment to your cousins, I am to be beggared for treating the public with the follies of your family, at your own request.

SMART: How can you think I would be such a dog? What the devil, then, are we to have nothing personal? Give us the actors, however.

FOOTE: Oh, that's stale. Besides, I think they have, of all men, the best right to complain.

SMART: How so?

FOOTE: Because, by rendering them ridiculous in their profession, you, at the same time, injure their pockets. Now, as to the other gentry, they have, providentially, something besides their understanding to rely on, and the only injury they can receive is that the whole town is then diverted with what was before only the amusement of private parties.

CANKER: Give us then a national portrait: a Scotchman or an Irishman.

FOOTE: If you mean merely the dialect of the two countries, I cannot think it either a subject of satire or of humour. It is an accidental unhappiness, for which a man is no more accountable than for the colour of his hair. Now, affectation I take to be the true comic object. If indeed a North Briton, struck with a scheme of refor-

---

battle of Minden: a British victory over the French in 1759, the Seven Years' War.

mation, should advance from the banks of the Tweed to teach the English the true pronunciation of their own language, he would, I think merit your laughter; nor would a Dublin mechanic, who, from heading the liberty-boys in a skirmish on Ormond Quay, should think he has the right to prescribe military laws to the first commander in Europe, be a less ridiculous object.

SMART: Are there such?

FOOTE: If you mean that the blunders of a few peasants, or the partial principles of a single scoundrel, are to stand as characteristic marks of a whole country, your pride may produce a laugh, but, believe me, it would be at the expense of your understanding.

CANKER: Heyday, what a system is here! Laws for laughing! And pray, sage sir, instruct us when may we laugh with propriety?

FOOTE: At an old beau, a superannuated beauty, a military coward, a stuttering orator, or a gouty dancer. In short, whoever affects to be what he is not, or strives to be what he cannot be, is an object worthy of the poet's pen, and your mirth.

SMART: Psha! I don't know what you mean by your is nots and cannots – damned abstruse jargon, eh, Canker?

CANKER: Well, but if you will not give us persons, let us have things. Treat us with a modern amour, and a state intrigue, or a . . .

FOOTE: And so amuse the public ear at the expense of private peace. You must excuse me.

CANKER: And with these principles, you expect to thrive on the spot?

SMART: No, no, it won't do. I tell thee the plain roast and boiled of the theatres will never do at this table. We must have high seasoned ragouts and rich sauces.

FOOTE: Why, perhaps, by way of dessert, I may produce something that may hit your palate.

SMART: Your bill of fare?

FOOTE: What think you of one of those itinerant field orators, who, although at declared enmity with common sense, have the address to poison the principles, and at the same time pick the pockets of half our industrious fellow subjects?

CANKER: Have a care. Dangerous ground. *Ludere cum sacris*, you know.

FOOTE: Now, I look upon it in a different manner. I consider those gentlemen in the light of public performers, like myself, and whether we exhibit at Tottenhamcourt or at the Haymarket, our purpose is the same, and the place is immaterial.

CANKER: Why, indeed, if it be considered . . .

FOOTE: Nay, more, I must beg leave to assert that ridicule is the only antidote against this pernicious poison. This is a madness that argument can never cure, and, should a little wholesome severity be applied, 'persecution' would be the immediate cry. Where, then, can we have recourse, but to the comic muse?

---

teach the English: a jibe at either Charles Macklin or Thomas Sheridan, who, although Irish, gave lectures on Elocution. Sheridan's were published in 1762.
Ormond Quay: 1759 had seen violent rioting in Dublin as a preliminary to the emergence of the Catholic 'Whiteboys' in the 1760s. *The Minor* was first performed in Dublin at the Crow St Theatre, 28 January 1760.
field orators: outdoor preachers such as Whitefield or Wesley.
Ludere cum sacris: to sport with the sacred.

Perhaps, the archness and severity of her smile may redress an evil that the laws cannot reach or reason reclaim.

CANKER: Why, if it does not cure those already distempered, it may be a means of stopping the infection.

SMART: But how is your scheme conducted?

FOOTE: Of that you may judge. We are just going upon a repetition of the piece. I should be glad to have your opinion.

SMART: We will gladly give it you.

FOOTE: One indulgence: as you are Englishmen, I think I need not beg that, as from necessity most of my performers are new, you will allow for their inexperience, and encourage their timidity.

SMART: Nought but reasonable.

FOOTE: Come then, prompter, begin.

PEARSE: Lord, sir, we are at a stand.

FOOTE: What's the matter?

PEARSE: Mrs O'Schohnesy has returned the part of the bawd. She says she is a gentlewoman and it would be a reflection on her family to do any such thing!

FOOTE: Indeed!

PEARSE: If it had been only a whore, says she, I should not have minded it, because no lady need be ashamed of doing that.

FOOTE: Well, there is no help for it; but these gentlemen must not be disappointed. Well, I'll do the character myself.

ACT I

SIR WILLIAM WEALTHY *and* MR RICHARD WEALTHY.

SIR WILLIAM: Come, come, brother, I know the world. People who have their attention eternally fixed upon one object cannot help being a little narrow in their notions.

RICHARD: A sagacious remark that, and highly probable that we merchants, who maintain a constant correspondence with the four quarters of the world, should know less of it than your fashionable fellows, whose whole experience is bounded by Westminster Bridge.

SIR WILLIAM: Nay, brother, as a proof that I am not blind to the benefit of travelling, George, you know, has been in Germany these four years.

RICHARD: Where he is well grounded in gaming and gluttony. France has furnished him with fawning and flattery; Italy equipped him with capriols and cantatas: and thus accomplished, my young gentleman is returned with a cargo of whores, cooks, valet de chambre, and fiddlesticks, a most valuable member of the British commonwealth.

SIR WILLIAM: You dislike, then, my system of education?

RICHARD: Most sincerely.

SIR WILLIAM: The whole?

---

most of my performers: the playbills for 28 July, advertising *The Minor* at the Haymarket, announced 'Most of the performers entirely new'.
capriols: capers, usually of horses, but here of dancing.

RICHARD: Every particular.

SIR WILLIAM: The early part, I should imagine, might merit your approbation.

RICHARD: Least of all. What, I suppose,because he has run the gauntlet through a public school, where, at sixteen, he had practised more vices than he would otherwise have heard of at sixty.

SIR WILLIAM: Ha, ha, prejudice!

RICHARD: Then, indeed, you removed him to the university, where, lest his morals should be mended, and his understanding improved, you fairly set him free from the restraint of the one and the drudgery of the other, by the privileged distinction of a silk gown and a velvet cap.

SIR WILLIAM: And all these evils, you think, a city education would have prevented?

RICHARD: Doubtless. – Proverbs, proverbs, brother William, convey wholesome instruction. Idleness is the root of all evil. Regular hours, constant employment and good example cannot fail to form the mind.

SIR WILLIAM: Why truly brother, had you stuck to your old civic vices, hypocrisy, cozenage and avarice, I don't know whether I might not have committed George to your care, but you cockneys now beat us suburbians at our own weapons. What, old boy, times are changed since the date of thy indentures, when the sleek, crop-eared prentice used to dangle after his mistress, with the great bible under his arm, to St Bride's on a Sunday, bring home the text, repeat the divisions of the discourse, dine at twelve, and regale, upon a gaudy day, with buns and beer at Islington or Mile End.

RICHARD: Wonderfully facetious!

SIR WILLIAM: Our modern lads are of a different metal. They have their gaming-clubs in the Garden, their little lodgings, the snug depositories of their rusty swords, and occasional bag-wigs, their horses for the turf, ay, and their commissions of bankruptcy too before they are well out of their time.

RICHARD: Infamous aspersion!

SIR WILLIAM: But the last meeting at Newmarket, Lord Lofty received at the hazard table the identical note from the individual tailor to whom he had paid it but the day before for a new set of liveries.

RICHARD: Invention!

SIR WILLIAM: These are anecdotes you will never meet with in your weekly travels from Cateaton Street to your boarded box in Clapham, brother.

RICHARD: And yet that boarded box, as your prodigal spendthrift proceeds, will soon be the only seat of the family.

SIR WILLIAM: Maybe not. Who knows what a reformation our project may produce!

RICHARD: I do. None at all.

SIR WILLIAM: Why so?

RICHARD: Because your means are so ill-proportioned to their ends. Were he my son, I would serve him . . .

---

silk gown and velvet cap: the privileged distinction of aristocratic undergraduates.
crop-eared: the short hair style typical of citizens, cf. the seventeenth-century 'Roundheads'.
gaudy day: the annual reunion festivities of a college or similar institution.
bankruptcy . . . out of their time: the premature declaration of bankruptcy to avoid the payment of debts.

SIR WILLIAM: As you have done your daughter. Discard him. But consider, I have but one.

RICHARD: That would weigh nothing with me, for, were Charlotte to set up a will of her own, and reject the man of my choice, she must expect to share the fate of her sister. I consider families as a smaller kind of kingdoms, and would have disobedience in the one as severely punished as rebellion in the other: cut off both from their respective societies.

SIR WILLIAM: Poor Lucy! But surely you begin to relent. Mayn't I intercede?

RICHARD: Lookye, brother, you know my mind. I will be absolute. If I meddle with the management of your son, it is at your own request, but if, directly or indirectly, you interfere with my banishment of that wilful, headstrong, disobedient hussy, all ties between us are broken, and I shall no more remember you as a brother than I do her as a child.

SIR WILLIAM: I have done. But to return. You think there is a probability in my plan?

RICHARD: I shall attend the issue.

SIR WILLIAM: You will lend your aid, however?

RICHARD: We shall see how you go on.
> (*Enter* SERVANT.)

SERVANT: A letter, sir.

SIR WILLIAM: Oh, from Capias, my attorney. Who brought it?

SERVANT: The person is without, sir.

SIR WILLIAM: Bid him wait. (*Exit* SERVANT. SIR WILLIAM *reads*.)
> 'Worthy sir,
>> The bearer is the person I promised to procure. I thought it was proper for you to examine him *in viva voce*. So, if you administer a few interrogatories, you will find, my cross-questioning him, whether he is a competent person to prosecute the cause you wot of. I wish you a speedy issue, and as there can be no default in your judgement, am of the opinion it should be carried into immediate execution. I am,
>> Worthy sir, etc.
>> TIMOTHY CAPIAS.
> P.S. The party's name is Samuel Shift. He is an admirable mime, or mimic, and most delectable company, as we experience every Tuesday night at our club, The Magpie and Horseshoe, Fetter Lane.'

Very methodical indeed, Mr Capias! – John! (*Enter* SERVANT.) Bid the person who brought this letter walk in. (*Exit* SERVANT.) Have you any curiosity, brother?

RICHARD: Not a jot. I must to the Change. In the evening you may find me in the counting-house, or at Jonathon's. (*Exit* RICHARD WEALTHY.)

SIR WILLIAM: You shall hear from me. (*Enter* SHIFT *and* SERVANT.) Shut the door, John, and remember, I am not at home. (*Exit* SERVANT.) You came from Mr Capias?

SHIFT: I did, sir.

SIR WILLIAM: Your name, I think, is Shift?

Change: Stock Exchange.
Jonathon's: a stock broker's coffee-house in Change Alley.

SHIFT: It is, sir.

SIR WILLIAM: Did Mr Capias drop any hint of my business with you?

SHIFT: None. He only said, with his spectacles on his nose and his hand upon his chin, 'Sir William Wealthy is a respectable personage, and my client. He wants to retain you in a certain affair and will open the case and give you your brief himself. If you adhere to his instructions and carry your cause, he is generous and will discharge your bill without taxation.'

SIR WILLIAM: Ha! ha! my friend Capias to a hair! Well, sir, this is no bad specimen of your abilities. But see that the door is fast. Now, sir, you are to . . .

SHIFT: A moment's pause, if you please. You must know, Sir William, I am a pro-digious admirer of forms. Now, Mr Capias tells me that it is always the rule to administer a retaining fee before you enter upon the merits.

SIR WILLIAM: Oh, sir, I beg your pardon!

SHIFT: Not that I question your generosity, but forms you know . . .

SIR WILLIAM: No apology, I beg. But as we are to have a closer connexion, it may not be amiss, by way of introduction, to understand one another a little. Pray, sir, where was you born?

SHIFT: At my father's.

SIR WILLIAM: Hum! And what was he?

SHIFT: A gentleman.

SIR WILLIAM: What was you bred?

SHIFT: A gentleman.

SIR WILLIAM: How do you live?

SHIFT: Like a gentleman.

SIR WILLIAM: Could nothing induce you to unbosom yourself?

SHIFT: Lookye, Sir William, there is a kind of something in your countenance, a certain openness and generosity, a *je ne scai* in your manner, that I will unlock. You shall see me all.

SIR WILLIAM: You will oblige me.

SHIFT: You must know then that fortune, which frequently delights to raise the noblest structures from the simplest foundations, who from a tailor made a pope, from a gin shop an empress, and many a prime minister from nothing at all, has thought fit to raise me to my present height from the humble employment of 'Light, your honour?' – A link boy.

SIR WILLIAM: A pleasant fellow! Who were your parents?

SHIFT: I was produced, sir, by a left-handed marriage, in the language of the news-papers, between an illustrious lamp-lighter and an eminent, itinerant cat and dog butcher. 'Cat's meat, and dog's meat!' I dare say, you have heard my mother, sir. But, as to this happy pair I owe little besides my being, I shall drop them where they dropped me – in the street.

SIR WILLIAM: Proceed.

SHIFT: My first knowledge of the world I owe to a school, which has produced many a great man, the avenues of the playhouse. There, sir, leaning on my extinguished

---

link boy: before street lighting, boys would carry 'links', or flaming torches, for pedestrians or coaches.

link, I learnt dexterity from pick-pockets, connivance from constables, politics and fashions from footmen, and the art of making and breaking a promise from their masters: 'Here, sirrah, light me across the kennel.' – I hope your honour will remember poor Jack. – 'You ragged rascal, I have no half-pence; I'll pay you the next time I see you.' But, lack-a-day, sir, that time I saw as seldom as his trades-men.

SIR WILLIAM: Very well.

SHIFT: To these accomplishments from without the theatre, I must add one that I obtained within.

SIR WILLIAM: How did you gain admittance there?

SHIFT: By my merit, sir, that, like my link, threw a radiance around me. A detachment from the headquarters here took possession, in the summer, of a country corpor-ation, where I did the honours of the barn by sweeping the stage and clipping the candles. There my skill and address was so conspicuous that it procured me the same office the ensuing winter at Drury Lane, where I acquired intrepidity, the crown of all my virtues.

SIR WILLIAM: How did you obtain that?

SHIFT: By my post. For I think, sir, he that dares stand the shot of the gallery in lighting, snuffing and sweeping the first night of a new play, may bid defiance to the pillory, with all its customary compliments.

SIR WILLIAM: Some truth in that.

SHIFT: But an unlucky crab-apple, applied to my right eye by a patriot gingerbread-baker from the Borough, who would not suffer three dancers from Switzerland, because he hated the French, forced me to a precipitate retreat.

SIR WILLIAM: Poor devil!

SHIFT: Broglio and Contades have done the same. But, as it happened, like a tennis ball, I rose higher by the rebound.

SIR WILLIAM: How so?

SHIFT: My misfortune, sir, moved the compassion of one of our performers, a whimsi-cal man. He took me into his service. To him I owe what I believe will make me useful to you.

SIR WILLIAM: Explain.

SHIFT: Why, sir, my master was remarkably happy in an art, which, however dis-esteemed at present, is, by Tully, reckoned amongst the perfections of an orator – mimicry.

SIR WILLIAM: Why, you are deeply read, Mr Shift!

SHIFT: A smattering – But, as I was saying, sir, nothing came amiss to my master. Bipeds or quadrupeds, rationals or animals, from the clamour of the bar to the cackle of the barn door, from the soporific twang of the Tabernacle of Tottenham-court to the melodious bray of their long-eared brethren in Bunhillfields, all were objects of his imitation, and my attention. In a word, sir, for two whole years,

---

kennel: open drainage ditch or sewer beside the road.
dancers . . . French: In 1755, at the height of the Seven Years' War, the Swiss ballet master Noverre's *The Chinese Festival* occasioned a riot at Drury Lane as the dancers were thought to be French.
Broglio, Contades: fashionable opera singers.

under this professor, I studied and starved, impoverished my body and pampered my mind, till, thinking myself pretty nearly equal to my master, I made him one of his own bows, and set up for myself.

SIR WILLIAM: You have been successful, I hope.

SHIFT: Pretty well; I can't complain. My art, sir, is a *passe-par-tout*. I seldom want employments. (*Pulls out a pocket-book.*) Hum – hum, oh! Wednesday, at Mrs Gammut's, near Hanover Square, there, there I shall make a meal upon the Mingotti, for her ladyship is in the opera interest, but, however, I shall revenge her cause upon her rival Mattei, Sunday evening, at Lady Sustinuto's concert. Thursday, I dine upon the actors, with ten Templars, at the Mitre, in Fleet Street. Friday, I am to give the amorous parley of two intriguing cats in the gutter, with the disturbing of a hen-roost, at Mr Deputy Sugarsops, near the Monument. So, sir, you see my hands are full. In short, Sir William, there is not a buck or a turtle devoured within the bills of mortality, but there I may, if I please, stick a napkin under my chin.

SIR WILLIAM: I'm afraid, Mr Shift, I must break in a little upon your engagements, but you shall be no loser by the bargain.

SHIFT: Command me.

SIR WILLIAM: Can you be secret as well as serviceable?

SHIFT: Mute as a mackerel.

SIR WILLIAM: Come hither, then. If you betray me to my son . . .

SHIFT: Scalp me.

SIR WILLIAM: Enough. – You must know then the hopes of our family are, Mr Shift, centred in one boy.

SHIFT: And, I warrant, he is a hopeful one.

SIR WILLIAM: No interruption, I beg. George has been abroad these four years, and, from his late behaviour, I have reason to believe that had a certain event happened, which I am afraid he wished, my death . . .

SHIFT: Yes, that's natural enough.

SIR WILLIAM: Nay, pray. – There would soon be an end to an ancient and honourable family.

SHIFT: Very melancholy, indeed. But families, like besoms, will wear to the stumps and finally fret out, as you say.

SIR WILLIAM: Prithee peace for five minutes.

SHIFT: I am tongue tied.

SIR WILLIAM: Now, I have projected a scheme to prevent this calamity.

SHIFT: Ay, I should be glad to hear that.

SIR WILLIAM: I am going to tell it you.

SHIFT: Proceed.

SIR WILLIAM: George, as I have contrived it, shall experience all the misery of real ruin, without running the least risk.

Mingotti, Mattei: fashionable opera singers.
Templars: lawyers from the Inner Temple.
cats in the gutter: Foote wrote a 'cat-duet' as a finale for *The Knights* (1748); it was sung by Ned Shuter and 'Cat' Harris.
bills of mortality: the metropolitan area as defined for registering births and deaths.

SHIFT: Aye, that will be a *coup de maître*.

SIR WILLIAM: I have prevailed upon his uncle, a wealthy citizen . . .

SHIFT: I don't like a city plot.

SIR WILLIAM: I tell thee it is my own.

SHIFT: I beg pardon.

SIR WILLIAM: My brother, I say, some time since wrote him a circumstantial account of my death, upon which he is returned in full expectation of succeeding to my estate.

SHIFT: Immediately?

SIR WILLIAM: No, when at age. In about three months.

SHIFT: I understand you.

SIR WILLIAM: Now, sir, guessing into what hands my heedless boy would naturally fall on his return, I have, in a feigned character, associated myself with a set of rascals, who will spread every bait that can flatter folly, inflame extravagance, allure inexperience, or catch credulity. And when, by their means, he thinks himself reduced to the last extremity, lost even to the most distant hope . . .

SHIFT: What then?

SIR WILLIAM: Then will I step in like his guardian-angel and snatch him from per-dition. If, mortified by misery, he becomes conscious of his errors, I have saved my son, but if, on the other hand, gratitude cannot bind, nor ruin reclaim him, I will cast him out, as an alien to my blood, and trust for the support of my name and family to a remote branch.

SHIFT: Bravely resolved. But what part am I to sustain in this drama?

SIR WILLIAM: Why, George, you are to know, is already stripped of what money he could command by two sharpers, but as I never trust them out of my sight they can't deceive me.

SHIFT: Out of your sight!

SIR WILLIAM: Why, I tell thee, I am one of the knot: an adept in their science, can slip, shuffle, cog or cut with the best of 'em.

SHIFT: How do you escape your son's notice?

SIR WILLIAM: His firm persuasion of my death, with the extravagance of my disguise. – Why, I would engage to elude your penetration when I am beaued out for the baron. But of that by and by. He has recourse, after his ill success, to the *cent per cent* gentry, the usurers, for a further supply.

SHIFT: Natural enough.

SIR WILLIAM: Pray, do you know – I forgot his name, a wrinkled old fellow in a thread-bare coat? He sits every morning from twelve will two in the left corner of Lloyd's coffee-house, and every evening from five till eight under the clock at the Temple Exchange.

SHIFT: What, little Transfer, the broker!

SIR WILLIAM: The same. Do you know him?

SHIFT: Know him! Ay, rot him! It was but last Easter Tuesday he had me turned out at a feast, at the Leathersellers' Hall, for singing 'Room for Cuckolds', like a parrot, and vowed it meant a reflection upon the whole body corporate.

SIR WILLIAM: You have reason to remember him.

SHIFT: Yes, yes, I recommended a minor to him myself, for the loan only of fifty pounds, and would you believe it, as I hope to be saved, we dined, supped and wetted five-and-thirty guineas upon tick, in meetings at the Crosskeys, in order to settle the terms, and after all, the scoundrel would not lend us a stiver.

SIR WILLIAM: Could you personate him?

SHIFT: Him! Oh, you shall see me shift into his shamble in a minute: and with a withered face, a bit of a purple nose, a cautionary stammer, and a sleek silver head, I would undertake to deceive even his banker. But, to speak the truth, I have a friend that can do this inimitably well. Have not you something of more consequence for me?

SIR WILLIAM: I have. Could not you, Master Shift, assume another shape? You have attended auctions.

SHIFT: Auctions! A constant puff. Deep in the mystery; a professed connoisseur, from a Niger to a nautilus, from the Apollo Belvidere to a butterfly.

SIR WILLIAM: One of those insinuating, oily orators, I will get you to personate, for we must have the plate and jewels in our possession, or they will soon fall into other hands.

SHIFT: I will do it.

SIR WILLIAM: Within: I will give you further instructions.

SHIFT: I'll follow you.

SIR WILLIAM: (*Going, returns.*) You will want materials.

SHIFT: Oh, my dress I can be furnished with in five minutes. (*Exit* SIR WILLIAM.) A whimsical old blade this. I shall laugh if this scheme miscarries. I have a strange mind to lend it a lift – never had a greater – Pho! a damned unnatural connexion this of mine! What have I to do with fathers and guardians! A parcel of preaching, careful, curmudgeonly – dead to pleasures themselves, and blasters of it in others – mere dogs in a manger. No, no, I'll veer, tack about, open my budget to the boy and join in a counter-plot. But hold, hold, friend Stephen, see first how the land lies. Who knows whether this Germanised genius has parts to comprehend, or the spirit to reward thy merit. There's danger in that, ay, marry is there. Egad, before I shift the helm, I'll first examine the coast, and then, if there be but a bold shore and a good bottom, have a care, old Square Toes, you will meet with your match. (*Exit.*)

(*Enter* SIR GEORGE WEALTHY, LOADER *and* SERVANT.)

SIR GEORGE: Let the Martin pannels for the *vis-a-vis* be carried to Long Acre, and the piebalds sent to Hall's to be bitted. You will give me leave to be in your debt till the evening, Mr Loader. I have just enough left to discharge the baron, and we must, you know, be punctual with him for the credit of the country.

LOADER: Fire him, a snub-nosed son of a bitch! Levant me, but he got enough last night to purchase a principality amongst his countrymen, the High-dutchians or Hussarians.

---

stiver: the smallest Dutch coin.
Niger: nigger or negro. Slavery was not illegal until the Somersett case of 1772.
nautilus: a sea-shell, indicative of the popularity of natural-history collections.
Martin pannels: saddles or harness. *OED* suggests Martin is a maker's name.
vis-a-vis: a small coach in which the passengers sit facing each other.
Levant me: to levant is to make a bet with the intention of absconding if lost.
High-dutchians: Southern Germans.
Hussarian: either Hessian from Hesse, or Hussite from Bohemia.

SIR GEORGE: You had your share, Mr Loader.

LOADER: Who, I! Lurch me at four, but I was marked to the top of your trick, by the baron, my dear. What, I am no *cinque and quatre* man. Come, shall we have a dip into the 'history of the Four Kings' this morning?

SIR GEORGE: Rather too early. Besides it is the rule abroad never to engage a-fresh, until our old scores are discharged.

LOADER: Capot me, but those lads abroad are pretty fellows, let 'em say what they will. Here, sir, they will vowel you from father to son to the twentieth generation. They would as soon nowadays pay a tradesman's bill, as a play debt. All sense of honour is gone, not a stiver stirring. They could as soon raise the dead as two pounds two. Nick me, but I have a great mind to tie up, and ruin the rascals. What, has Transfer been here this morning?

(Enter DICK.)

SIR GEORGE: Anybody here this morning, Dick?

DICK: Nobody, your honour.

LOADER: Repique the rascal. He promised to be here before me.

DICK: I beg your honour's pardon. Mrs Cole from the Piazza was here, between seven and eight.

SIR GEORGE: An early hour for a lady of her calling.

DICK: Mercy on me! The poor gentlewoman is mortally altered since we used to lodge there, in our jaunts from Oxford; wrapt up in flannels, all over the rhematise.

LOADER: Ay, ay, old Moll is at her last stake.

DICK: She bade me say, she just stopped in her way to the tabernacle; after the exhortation, she says, she'll call again.

SIR GEORGE: Exhortation! Oh, I recollect. Well, whilst they only make proselytes from that profession, they are heartily welcome to them. She does not mean to make me a convert?

DICK: I believe she has some such design upon me, for she offered me a book of hymns, a shilling and a dram, to go along with her.

SIR GEORGE: No bad scheme, Dick. Thou hast a fine, sober, psalm-singing countenance, and, when thou hast been some time in their trammels, may'st make as able a teacher as the best of 'em.

DICK: Laud, sir, I want learning.

SIR GEORGE: Oh, the spirit, the spirit will supply all that, Dick, never fear.

(Enter SIR WILLIAM, *as a German baron.)*

SIR GEORGE: My dear baron, what news from the Haymarket? What says the Florenza? Does she yield? Shall I be happy? Say yes, and command my fortune.

SIR WILLIAM: I was never did see so fine a woman since I was leave Hamburg. Dere

---

Lurch me at four: beat me in a four-handed card game.

cinque and quatre: a dice game.

Capot: decisively beat at piquet.

vowel: to pay by IOU.

tie up: foreclose on the debt.

Repique: in piquet, to score from the cards before play starts.

the Piazza: Covent Garden market.

Haymarket: the King's Theatre or opera house in the Haymarket, as opposed to Foote's own Little Theatre in the Haymarket.

was all de colour, all red and white, dat was quite natural; *point d'artifice*. Then she was dance and sing – I vow to heaven, I was never see de like!

SIR GEORGE: But how did she receive my embassy? What hopes?

SIR WILLIAM: Why, dere was, *monsieur le chevalier*, when I first enter, dree or four damned queer people. Ah, ah, dought I, by gar I guess your business. Dere was one fat big woman's, dat I know long time: *le valet de chambre* was tell me dat she came from a grand merchand. Ha, ha, dought I, by your leave, stick to your shop, or, if you must have de pretty girl, dere is de playhouse, dat do very well for you, but for de opera, *pardonnez*, by gar, dat is meat for your master.

SIR GEORGE: Insolent mechanic! – But she despised him?

SIR WILLIAM: Ay, may foy, he is damn rich, has *beaucoup de* guineas; but after de fat woman was go, I was tell the signora, madam, dere is one certain *chevalier* of dis country, who has travelled, see de world, *bien fait*, well made, *beaucoup d'espirit*, a great deal of monies, who beg, by gar, to have de honour to drow himself at your feet.

SIR GEORGE: Well, well, baron.

SIR WILLIAM: She aska your name. As soon as I tell her, aha, by gar, dans an instant, she melt like de lomp of sugar. She run to her bureau, and, in de minute, return wid de paper.

SIR GEORGE: Give it me. (*Reads.*) '*Les preliminaires d'une traite entre le Chevalier Wealthy, and la Signora Diamenti* . . . ' A bagatelle, a trifle, she shall have it.

LOADER: Harkye, knight, what is all that there outlandish stuff?

SIR GEORGE: Read, read! The eloquence of angels, my dear baron!

LOADER: Slam me, but the man's mad! I don't understand their gibberish. What is it in English?

SIR GEORGE: The preliminaries of a subsidy treaty between Sir G. Wealthy and Signora Florenza. That the said signora will resign the possession of her person to the said Sir George, on the payment of three hundred guineas monthly, for equipage, table, domestics, dress, dogs and diamonds; her debts to be duly discharged, and a note advanced of five hundred by way of entrance.

LOADER: Zounds, what a cormorant! She must be devilish handsome.

SIR GEORGE: I am told so.

LOADER: Told so! Why, have you never seen her?

SIR GEORGE: No; and possibly never may, but from my box at the opera.

LOADER: Heyday! Why, what the devil . . .

SIR GEORGE: Ha, ha, you stare! I don't wonder at it. This is an elegant refinement, unknown to the gross voluptuaries of this part of the world. This is, Mr Loader, what may be called a debt to your dignity, for an opera girl is as essential a piece of equipage for a man of fashion as his coach.

LOADER: The devil!

SIR GEORGE: 'Tis for the vulgar only to enjoy what they possess: the distinction of ranks and conditions are to have hounds and never hunt, cooks and dine at taverns, houses you never inhabit, mistresses you never enjoy . . .

LOADER: And debts you never pay. Egad, I am not surprised at it, if this be your trade, no wonder that you want money for necessaries, when you give such a damned deal for nothing at all.

(*Enter* SERVANT.)

SERVANT: Mrs Cole, to wait upon your honour.

SIR GEORGE: My dear baron, run, despatch my affairs, conclude my treaty, and thank her for the very reasonable conditions.

SIR WILLIAM: I sall.

SIR GEORGE: Mr Loader, shall I trouble you to introduce the lady? She is, I think, your acquaintance.

LOADER: Who, old Moll? Ay, ay, she's your market-woman. I would not give six-pence for your signoras. One armful of good, wholesome British beauty is worth a ship-load of their trapesing, tawdry trollops. But, harkye, baron, how much for the table? Why she must have a devilish large family, or a monstrous stomach.

SIR WILLIAM: Ay, ay, dere is her mother, *la complaisante* to walk in de Park, and to go to de play, two broders, *deux valets*, dree Spanish lap-dogs and de monkey.

LOADER: Strip me, if I would set five shillings against the whole gang. May my partner renounce with the game in his hand, if I were you, knight, if I would not . . . (*Exit* SIR WILLIAM.)

SIR GEORGE: But the lady waits. (*Exit* LOADER.) A strange fellow this! What a whimsical jargon he talks! Not an idea abstracted from play! To say truth, I am sincerely sick of my acquaintance; but, however, I have the first people in the kingdom to keep me in countenance. Death and the dice level all distinctions.

(*Enter* MRS COLE, *supported by* LOADER *and* DICK.)

MRS COLE: Gently, gently, good Mr Loader.

LOADER: Come along, old Moll. Why, you jade, you look as rosy this morning – I must have a smack at your muns. Here, taste her, she is as good as old hock to get you a stomach.

MRS COLE: Fie, Mr Loader, I thought you had forgot me.

LOADER: I forget you! I would as soon forget what is trumps.

MRS COLE: Softly, softly, young man. There, there mighty well. And how does your honour do? I haven't seen your honour, I can't tell the – Oh! mercy upon me, there's a twinge.

SIR GEORGE: What is the matter, Mrs Cole?

MRS COLE: My old disorder, my rheumatise; I haven't been able to get a wink of – Oh, la! What, you have been in town these two days?

SIR GEORGE: Since Wednesday.

MRS COLE: And never once called upon old Cole. No, no, I am worn out, thrown by and forgotten, like a tattered garment, as Mr Squintum says. Oh, he is a dear man! But for him I had been a lost sheep; never known the comforts of the *new birth*, no. There's your old friend, Kitty Carrot, at home still. What, shall we see you this evening? I have kept the green-room for you ever since I heard you were in town.

LOADER: What, shall we take a snap at old Moll's? Hey, beldame, have you a good batch of Burgundy abroach?

MRS COLE: Bright as a ruby; and for flavour! You know the colonel – he and Jenny Cummins drank three flasks, hand to fist, last night.

LOADER: What, and bilk thee of thy share?

---

smack at your muns: kiss you on the mouth.

MRS COLE: Ah, don't mention it, Mr Loader. No, that's all over with me. The time has been when I could have earned thirty shillings a day by my own drinking, and the next morning was neither sick nor sorry. But now, Oh laud! a thimbleful turns me topsy-turvy.

LOADER: Poor old girl!

MRS COLE: Ay, I have done with these idle vanities; my thoughts are fixed upon a better place. What, I suppose, Mr Loader, you will be for your old friend the black-eyed girl from Rosemary Lane. Ha, ha! Well, 'tis a merry little tit. A thousand pities she's such a reprobate! But she'll mend. Her time is not come. All shall have their call, as Mr Squintum says, sooner or later. Regeneration is not the work of a day. No, no, no, – Oh!

SIR GEORGE: Not worse, I hope.

MRS COLE: Rack, rack, gnaw, gnaw, never easy; a-bed or up, all's one. Pray, honest friend, have you any clary or mint water in the house?

DICK: A case of French drams.

MRS COLE: Heaven defend me! I would not touch a dram for the world.

SIR GEORGE: They are but cordials, Mrs Cole. Fetch 'em, you blockhead. (*Exit* DICK.)

MRS COLE: Ay, I am a-going. A-wasting and a-wasting, Sir George. What will become of the house when I am gone, heaven knows. No. When people are missed, then they are mourned. Sixteen years have I lived in the Garden, comfortably and creditably; and, though I say it, could have got bail any hour of the day: reputable tradesmen, Sir George, neighbours, Mr Loader knows; no knock-me-down doings in my house. A set of regular, sober customers. No rioters. Sixteen, did I say? Ay, eighteen years I have paid scot and lot in the parish of St Paul's, and, during the whole time, nobody have said, 'Mrs Cole, why do you so?' Unless twice that I was before Sir Thomas De Val, and three times in the round-house. (*She cries.*)

SIR GEORGE: Nay, don't weep, Mrs Cole.

LOADER: May I lose deal, with an honour at bottom, if old Moll does not bring tears into my eyes.

MRS COLE: However, it is a comfort after all, to think one has passed through the world with credit and character. Ay, a good name, as Mr Squintum says, is better than a gallipot of ointment.

> (*Enter* DICK *with a dram.*)

LOADER: Come, haste, Dick, haste; sorrow is dry. Here, Moll, shall I fill thee a bumper?

MRS COLE: Hold, hold, Mr Loader! Heaven help you, I could as soon swallow the Thames. Only a sip, to keep the gout out of my stomach.

LOADER: Why then, here's to thee. – Levant me, but it is supernaculum. – Speak when you have enough.

MRS COLE: I won't trouble you for the glass; my hands do so tremble and shake, I shall but spill the good creature.

---

clary or mint water: herb teas.
Sir Thomas De Val: Thomas De Veil was a Bow Street magistrate.
supernaculum: drained to the last drop.

LOADER: Well pulled! But now to business. Prythee, Moll, did not I see a tight young wench, in a linen gown, knock at your door this morning?

MRS COLE: Ay, a young thing from the country.

LOADER: Could we not get a peep at her this evening?

MRS COLE: Impossible! She is engaged to Sir Timothy Trotter. I have taken earnest for her three months.

LOADER: Pho, what signifies such a fellow as that! Tip him an old trader, and give her to the knight.

MRS COLE: 'Tip him an old trader!' Mercy on us, where do you expect to go when you die, Mr Loader?

LOADER: Crop me, but this Squintum has turned her brains.

SIR GEORGE: Nay, Mr Loader, I think the gentleman has wrought a most happy reformation.

MRS COLE: Oh, it was a wonderful work. There had I been tossing in the sea of sin, without rudder or compass. And had not the good gentleman piloted me into the harbour of grace, I must have struck against the rocks of reprobation, and have been quite swallowed up in the whirlpool of despair. He was the precious instrument of my spiritual sprinkling. – But, however, Sir George, if your mind be set on a young country thing, tomorrow night I believe I can furnish you.

LOADER: As how?

MRS COLE: I have advertised this morning, in the register office, for servants under seventeen, and ten to one but I light on something that will do.

LOADER: Pillory me, but it has a face!

MRS COLE: Truly, consistently with my conscience, I would do anything for your honour.

SIR GEORGE: Right, Mrs Cole, never lose sight of that monitor. But, pray, how long has this heavenly change been wrought in you?

MRS COLE: Ever since my last visitation of the gout. Upon my first fit, seven years ago, I began to have my doubts and my waverings; but I was lost in a labyrinth, and nobody to show me the road. One time, I thought of dying a Roman, which is truly a comfortable communion enough for one of us, but it would not do.

SIR GEORGE: Why not?

MRS COLE: I went one summer over to Boulogne to repent, and, would you believe it, the bare-footed, bald-pated beggars would not give me absolution, without I quitted my business. Did you ever hear of such a set of scabby – Besides, I could not bear their barbarity. Would you believe it, Mr Loader, they lock up, for their lives, in a nunnery, the prettiest, sweetest, tender young things! Oh, six of them, for a season, would finish my business here, and then I should have nothing to do, but to think of hereafter.

LOADER: Brand me, what a country!

SIR GEORGE: Oh, scandalous!

MRS COLE: Oh no, it would not do. So, in my last illness, I was wished to Mr Squintum, who stepped in with his saving grace, got me with the new birth, and I became, as you see, regenerate and another creature.

---

register office: where newcomers to London could advertise for employment. Its use by pimps and prostitutes had become scandalous. See Joseph Reed's play *The Register Office*.

(*Enter* DICK.)

DICK: Mr Transfer, sir, has sent to know if your honour be at home.

SIR GEORGE: Mrs Cole, I am mortified to part with you. But business, you know . . .

MRS COLE: True, Sir George. Mr Loader, your arm – gently, oh, oh!

SIR GEORGE: Would you take another thimbleful, Mrs Cole?

MRS COLE: Not a drop. I shall see you this evening?

SIR GEORGE: Depend upon me.

MRS COLE: Tomorrow I hope to suit you. We are to have, at the tabernacle, an occasional hymn, with a thanksgiving sermon for my recovery. After which, I shall call at the register office, and see what goods my advertisement has brought in.

SIR GEORGE: Extremely obliged to you, Mrs Cole.

MRS COLE: Or, if that should not do, I have a tid-bit at home will suit your stomach; never brushed by a beard. Well, heaven bless you – Softly, have a care, Mr Loader – Richard, you may as well give me the bottle into the chair, for fear I should be taken ill on the road. Gently – so, so! (*Exit* MRS COLE *and* LOADER.)

SIR GEORGE: Dick, show Mr Transfer in. – Ha, ha, what a hodge-podge! How the jade has jumbled together the carnal and the spiritual! With what ease she reconciles her new birth to her old calling! No wonder these preachers have plenty of proselytes, whilst they have the address so comfortably to blend the hitherto jarring interests of the two worlds.

(*Enter* LOADER.)

LOADER: Well, knight, I have housed her; but they want you within, sir.

SIR GEORGE: I'll go to them immediately. (*Exit.*)

ACT II

Enter DICK, *introducing* TRANSFER.

DICK: My master will come to you presently. (*Exit.*)

(*Enter* SIR GEORGE.)

SIR GEORGE: Mr Transfer, your servant.

TRANSFER: You honour's very humble. I thought to have found Mr Loader here.

SIR GEORGE: He will return immediately. Well, Mr Transfer – but take a chair – you have had a long walk. Mr Loader, I presume, opened to you the urgency of my business.

TRANSFER: Ay, ay, the general cry, 'Money, money!' I don't know, for my part, where all the money is flown to. Formerly a note, with a tolerable endorsement, was as current as cash. If your uncle Richard now would join in this security . . .

SIR GEORGE: Impossible.

TRANSFER: Ay, like enough. I wish you were of age.

SIR GEORGE: So do I. But as that will be considered in the premium . . .

TRANSFER: True, true. I see you understand business. And what sum does your honour lack at present?

SIR GEORGE: Lack! How much have you brought?

TRANSFER: Who, I? Dear me! None.

SIR GEORGE: Zounds, none!

TRANSFER: Lack-a-day, none to be had, I think. All the morning have I been upon the hunt. There, Ephraim Barebones, the tallow-chandler, in Thames Street, used to be a never-failing chap; not a guinea to be got there. Then I tottled away to Nebuchadnezzar Zebulon, in the Old Jewry, but it happened to be Saturday, and they never touch on the Sabbath, you know.

SIR GEORGE: Why, what the devil can I do?

TRANSFER: Good me, I did not know your honour had been so pressed.

SIR GEORGE: My honour pressed! Yes, my honour is not only pressed, but ruined, unless I can raise money to redeem it. That blockhead Loader, to depend upon this old doating . . .

TRANSFER: Well, well, now I declare, I am quite sorry to see your honour in such a taking.

SIR GEORGE: Damn your sorrow!

TRANSFER: But come, don't be cast down. Though money is not to be had, money's worth may, and that's the same thing.

SIR GEORGE: How, dear Transfer?

TRANSFER: Why I have, at my warehouse in the City, ten casks of whale-blubber, a large cargo of Dantzig dowlas, with a curious sortment of Birmingham hafts and Whitney blankets, for exportation.

SIR GEORGE: Hey!

TRANSFER: And, stay, stay, then again, at my country house, the bottom of Gray's Inn Lane, there's a hundred tun of fine old hay, only damaged a little last winter, for want of thatching; with forty load of flint-stones.

SIR GEORGE: Well.

TRANSFER: Your honour may have all these for a reasonable profit, and convert them into cash.

SIR GEORGE: Blubber and blankets? Why, you old rascal, do you banter me?

TRANSFER: Who I? Oh law! Marry, heaven forbid.

SIR GEORGE: Get out of my – You stuttering scoundrel.

TRANSFER: If your honour would but hear me . . .

SIR GEORGE: Troop, I say, unless you have a mind to go a shorter way than you came. (*Exit* TRANSFER.) And yet there is something so uncommonly ridiculous in his proposal, that were my mind more at ease . . . (*Enter* LOADER.) So, sir, you have recommended me to a fine fellow.

LOADER: What's the matter?

SIR GEORGE: He can't supply me with a shilling! And wants, besides, to make me a dealer in dowlas.

LOADER: Ay, and a very good commodity too. People that are upon the ways and means must not be nice, knight. A pretty piece of work you have made here! Thrown up the cards, with the game in your hands.

SIR GEORGE: Why, prithee, of what use would his . . .

LOADER: Use! Of every use. Procure you the spankers, my boy. I have a broker that, in a twinkling, shall take off your bargain.

SIR GEORGE: Indeed?

LOADER: Indeed! Ay, indeed. You sit down to hazard and not know the chances! I'll

---

dowlas: strong calico or linen.

call him back. Hello, Transfer! A pretty little, busy, bustling – You may travel miles before you will meet with his match. If there is one pound in the City, he will get it. He creeps, like a ferret, into their bags, and makes the yellow-boys bolt again. (*Enter* TRANSFER.) Come hither, little Transfer. What, man, our Minor was a little too hasty. He did not understand trap. Know nothing of the game, my dear.

TRANSFER: What I said, was to serve Sir George, as he seemed . . .

LOADER: I told him so. Well, well, we will take thy commodities, were they as many more. But try, prithee, if thou couldst not procure us some of the ready, for present spending.

TRANSFER: Let me consider.

LOADER: Ay, do come, shuffle thy brains. Never fear the baronet. To let a lord of lands want shiners! 'Tis a shame.

TRANSFER: I do recollect, in this quarter of the town, an old friend, that used to do things in this way.

LOADER: Who?

TRANSFER: Statute, the scrivener.

LOADER: Slam me, but he has nicked the chance.

TRANSFER: A hard man, Master Loader.

SIR GEORGE: No matter.

TRANSFER: His demands are exorbitant.

SIR GEORGE: That is no fault of ours.

LOADER: Well said, knight!

TRANSFER: But to save time, I had better mention his terms.

LOADER: Unnecessary.

TRANSFER: Five per cent legal interest.

SIR GEORGE: He shall have it.

TRANSFER: Ten, the premium.

SIR GEORGE: No more words.

TRANSFER: Then, as you are not of age, five more for insuring your life.

LOADER: We will give it.

TRANSFER: As for what he will demand for the risk . . .

SIR GEORGE: He will be satisfied.

TRANSFER: You pay the attorney.

SIR GEORGE: Amply, amply. Loader, despatch him.

LOADER: There, there, little Transfer, now everything is settled. All terms shall be complied with, reasonable or unreasonable. What, our principal is a man of honour. (*Exit* TRANSFER.) Hey, my knight, this is doing business. This pinch is a sure card.

        (*Re-enter* TRANSFER.)

TRANSFER: I had forgot one thing. I am not the principal, you pay the brokerage.

LOADER: Ay, ay, and a handsome present into the bargain, never fear.

TRANSFER: Enough, enough.

LOADER: Harkye, Transfer, we'll take the Birmingham hafts and Whitney wares.

TRANSFER: They shall be forthcoming. You would not have the hay and flints?

LOADER: Every pebble of 'em. The magistrates of the baronet's borough are infirm

---

understand trap: recognise his own interest.

and gouty. He shall deal for them for a new pavement. (*Exit* TRANSFER.) So, that's settled. I believe, knight, I can lend you a helping hand as to the last article. I know some traders that will truck, fellows with finery. Not commodities of such clumsy conveyance as old Transfer's.

SIR GEORGE: You are obliging.

LOADER: I'll do it, boy, and get you, into the bargain, a bonny auctioneer, that shall dispose of 'em in a crack. (*Exit.*)

(*Enter* DICK.)

DICK: Your uncle, sir, has been waiting some time.

SIR GEORGE: He comes in a lucky hour. Show him in. (*Exit* DICK.) Now for a lecture. My situation shall not sink my spirits, however. Here comes the musty trader, running over with remonstrances. I must banter the cit.

(*Enter* RICHARD WEALTH.)

RICHARD: So, sir, what, I suppose this is a spice of your foreign breeding, to let your uncle kick his heels in your hall, whilst your presence chamber is crowded with pimps, bawds and gamesters.

SIR GEORGE: Oh, a proof of my respect, dear nuncle. Would it have been decent, now, nuncle, to have introduced you into such company?

RICHARD: Wonderfully considerate! Well, young man, and what do you think will be the end of all this? Here I have received by the last mail a quire of your draughts from abroad. I see you are determined our neighbours should taste of your magnificence.

SIR GEORGE: Yes, I think I did some credit to my country.

RICHARD: And how are these to be paid?

SIR GEORGE: That I submit to you, dear nuncle.

RICHARD: From me! Not a sous to keep you from the counter.

SIR GEORGE: Why then let the scoundrels stay. It is their duty. I have other demands, debts of honour, which must be discharged.

RICHARD: Here's a diabolical distinction! Here's a prostitution of words! Honour! 'Sdeath, that a rascal, who has picked your pocket, shall have his crime gilded with the most sacred distinction, and his plunder punctually paid, whilst the industrious mechanic, who ministers to your very wants, shall have his debt delayed and his demand treated as insolent.

SIR GEORGE: Oh! A truce to this threadbare trumpery, dear nuncle.

RICHARD: I confess my folly. But make yourself easy, you won't be troubled with many more of my visits. I own I was weak enough to design a short expostulation with you, but as we in the City know the true value of time, I shall take care not to squander away any more of it upon you.

SIR GEORGE: A prudent resolution.

RICHARD: One commission, however, I cannot dispense with myself from executing. It was agreed between your father and me that as he had but one son and I one daughter . . .

SIR GEORGE: Your gettings should be added to his estate, and my cousin Margery and I squat down together in the comfortable state of matrimony.

RICHARD: Puppy! Such was our intention. Now his last will claims this contract.

SIR GEORGE: Dispatch, dear nuncle.

Counter: a City law court.

RICHARD: Why then, in a word, see me here demand the execution.

SIR GEORGE: What d'ye mean? For me to marry Margery?

RICHARD: I do.

SIR GEORGE: What, *moi* – me?

RICHARD: You, you – Your answer, ay or no?

SIR GEORGE: Why then, concisely and briefly, without equivocation, or further circumlocution – No.

RICHARD: I am glad of it.

SIR GEORGE: So am I.

RICHARD: But pray, if it would not be too great a favour, what objections can you have to my daughter? Not that I want to remove them, but merely out of curiosity. What objections?

SIR GEORGE: None. I neither know her, have seen her, inquired after her, or ever intended it.

RICHARD: What, perhaps I am the stumbling block?

SIR GEORGE: You have hit it.

RICHARD: Ay, now we come to the point. Well and pray . . .

SIR GEORGE: Why, it is not so much a dislike to your person, though that is exceptionable enough, but your profession, dear nuncle, is an insuperable obstacle.

RICHARD: Good lack! And what harm has that done, pray?

SIR GEORGE: Done! So stained, polluted and tainted the whole mass of your blood, thrown such a blot on your 'scutcheon, as ten regular successions can hardly efface.

RICHARD: The deuce!

SIR GEORGE: And could you now, consistently with your duty as a faithful guardian, recommend my union with the daughter of a trader?

RICHARD: Why indeed, I ask pardon. I am afraid I did not weigh the matter so maturely as I ought.

SIR GEORGE: Oh, a horrid barbarous scheme!

RICHARD: But then, I thought her having the honour to partake in the same flesh and blood with yourself might prove, in some measure, a kind of fuller's earth, to scour out the dirty spots contracted by commerce.

SIR GEORGE: Impossible!

RICHARD: Besides, here it has been the practice even of peers.

SIR GEORGE: Don't mention the unnatural intercourse! Thank heaven, Mr Richard Wealthy, my education has been in another country, where I have been too well instructed in the value of nobility, to think of intermixing it with the offspring of a bourgeois. Why, what apology could I make to my children for giving them such a mother?

RICHARD: I did not think of that. Then I must despair, I am afraid.

SIR GEORGE: I can afford but little hopes. Though upon reflection – is the *grisette* pretty?

RICHARD: A parent may be partial. She is thought so.

SIR GEORGE: Ah, *la jolie petite bourgeoise*! Poor girl, I sincerely pity her. And, I suppose, to procure her emersion from the mercantile mud, no consideration would be spared.

RICHARD: Why to be sure, for such an honour, one would strain a point.

SIR GEORGE: Why then, not totally to destroy your hopes, I do recollect an edict in favour of Brittany: that when a man of distinction engages in commerce, his nobility is suffered to sleep.

RICHARD: Indeed!

SIR GEORGE: And upon his quitting the contagious connection, he is permitted to resume his rank.

RICHARD: That's fortunate.

SIR GEORGE: So, nuncle Richard, if you will sell out of the stocks, shut up your counting-house, and quit St Mary-Axe for Grosvenor Square . . .

RICHARD: What then?

SIR GEORGE: Why, when your rank has had time to rouse itself (for I think your nobility, nuncle, has had a pretty long nap), if the girl's person is pleasing, and the purchase-money is adequate to the honour, I may in time be prevailed upon to restore her to the right of her family.

RICHARD: Amazing condescension!

SIR GEORGE: Good nature is my foible. But, upon my soul, I would not have gone so far for anybody else.

RICHARD: I can contain no longer. Hear me, spendthrift, prodigal, do you know that in ten days your whole revenue won't purchase you a feather to adorn your empty head . . .

SIR GEORGE: Heyday, what's the matter now?

RICHARD: And that you derive every acre of your boasted patrimony from your great uncle, a soap-boiler!

SIR GEORGE: Infamous aspersion!

RICHARD: It was his bags, the fruit of his honest industry, that preserved your lazy, beggarly nobility. His wealth repaired your tottering hall, from the ruins of which even the rats had run.

SIR GEORGE: Better our name had perished! Insupportable! Soap-boiling, uncle!

RICHARD: Traduce a trader in a country of commerce! It is treason against the community, and, for your punishment, I would have you restored to the sordid condition from whence we drew you, and, like your predecessors the Picts, stripped, painted and fed upon hips, haws and blackberries.

SIR GEORGE: A truce, dear haberdasher.

RICHARD: One pleasure I have, that to this goal you are upon the gallop. But have a care, the sword hangs but by a thread. When next we meet, know me for the master of your fate. (*Exit.*)

SIR GEORGE: Insolent mechanic! But that his bourgeois blood would have soiled my sword . . .

(*Enter* SIR WILLIAM *as the* BARON *and* LOADER.)

SIR WILLIAM: What is de matter?

SIR GEORGE: A fellow here, upon the credit of a little affinity, has dared to upbraid me with being sprung from a soap-boiler.

SIR WILLIAM: Vat, you from the boiler of soap!

SIR GEORGE: Me.

SIR WILLIAM: Aha, by gar, dat is anoder ting. And harka you, mister monsieur, ha – how dare you have d' affrontary . . .

SIR GEORGE: How!

SIR WILLIAM: De impertinence to sit down, play wid me?

SIR GEORGE: What is this?

SIR WILLIAM: A beggarly bourgeois *vis-à-vis* a baron of twenty descents.

LOADER: But baron . . .

SIR WILLIAM: By gar, I am almost ashamed to win of such a low, dirty – Give me my monies and let me never see your face.

LOADER: Why, but, baron, you mistake this thing. I know the old buck this fellow prates about.

SIR WILLIAM: Maybe.

LOADER: Pigeon me, as true a gentleman as the Grand Signior. He was, indeed, a good-natured, obliging, friendly fellow, and being a great judge of soap, tar and train-oil, he used to have it home to his house, and sell it to his acquaintance for ready money to serve them.

SIR WILLIAM: Was dat all?

LOADER: Upon my honour.

SIR WILLIAM: Oh, dat, dat is anoder ting. By gar, I was afraid he was negotiant.

LOADER: Nothing like it.

> (*Enter* DICK.)

DICK: A gentleman to inquire for Mr Loader.

LOADER: I come. – A pretty son of a bitch, this baron! Pimps for a man, picks his pocket, and then wants to kick him out of company, because his uncle was an oilman. (*Exit.*)

SIR WILLIAM: I beg pardon, *chevalier*, I was mistake.

SIR GEORGE: Oh, don't mention it. Had the flam been fact, your behaviour was natural enough.

> (*Enter* LOADER.)

LOADER: Mr Smirk, the auctioneer.

SIR GEORGE: Show him in, by all means. (*Exit* LOADER.)

SIR WILLIAM: You have an affair.

SIR GEORGE: If you'll walk into the next room, they will be finished in five minutes.
> (*Exit* SIR WILLIAM.)

> (*Enter* LOADER, *with* SHIFT *as* SMIRK.)

LOADER: Here, Master Smirk, this is the gentleman. Harkye, knight, did not I tell you old Moll was your mark? Here she had brought a pretty piece of man's meat already, as sweet as a nosegay and as ripe as a cherry, you rogue. Despatch him, meantime we'll manage the girl. (*Exit.*)

SHIFT: You are the principal.

SIR GEORGE: Even so. I have, Mr Smirk, some things of considerable value, which I want to dispose of immediately.

SHIFT: You have?

SIR GEORGE: Could you assist me?

SHIFT: Doubtless.

SIR GEORGE: But, directly?

SHIFT: We have an auction at twelve. I'll add your cargo to the catalogue.

---

negotiant: merchant (French).

SIR GEORGE: Can that be done?

SHIFT: Every day's practice. It is for the credit of the sale. Last week, amongst the valuable effects of a gentleman going abroad, I sold a choice collection of china, with a curious service of plate, though the real party was never master of above two delft dishes, and a dozen of pewter, in all his life.

SIR GEORGE: Very artificial. But this must be concealed.

SHIFT: Buried here. Oh, many an aigrette and solitaire have I sold to discharge a lady's play debt. But then we must know the parties, otherwise it might be knocked down to the husband himself. Ha, ha – heigh-ho!

SIR GEORGE: True. Upon my word, your profession requires parts.

SHIFT: Nobody's more. Did you ever hear, Sir George, what first brought me into the business?

SIR GEORGE: Never.

SHIFT: Quite an accident, as I may say. You must have known my predecessor, Mr Prig, the greatest man in the world, in his way, ay, that ever was or ever will be; quite a jewel of a man; he would touch you up a lot; there was no resisting him. He would force you to bid, whether you would or no. I shall never see his equal.

SIR GEORGE: You are modest, Mr Smirk.

SHIFT: No, no, but his shadow. Far be it from me to vie with so great a man. But, as I was saying, my predecessor, Mr Prig, was to have a sale, as it might be, on a Saturday. On Friday at noon (I shall never forget the day) he was suddenly seized with a violent cholic. He sent for me to his bed-side, squeezed me by the hand, 'Dear Smirk,' said he, 'what an accident! You know what is tomorrow: the greatest show this season; prints, pictures, bronzes, butterflies, medals and mignonettes; all the world will be there, Lady Dy Joss, Mrs Nankyn, the Duchess of Dupe and everybody at all. You see my state, it will be impossible for me to mount. What can I do?' It was not for me, you know, to advise that great man.

SIR GEORGE: No, no.

SHIFT: At last, looking wistfully at me, 'Smirk,' says he, 'do you love me?' 'Mr Prig, can you doubt it?' 'I'll put it to the test', says he, 'Supply my place tomorrow.' I, eager to show my love, rashly and rapidly replied, 'I will.'

SIR GEORGE: That was bold.

SHIFT: Absolute madness. But I had gone too far to recede. The point was, to prepare for the awful occasion. The first want that occurred to me was a wig. But this was too material an article to depend on my own judgement. I resolved to consult my friends. I told them the affair: 'You hear, gentlemen, what has happened: Mr Prig, one of the greatest men in his way the world ever saw, or ever will, quite a jewel of a man, taken with a violent fit of the cholic; tomorrow, the greatest show this season; prints, pictures, bronzes, butterflies, medals and mignonettes; everybody in the world to be there; Lady Dy Joss, Mrs Nankyn, Duchess of Dupe and all mankind; it being impossible he should mount, I have consented to sell –' They stared. 'It is true, gentlemen. Now I should be glad to have your opinions as to a wig.' They were divided; some recommended a tye, others a bag; one mentioned a bob, but was soon over-ruled. Now, for my part, I own, I rather inclined

---

Mr Prig: Christopher Cock, Abraham Langford's predecessor as auctioneer. Foote had mimicked him in *The Diversions of the Morning*.

to the bag, but to avoid the imputation of rashness, I resolved to take Mrs Smirk's judgement, my wife, a dear good woman, fine in figure, high in taste, a superior genius, and knows old china like a Nabob.

SIR GEORGE: What was her decision?

SHIFT: I told her the case. 'My dear, you know what has happened. My good friend, Mr Prig, the greatest man in the world, in his way, that ever was, or ever will be, quite a jewel of a man, a violent fit of cholic – the greatest show this season tomorrow, pictures and everything in the world; all the world will be there. Now, as it is impossible he should, I mount in his stead. You know the importance of a wig; I have asked my friends – some recommended a tye, others a bag – what is your opinion?' 'Why, to deal freely, Mr Smirk,' says she, 'a tye for your round, regular, smiling face would be rather too formal, and a bag too boyish, deficient in dignity for the solemn occasion. Were I worthy to advise you, you should wear a something between both.' 'I'll be hanged if you don't mean a major.' I jumped at the hint, and a major it was.

SIR GEORGE: So, that was fixed.

SHIFT: Finally. But the next day, when I came to mount the rostrum, then was the trial. My limbs shook and my tongue trembled. The first lot was a chamber utensil, in Chelsea china, of the pea-green pattern. It occasioned a great laugh, but I got through it. Her grace, indeed, gave me great encouragement. I overheard her whisper to Lady Dy, 'Upon my word, Mr Smirk does it very well.' 'Very well indeed, Mr Smirk,' addressing herself to me. I made an acknowledging bow to her grace, as in duty bound. But, one flower flounced involuntarily from me that day, as I may say. I remember, Dr Trifle called it enthusiastic, and pronounced it a presage of my future greatness.

SIR GEORGE: What was that?

SHIFT: Why, sir, the lot was a Guido; a single figure, a marvellous fine performance, well preserved and highly finished. It stuck at five-and-forty. I charmed with the picture and piqued at the people, 'A-going for five-and-forty, nobody more than five-and-forty – Pray, ladies and gentlemen, look at this piece, quite flesh and blood, and only wants a touch from the torch of Prometheus, to start from the canvas and fall a-bidding.' A general plaudit ensued. I bowed, and in three minutes knocked it down at sixty-three ten.

SIR GEORGE: That was a stroke at least equal to your master.

SHIFT: Oh dear me! You did not know the great man – alike in everything. He had as much to say upon a ribbon as a Raphael. His manner was inimitably fine. I remember, they took him off at the playhouse, some time ago. Pleasant, but wrong. Public characters should not be sported with. They are sacred. But we lose time.

SIR GEORGE: Oh, in the lobby, on the table, you will find the particulars.

SHIFT: We shall see you. There will be a world of company. I shall please you. But the great nicety of our art is the eye. Mark how mine skims round the room. Some bidders are shy, and only advance with a nod; but I nail them. One, two, three, four, five. You will be surprised – Ha, ha, ha, – heigh-ho! (*Exeunt.*)

ACT III

Enter SIR GEORGE *and* LOADER.

SIR GEORGE: A most infernal run. Let's see (*Pulls out a card.*), Loader a thousand, the baron two, tally – enough to beggar a banker. Every shilling of Transfer's supply exhausted! Nor will even the sale of my moveables prove sufficient to discharge my debts. Death and the devil! In what a complication of calamities has a few days plunged me! And no resource?

LOADER: Knight, here's old Moll, come to wait on you. She has brought the tid-bit I spoke of. Shall I bid her send her in?

SIR GEORGE: Pray do. (*Exit* LOADER.)

(*Enter* MRS COLE *and* LUCY.)

MRS COLE: Come along Lucy. You bashful baggage. I thought I had silenced your scruples. Don't you remember what Mr Squintum said? 'A woman's not worth saving, that won't be guilty of a swinging sin; for then they have matter to repent upon.' Here, your honour, I leave her to your management. She is young, tender and timid, does not know what is for her own good; but your honour will soon teach her. I would willingly stay, but I must not lose the lecture. (*Exit.*)

SIR GEORGE: Upon my credit, a fine figure! Awkward – can't produce her publicly as mine. But she will do for private amusement. – Will you be seated, miss? – Dumb! Quite a picture! She too wants a touch of the Promethean torch. – Will you be so kind, ma'am, to walk from your frame and take a chair? – Come, prithee, why so coy? Nay, I am not adroit in the custom of this country. I suppose I must conduct you. – Come, miss.

LUCY: Oh, sir.

SIR GEORGE: Child!

LUCY: If you have any humanity, spare me.

SIR GEORGE: In tears! What can this mean? Artifice. A project to raise the price, I suppose. Lookye, my dear, you may save this piece of pathetic for another occasion. It won't do with me. I am no novice. So, child, a truce to your tragedy, I beg.

LUCY: Indeed you wrong me, sir; indeed you do.

SIR GEORGE: Wrong you! How came you here, and for what purpose?

LUCY: A shameful one. I know it all, and yet believe me, sir, I am innocent.

SIR GEORGE: Oh, I don't question that. Your pious patroness is a proof of your innocence.

LUCY: What can I say to gain your credit? And yet, sir, strong as appearances are against me, by all that's holy, you see me here, a poor distressed, involuntary victim.

SIR GEORGE: Her style's above the common class, her tears are real. – Rise child. – How the poor creature trembles!

LUCY: Say, then, I am safe.

SIR GEORGE: Fear nothing.

LUCY: May heaven reward you; I cannot.

SIR GEORGE: Prithee, child, collect yourself, and help me unravel this mystery. You came hither willingly? There was no force?

LUCY: None.

SIR GEORGE: You know Mrs Cole.

LUCY: Too well.

SIR GEORGE: How came you then to trust her?

LUCY: Mine, sir, is a tedious, melancholy tale.

SIR GEORGE: And artless too?

LUCY: As innocence.

SIR GEORGE: Give it me.

LUCY: It will tire you.

SIR GEORGE: Not if it be true. Be just and you will find me generous.

LUCY: On that, sir, I relied in venturing hither.

SIR GEORGE: You did me justice. Trust me with all your story. If you deserve, depend upon my protection.

LUCY: Some months ago, sir, I was considered as the joint heiress of a respectable, wealthy merchant; dear to my friends, happy in my prospects, and my father's favourite.

SIR GEORGE: His name?

LUCY: There you must pardon me. Unkind and cruel though he has been to me, let me discharge the duty of a daughter, suffer in silence, nor bring reproach on him who gave me being.

SIR GEORGE: I applaud your piety.

LUCY: At this happy period, my father, judging an addition of wealth must bring an increase of happiness, resolved to unite me with a man, sordid in his mind, brutal in his manners, and riches his only recommendation. My refusal of this ill-suited match, though mildly given, inflamed my father's temper, naturally choleric, alienated his affection, and banished me his house, distressed and destitute.

SIR GEORGE: Would no friend receive you?

LUCY: Alas, how few are friends to the unfortunate! Besides, I knew, sir, such a step would be considered by my father as an appeal from his justice. I therefore retired to a remote corner of the town, trusting, as my only advocate, to the tender calls of nature, in his cool, reflecting hours.

SIR GEORGE: How came you to know this woman?

LUCY: Accident placed me in a house, the mistress of which professed the same principles with my infamous conductress. There, as enthusiasm is the child of melancholy, I caught the infection. A constant acquaintance on their assemblies procured me the acquaintance of this woman, whose extraordinary zeal and devotion first drew my attention and confidence. I trusted her with my story, and, in return, received the warmest invitation to take the protection of her house. This I unfortunately accepted.

SIR GEORGE: Unfortunately indeed!

LUCY: By the decency of appearances, I was some time imposed upon. But an accident, which you will excuse my repeating, revealed all the horror of my situation. I will not trouble you with a recital of all the arts used to seduce me. Happily they hitherto have failed. But this morning I was acquainted with my destiny, and no other election left me, but immediate compliance, or a jail. In this desperate condition, you cannot wonder, sir, at my choosing rather to rely on the generosity of a gentleman, than the humanity of a creature insensible to pity, and void of every virtue.

SIR GEORGE: The event shall justify your choice. You have my faith and honour for
   your security. For, although I cannot boast of my own goodness, yet I have an
   honest feeling for afflicted virtue, and, however unfashionable, a spirit that dares
   afford it protection. Give me your hand. As soon as I have despatched some
   pressing business here, I will lodge you in an asylum, sacred to the distresses of
   your sex, where indigent beauty is guarded from temptation, and deluded
   innocence rescued from infamy. (*Exeunt.*)
        (*Enter* SHIFT.)
SHIFT: Zooks, I have toiled like a horse; quite tired by Jupiter. And what shall I get
   for my pains? The odd fellow here talks of making me easy for life. Easy! And
   what does he mean by easy? He'll make me an exciseman, I suppose, and so, with
   an ink-horn at my button-hole, and a taper switch in my hand, I shall run about
   gauging of beer-barrels. No, that will never do. This lad here is no fool. Foppish
   indeed. He does not want parts. No, nor principles neither. I overheard his scene
   with the girl. I think I may trust him. I have a great mind to venture it. It is a shame
   to have him duped by this old don. It must not be. I'll in and unfold – Ha! – Egad,
   I have a thought too, which, if my heir apparent can execute, I shall still lie
   concealed, and perhaps be rewarded on both sides.
        I have it, – 'tis engendered, piping hot,
        And now, Sir Knight, I'll match you with a plot. (*Exit.*)
        (*Enter* SIR WILLIAM *and* RICHARD WEALTHY.)
RICHARD: Well, I suppose by this time, you are satisfied what a scoundrel you have
   brought into the world, and are ready to finish your foolery.
SIR WILLIAM: Go to the catastrophe, good brother.
RICHARD: Let us have it over, then.
SIR WILLIAM: I have already alarmed all his tradesmen. I suppose we shall soon have
   him here, with a legion of bailiffs and constables. – Oh, you have my will about
   you?
RICHARD: Yes, yes.
SIR WILLIAM: It is almost time to produce it, or read him the clause that relates to his
   rejecting your daughter. That will do the business. But they come. I must return
   to my character.
        (*Enter* SHIFT.)
SHIFT: Sir, sir, we are all in the wrong box. Our scheme is blown up, your son has
   detected Loader and Tally, and is playing the very devil within.
SIR WILLIAM: Oh, the bunglers!
SHIFT: Now for it, youngster.
        (*Enter* SIR GEORGE, *driving in* LOADER *and another.*)
SIR GEORGE: Rascals, robbers, that, like locusts, mark the road you have taken by
   the ruin and desolation you have left behind you.
LOADER: Sir George!
SIR GEORGE: And can youth, however cautious, be guarded against such deep-laid,
   complicated villainy? Where are the rest of your diabolical crew? Your
   auctioneer, usurer, and – Oh sir, are you here? I am glad you have not escaped
   us, however.
SIR WILLIAM: What de devil is de matter?
SIR GEORGE: Your birth, which I believe an imposition, preserves you, however,

from the discipline these rogues have received. A baron, a nobleman, a sharper! Oh shame! It is enough to banish all confidence from the world. On whose faith can we rely, when those whose honour is held as sacred as an oath, unmindful of their dignity, descend to rival pick-pockets in their infamous arts? What are these (*Pulls out dice.*) pretty implements? The fruit of your leisure hours! They are dexterously done. You have a fine mechanical turn. – Dick, secure the door.

    (MRS COLE, *speaking as entering*)

MRS COLE: Here I am, at last. Well, and how is your honour and the little gentlewoman? – Bless me! What is the matter here?

SIR GEORGE: I am, madam, treating your friends with a cold collation, and you are opportunely come for your share. The little gentlewoman is safe, and in much better hands than you designed her. Abominable hypocrite! who, tottering under the load of irreverend age and infamous diseases, inflexibly proceed in the practice of every vice, impiously prostituting the most sacred institutions to the most infernal purposes.

MRS COLE: I hope your honour . . .

SIR GEORGE: Take her away. As you have been singular in your penitence, you ought to be distinguished in your penance, which I promise you shall be most publicly and plentifully bestowed. (*Exit* MRS COLE.)

    (*Enter* DICK, *with constables.*)

DICK: The constables, sir.

SIR GEORGE: Let them come in, that I may consign these gentlemen to their care. (*to* SIR WILLIAM) Your letters of nobility you will produce in a court of justice. Though, if I read you right, you are one of those indigent, itinerant nobles of your own creation, which our reputation for hospitality draws here in shoals, to the shame of our understanding, the impairing of our fortunes, and, when you are trusted, the betraying of our designs. Officers, do your duty.

SIR WILLIAM: Why, don't you know me?

SIR GEORGE: Just as I guessed. An imposter! He has recovered the free use of his tongue already.

SIR WILLIAM: Nay, but George.

SIR GEORGE: Insolent familiarity! Away with him.

SIR WILLIAM: Hold, hold a moment. Brother Richard, set this matter to rights.

RICHARD: Don't you know him?

SIR GEORGE: Know him! The very question is an affront.

RICHARD: Nay, I don't wonder at it. 'Tis your father, you fool.

SIR GEORGE: My father! Impossible!

SIR WILLIAM: That may be, but 'tis true.

SIR GEORGE: My father alive! Thus let me greet the blessing.

SIR WILLIAM: Alive! Ay, and I believe I shall not be in a hurry to die again.

SIR GEORGE: But, dear sir, the report of your death – and this disguise – to what . . .

SIR WILLIAM: Don't ask any questions. Your uncle will tell you all. For my part, I am sick of the scheme.

RICHARD: I told you what would come of your politics.

SIR WILLIAM: You did so. But if it had not been for those clumsy scoundrels, the plot was as good a plot – Oh George, such discoveries I have to make! Within I'll unravel the whole.

SIR GEORGE: Perhaps, sir, I may match 'em.

SHIFT: Sir. (*Pulls him by the sleeve.*)

SIR GEORGE: Never fear. It is impossible, gentlemen, to determine your fate, till this matter is more fully explained. Till when, keep them in safe custody. Do you know them, sir?

SIR WILLIAM: Yes, but that's more than they did me. I can cancel your debts there, and, I believe, prevail on those gentlemen to refund too. – But you have been a sad profligate young dog, George.

SIR GEORGE: I cannot boast of my goodness, sir, but I think I could produce you a proof that I am not so totally destitute of . . .

SIR WILLIAM: Ay, why then prithee do.

SIR GEORGE: I have, sir, this day resisted a temptation that greater pretenders to morality might have yielded to. But I will trust myself no longer, and must crave your interposition and protection.

SIR WILLIAM: To what?

SIR GEORGE: I will attend you with the explanation in an instant. (*Exit.*)

SIR WILLIAM: Prithee, Shift, what does it mean?

SHIFT: I believe I can guess.

SIR WILLIAM: Let us have it.

SHIFT: I suppose the affair I overheard just now. A prodigious fine elegant girl, faith, that, discarded by her family for refusing to marry her grandfather, fell into the hands of the venerable lady you saw, who, being the kind caterer for your son's amusements, brought her hither for a purpose obvious enough. But the young gentleman, touched with her story, truth, and tears, was converted from the spoiler of her honour to the protector of her innocence.

SIR WILLIAM: Lookye there, brother, did I not tell you that George was not so bad at the bottom!

RICHARD: This does indeed atone for half the – But here they are.

(*Enter* SIR GEORGE *and* LUCY.)

SIR GEORGE: Fear nothing, madam, you may safely rely on the . . .

LUCY: My father!

RICHARD: Lucy!

LUCY: Oh sir, can you forgive your poor distressed unhappy girl? You scarce can guess how hardly I have been used since my banishment from your paternal roof. Want, pining want, anguish and shame have been my constant partners.

SIR WILLIAM: Brother!

SIR GEORGE: Sir!

LUCY: Father!

RICHARD: Rise, child, 'tis I must ask thee for forgiveness. Can'st thou forget the woes I have made thee suffer? Come to my arms once more, thou darling of my age. What mischief had my rashness nearly completed. Nephew, I scarce can thank you as I ought, but . . .

SIR GEORGE: I am richly paid, in being the happy instrument – Yet, might I urge a wish . . .

SHIFT: no stage direction is given for the exit and re-entrance of SHIFT, which would have been necessary for Foote when he was doubling SHIFT and MRS COLE.

RICHARD: Name it.

SIR GEORGE: That you would forgive my follies of today, and, as I have been providentially the occasional guardian of your daughter's honour, that you would
bestow on me that right for life.

RICHARD: That must depend on Lucy. Her will, not mine, shall now direct her
choice. – What says your father?

SIR WILLIAM: Me! Oh, I'll show you in an instant. Give me your hands. There,
children, now you are joined, and the devil take him that wishes to part you.

SIR GEORGE: I thank you for us both.

RICHARD: Happiness attend you.

SIR WILLIAM: Now, brother, I hope you will allow me to be a good plotter. All this
was brought to bear by my means.

SHIFT: With my assistance, I hope you will own, sir.

SIR WILLIAM: That's true, honest Shift, and thou shalt be richly rewarded. Nay,
George shall be your friend too. This Shift is an ingenious fellow, let me tell you,
son.

SIR GEORGE: I am no stranger to his abilities, sir. But if you please, we will retire.
The various struggles of this fair sufferer require the soothing softness of a sister's
love. And now, sir, I hope your fears for me are over, for had I not this motive to
restrain my follies, yet I now know the town too well to be ever its bubble, and
will take care to preserve, at least,

> Some more estate, and principles and wit,
> Than brokers, bawds, and gamesters shall think fit.

EPILOGUE

SHIFT, *addressing himself to* SIR GEORGE

> And what becomes of your poor servant, Shift?
> Your father talks of lending me a lift –
> A great man's promise, when his turn is serv'd!
> Capons on promises would soon be starv'd:
> No, on myself alone, I'll now rely:
> 'Gad I've a thriving traffic in my eye –
> Near the mad mansions of Moorfields I'll bawl;
> 'Friends, fathers, mothers, sisters, sons, and all,
> Shut up your shops, and listen to my call.
> With labour, toil, all second means dispense,
> And live a rent-charge upon Providence.
> Prick up your ears; a story now I'll tell,
> Which once a widow, and her child befel –
> I knew the mother, and her daughter well.
> Poor, it is true, they were; but never wanted,
> For whatsoe'er they ask'd, was always granted:

---

in my eye: Foote may have pointed a double meaning here, by adopting the squint needed for his
take-off of Squintum/Whitefield.

One fatal day, the matron's truth was tried,
She wanted meat and drink, and fairly cried.
(*Child*) Mother you cry! (*Mother*) Oh, child, I've got no bread.
(*Child*) What matters that? Why Providence an't dead!
With reason good, this truth the child might say,
For there came in at noon, that very day,
Bread, greens, potatoes, and a leg of mutton,
A better sure a table ne'er was put on:
Ay, that may be, ye cry, with those poor souls;
But ne'er had we a rasher for the coals.
And d'ye deserve it? How d'ye spend your days?
In pastimes, prodigality, and plays!
Let's go see Foote! Ah, Foote's a prcious limb!
Old Nick will soon a football make of him!
For foremost rows in side-boxes you shove,
Think you to meet with side-boxes above?
Where giggling girls and powdered fops may sit, – ⎫
No, you'll be cramm'd together in the Pit,   ⎬
And crowd the house for Satan's benefit.   ⎭
Oh, what, you snivel! Well, do so no more; ⎫
Drop, to atone, your money at the door,   ⎬
And (if I please) – I'll give it to the poor.'   ⎭

THE NABOB

A comedy in three acts

by SAMUEL FOOTE

First performed at the Theatre Royal, Haymarket, on 29 June 1772, with the following cast:

SIR MATTHEW MITE	Mr Foote
SIR JOHN OLDHAM	Mr Gentleman
MR THOMAS OLDHAM	Mr Aicken
YOUNG OLDHAM	Mr DuBellamy
MR MAYOR	Mr Parsons
TOUCHIT	Mr Baddeley
FIRST ANTIQUARIAN	Mr Loyd
SECOND ANTIQUARIAN	Mr Hamilton
SECRETARY	Mr Davis
RAPINE	Mr Lings
NATHAN	Mr Castle
MOSES	Mr Jacobs
JANUS PUTTY	Mr Weston
CONSERVE	Mr Fearon
WAITER	Mr Ward
LADY OLDHAM	Mrs Egerton
SOPHY	Miss Ambrose
MRS MATCH'EM	Mrs Gardner
CROCUS	Miss Craven
Beadles, servants etc.	

SCENE: A borough lying to the westward of the Metropolis.

PROLOGUE

Spoken at the Theatre Royal, Dublin, by Mr Foote, on 19 November 1773.

Upwards of twenty years are fled and wasted
Since in this spot your favours first I tasted.
Urg'd by your smiles through various realms to roam,
The Muse now brings her motley cargo home;
For frugal Nature, with an equal hand,
Bestows peculiar gifts on every land.
To France she gave her rapid repartee,   ⎱
Bows, and *bon mots*, fibs, fashions, flattery, ⎬
Shrugs, grins, grimace, and sportive gaiety: ⎰
Armed with the whole artillery of love,
Latium's soft sons possess the powers to move;
Humour, the foremost of the festive crew,
Source of the comic scene, she gave to you;
Humour, with arched brow, and leering eye,
Shrewd, solemn, sneering, subtle, slow, and sly;
Serious herself, yet laughter still provoking,
By teasing, tickling, jeering, gibing, joking:
Impartial gift, that owns nor rank nor birth!
'Tis theirs who rule the realm, or till the earth;
Theirs who in senates wage the wordy war,
And theirs whose humble lot conducts the car.
If aught deriv'd from her adorns my strain,
You have, at least discover'd first, the vein.
Should wide experience, or maturing age,
Have brought or mirth or moral to the stage,
To you, the patrons or the wilder song,
The chaster notes in justice must belong:
But should infirmities with time conspire,
My force to weaken or abate my fire,
Less entertainment may arise to you,
But to myself less danger will ensue.
If age contracts my muscles, shrills my tone,
No man will claim those foibles as his own;
Nor, if I halt or hobble through the scene,
Malice point out what citizen I mean:
No foe I fear more than a legal fury,
Unless I gain this circle for my jury.

ACT 1

SCENE 1.   *A chamber. Enter* LADY OLDHAM *and* SIR JOHN OLDHAM.
LADY OLDHAM: Not a syllable more will I hear!
SIR JOHN: Nay, but, my dear . . .
LADY OLDHAM: I am amazed, Sir John, at your meanness! Or that you could submit
    to give his paltry proposals so much as a reading!
SIR JOHN: Nay, my dear, what would you have had me done?
LADY OLDHAM: Done? Returned them with the contempt they deserved.
SIR JOHN: Nay, but consider, my love . . .
LADY OLDHAM: The subject neither demands nor deserves it.
SIR JOHN: If you would condescend but for five minutes to give me a hearing, I think
    I could satisfy you that . . .
LADY OLDHAM: You have neither feeling nor spirit, of that I am already convinced.
    But come, unfold! I am calm. Reveal the pretty project your precious head has
    produced.
SIR JOHN: Nay, my dear, as to – that my head produced – To be sure, I don't pretend
    that – I only wished to, that is, ah, ah . . .
LADY OLDHAM: Nay, I don't wonder that shame has tied up your tongue! But,
    come, I will spare the confusion, and tell you what you would say: 'Here, Lady
    Oldham, Sir Matthew Mite has just sent me a letter, modestly desiring that, in
    return for the ruin he has brought upon me and my house, I would be so kind as
    to bestow upon him my darling daughter, the hopes of my –' And is it possible you
    can be mean enough to think of such an alliance?
SIR JOHN: I think, my dear, you are totally wrong, but you are so impetuous. I only
    wanted you just to peruse the contents, that is, only by way of seeing, my love,
    what the man would be at.
LADY OLDHAM: Ah, can there be the least doubt of his meaning? Had not your
    spirit been sunk to the lowest pitch of – but I will be cool. Will you, Sir John,
    oblige me with an answer to a few short questions?
SIR JOHN: Without doubt.
LADY OLDHAM: I suppose you consider yourself as sprung from a family, at least as
    ancient as any in the county you live in?
SIR JOHN: That, I fancy, will not be denied.
LADY OLDHAM: Nor was it, I flatter myself, dishonoured by an alliance with mine?
SIR JOHN: My lady, the very reverse.
LADY OLDHAM: Very well, you succeeded, sir, to a patrimony which, though the
    liberal and hospitable spirit of your predecessors would not suffer to increase, yet
    their prudence took care should never be diminished?
SIR JOHN: True.
LADY OLDHAM: From the public and private virtues of your ancestors, the inhabi-
    tants of the neighbouring borough thought their best and dearest interests in no
    hands so secure as in theirs?
SIR JOHN: Right.
LADY OLDHAM: Nor till lately were they so tainted by the fashions of the times, as
    to adopt the egregious absurdity, that, to be faithfully served and protected
    above, it was necessary to be largely bribed and corrupted below?

SIR JOHN: Why, I can't say, except now and then a bit of venison, or an annual dinner, they have ever put me to any great . . .

LADY OLDHAM: Indulge me yet a moment, Sir John! In this happy situation, did the last year cheerfully close; our condition, though not opulent, affluent, and you happy in the quiet possession of your family honours.

SIR JOHN: There's no gainsaying of that.

LADY OLDHAM: Now, look at the dismal, shocking reverse!

SIR JOHN: There is but too much reason in what your ladyship says.

LADY OLDHAM: And consider, at the same time, to whom you are obliged.

SIR JOHN: Why, what could we do? Your ladyship knows there was nobody more against my giving up than yourself.

LADY OLDHAM: Let me proceed. At this crisis, preceded by all the pomp of Asia, Sir Matthew Mite, from the Indies, came thundering amongst us, and, profusely scattering the spoils of ruined provinces, corrupted the virtue and alienated the affections of all the old friends to the family.

SIR JOHN: That is nothing but truth.

LADY OLDHAM: Compelled by the same means to defend those that were employed in securing your interest, you have been obliged deeply to encumber your fortune; his superior address has procured a return; and probably your petition will complete the ruin his opposition began.

SIR JOHN: Let us hope all for the best.

LADY OLDHAM: And who can tell, but you may be soon forced to part with your patrimony, to the very insolent, worthless individual who has been the author of your distress?

SIR JOHN: I would sooner perish, my lady!

LADY OLDHAM: Parallel instances may be produced. Nor is it at all unlikely, but Sir Matthew, taking a fancy to your family mansion, has pursued this very method to compel you to sell it.

SIR JOHN: It is, my dear, to avoid this necessity that I wish you to give his letter a reading.

LADY OLDHAM: Is it possible, not to mention the meanness, that you can be weak enough to expect any real service from that infamous quarter?

SIR JOHN: Who can tell, my love, but a consciousness of the mischief he has done us may have roused some feelings that . . .

LADY OLDHAM: His feelings! Will he listen to a private complaint, who has been deaf to the cries of a people? Or drop a tear for particular distress, who owes his rise to the ruin of thousands?

SIR JOHN: Well, Lady Oldham, I find all that I say just signifies nothing. But here comes brother Thomas. Two heads are better than one; let us take his opinion, my love.

LADY OLDHAM: What need of any opinion? The case is too clear; nor, indeed, if

---

your petition: Sir John is petitioning parliament to annul the election of Sir Matthew Mite, on the grounds of corruption, but obviously Sir John himself has dissipated his own fortune in the campaign. If the petition fails, the costs will ruin him completely. Such petitions were a common feature of the Patriot reform movement.

there had been a necessity for consulting another, should I have thought your brother the properest man to advise with on the occasion.

SIR JOHN: And why not? There is not a merchant on Change whose judgement would be sooner taken.

LADY OLDHAM: Perhaps not, on the value of merchandise, or the goodness of a bill of exchange: but there is a nicety, a delicacy, an elevation of sentiment, in this case, which people who have narrowed their notions with commerce, and considered during the course of their lives their interest alone, will scarcely comprehend.

(*Enter* MR THOMAS OLDHAM.)

THOMAS: So, sister! What! Upon your old topic, I find?

LADY OLDHAM: Sir!

THOMAS: Some pretty comparisons, I suppose, not much to the honour of trade.

LADY OLDHAM: Nay, brother, you know I have always allowed merchants to be a useful body of men, and considered commerce, in this country, as a pretty resource enough for the younger shoots of a family.

THOMAS: Exceedingly condescending, indeed! And yet, sister, I could produce you some instances where the younger shoots have flourished and throve, when the reverend trunk has decayed.

LADY OLDHAM: Perhaps, brother Thomas, in your sense of the word, but let me tell you there is a very material difference between . . .

THOMAS: Nay, nay, do not let us revive our ancient disputes! You seem warm; no misunderstanding, I hope?

SIR JOHN: No, no. None in the least. You know my lady's temper is apt to be lively now and then, a little hasty or so, but when her ladyship is cool, no mortal can reason more justly.

LADY OLDHAM: Do you expect my thanks for this flattering picture?

THOMAS: Nay, sister. – But come! What has occasioned this mighty debate?

SIR JOHN: You know, brother, how affairs stand at present between Sir Matthew and us.

THOMAS: Well.

SIR JOHN: He has sent us here a kind of compromise – I don't know well what to call it – a sort of treaty.

THOMAS: That in your hand?

SIR JOHN: Yes, and I can't prevail on my lady to give it a reading.

THOMAS: And why not?

LADY OLDHAM: To what end?

THOMAS: A very natural one: in order to know the contents.

LADY OLDHAM: Of what importance can they be to us?

THOMAS: That the letter will tell you. But, surely, Lady Oldham, you are rather too nice. Give it to me!

SIR JOHN: Is it your ladyship's pleasure?

---

on Change: member of the Stock Exchange.

treaty: much of the pillage of India by the East India Company had been done under the pretext or title of Trade Treaties.

THOMAS: Psha! Here's a rout, indeed! One would be apt to suspect that the packet were pestilential, and came from the Archipelago, instead of the Indies. Now let us see what this formidable memorial contains! (*Opens the letter.*) 'To Sir John Oldham. Sir Matthew Mite having lately seen, at Lady Levant's rout, the eldest Miss Oldham, and being struck with her personal charms, proposes to her father the following treaty.'

LADY OLDHAM: A very monarchial address!

THOMAS: '*Imprimis*: Upon a matrimonial union between the young lady and him, all hostilities and contention shall cease, and Sir John be suffered to take his seat in security.'

LADY OLDHAM: That he will do, without any obligation to him.

THOMAS: Are you, sister, sure of that?

LADY OLDHAM: You don't harbour the least doubt of our merits?

THOMAS: But do they always prevail?

LADY OLDHAM: There is now, brother Thomas, no danger to dread. The restraint the popular part of government has in this instance laid on itself, at the same time that it does honour to them, distributes equal justice to all.

THOMAS: And are you aware what the expense will be to obtain it? – But, pray, let me proceed! 'Secondly, as Sir Matthew is bent upon a large territorial acquisition in England, and Sir John Oldham's finances are at present a little out of repair, Sir Matthew Mite will make up the money already advanced in another name, by way of future mortgage upon his estate, for the entire purchase, five lacks of rupees.'

SIR JOHN: Lacks of rupees?

LADY OLDHAM: Now, Sir John! Was I right in my guess?

SIR JOHN: Your ladyship is never out. But brother Thomas, these same lacks – to what may they amount?

THOMAS: Sixty thousand at least.

SIR JOHN: No inconsiderable offer, my lady.

LADY OLDHAM: Contemptible! But pray, sir, proceed.

THOMAS: 'Or, if it should be more agreeable to the parties, Sir Matthew will settle upon Sir John and his lady, for their joint lives, a jagghire.'

SIR JOHN: A jagghire?

THOMAS: The term is Indian, and means an annual income.

LADY OLDHAM: What strange jargon he deals in!

THOMAS: His style is a little oriental, I must own, but most exceedingly clear.

LADY OLDHAM: Yes, to Cossim Ali-Khan, or Mihir Jaffier. I hope you are near the conclusion.

THOMAS: But two articles more. (*Reads.*) 'And that the principals may have no cares for the younger parts of their family, Sir Matthew will, at his own expense, transport the two young ladies, Miss Oldham's two sisters, to Madras or Calcutta, and there procure them suitable husbands.'

---

the popular part of government: Lord North, prime minister since 1770, had tried to defuse the anti-corruption clamour of John Wilkes and Edmund Burke, by adopting an unaggressive policy of supporting individual complaints against corrupt elections, whilst blocking any moves toward general parliamentary reform.

LADY OLDHAM: Madras, or Calcutta!

THOMAS: Your patience, dear sister – 'And as for the three boys, they shall be either made super-cargoes, ships' husbands, or go out cadets and writers in the Company's service.'

LADY OLDHAM: Why, he treats my children like a parcel of convicts. Is this their method of supplying their settlements?

THOMAS: This, with now and then a little kidnapping, dear sister. – Well, madam, you have now the means of getting rid of all your offspring at once. Did I not tell you the paper was worth your perusal? You will reply to his wish: you can have no doubts, I suppose.

LADY OLDHAM: Not the least, as I will show you. (*Tears the letter.*) And if Sir John has the least spirit or pride, he will treat the insolent principal as I do his proposals.

THOMAS: But that method, as things stand, may not be altogether so safe. I am sorry you were so hasty in destroying the letter. If I remember rightly, there is mention made of advancing money in another man's name.

LADY OLDHAM: We have been compelled to borrow, I own; but I had no conception that he was the lender.

THOMAS: That's done by a common contrivance. Not a country lawyer but knows the doctrine of transfer. How much was the sum?

SIR JOHN: Ten thousand pounds.

THOMAS: And what, Sir John, were the terms?

SIR JOHN: As I could give no real security, my estate being settled till my son John comes of age, I found myself obliged to comply with all that was asked.

THOMAS: A judgement, no doubt.

SIR JOHN: They divided the sum, and I gave them a couple.

THOMAS: Which will affect not only your person, but personal property. So they are both in his power.

SIR JOHN: Too true, I am afraid!

THOMAS: And you may be sent to gaol, and your family turned into the streets, whenever he pleases.

LADY OLDHAM: How! Heaven forbid!

THOMAS: Not the least doubt can be made. This is an artful project. No wonder so much contrivance and cunning has been an over-match for a plain English gentleman or an innocent Indian. And what is now to be done? Does your daughter Sophy know of this letter?

LADY OLDHAM: Sir John?

SIR JOHN: It reached my hands not ten minutes ago.

THOMAS: I had some reason to think that, had you complied, you would not have found her very eager to second your wishes.

LADY OLDHAM: I don't know that, brother. Young girls are easily caught with titles and splendour; magnificence has a kind of magic for them.

THOMAS: I have a better opinion of Sophy. You know, Lady Oldham, I have often hinted that my boy was fond of his cousin, and, possibly, my niece not totally

---

judgement: under a judgement debt the debtor waived from the outset all his legal rights against immediate foreclosure. His chattels could be seized and himself imprisoned.

averse to his wish; but you have always stopped me short, under a notion that the children were too nearly allied.

LADY OLDHAM: Why, brother, don't you think . . .

THOMAS: But that, sister, was not the right reason. You could have easily digested the cousins, but the counting-house stuck in his way. Your favourite maxim has been that citizens are a distinct race, a sort of creatures that should not mix with each other.

LADY OLDHAM: Bless me, brother, you can't conceive that I . . .

THOMAS: Nay, no apology, good Lady Oldham! Perhaps you have a higher alliance in view, and I promise you my boy shall never enter into any family but with the hearty concurrence of all the parties concerned. But a truce to this topic. Let us now consider what is to be done. You are totally averse to this treaty?

LADY OLDHAM: Can that be a question?

THOMAS: Some little management is necessary as to the mode of rejection. As matters now stand, it would not be prudent to exasperate Sir Matthew.

LADY OLDHAM: Let Sir John discharge the debt due to him at once.

THOMAS: But where shall we get materials?

LADY OLDHAM: Can that be a difficult task?

THOMAS: Exceedingly so, as I apprehend. But few can be found to advance so large a sum on such slender security, nor is it to be expected, indeed, unless from a friend to relieve, or a foe to ruin.

LADY OLDHAM: Is it possible Sir Matthew can have acted from so infernal a motive, to have advanced the money with a view of distressing us deeper?

THOMAS: Sir Matthew is a profound politician, and will not stick at trifles to carry his point.

LADY OLDHAM: With the wealth of the East, we have, too, imported the worst of its vices. What a horrid crew!

THOMAS: Hold, sister! don't gratify your resentment at the expense of your justice. A general conclusion from a single instance is but indifferent logic.

LADY OLDHAM: Why, is not this Sir Matthew . . .

THOMAS: Perhaps as bad a subject as your passion can paint him, but there are men from the Indies, and many too, with whom I have the honour to live, who dispense nobly and with hospitality here what they have acquired with honour and credit elsewhere; and, at the same time that they have increased the dominions and wealth, have added virtues, too, to their country.

LADY OLDHAM: Perhaps so. But what is to be done? Suppose I were to wait on Sir Matthew myself.

THOMAS: If your ladyship is secure of commanding your temper.

SIR JOHN: Mercy on us, brother Thomas, there's no such thing as trusting to that!

LADY OLDHAM: You are always very obliging, Sir John! If the embassy was to be executed by you . . .

THOMAS: Come, come, to end the dispute, I will undertake the commission myself.

LADY OLDHAM: You will take care, brother, to make no concessions that will derogate from . . .

THOMAS: Your dignity. In my hands it will have nothing to fear. But should I not see my niece first? She ought to be consulted, I think.

SIR JOHN: By all means.

THOMAS: For, if she approved of the knight, I don't see anything in the alliance so much to be dreaded.

SIR JOHN: I will fetch her this instant.

LADY OLDHAM: And so with your usual delicacy come pop on the poor girl without the least preparation.

SIR JOHN: Well, my dear, I submit.

LADY OLDHAM: I will send Sophy to her uncle directly. But I desire the girl may be left to herself – no undue influence! (*Exit.*)

THOMAS: The caution was needless.

SIR JOHN: Why, really, now, brother, but that my lady is too warm, I don't see anything so very unreasonable in this same paper here that lies scattered about. But, I forget, did he mention anything of any fortune he was to have with the girl?

THOMAS: Pho! A paltry consideration, below his concern.

SIR JOHN: My lady herself must own there is something generous in that, and, indeed, if we could by the means of the girl stop the gap that has been made in my Rent, Roll, and set all our little matters to rights . . .

THOMAS: Will you stay and represent the case to Sophy yourself?

SIR JOHN: Not a syllable! My lady would never forgive me should I drop the least hint. No, no, let it all come from yourself. (*Enter* SOPHY.) Your uncle, child, has something to say to you. You know he loves you, my dear, and will advise you for the best. But remember if your mother asks you, I have not mentioned a word. (*Exit.*)

THOMAS: Come hither, Sophy, my love! Don't be alarmed. I suppose my lady has opened to you that Sir Matthew has sent a strange kind of romantic letter.

SOPHY: But she did not seem, sir, to suppose that it deserved much attention.

THOMAS: As matters now stand, perhaps more than she thinks. But come, my good girl, be explicit: suppose the affairs of your family should demand a compliance with this whimsical letter, should you have any reluctance to the union proposed?

SOPHY: Me, sir? I never saw the gentleman but once in my life.

THOMAS: And I do not think that would interest you much in his favour. His personal attractions are not very alluring, I own, but is there no other bar in the way?

SOPHY: Sir!

THOMAS: No prepossession? No prior object that has attracted your notice?

SOPHY: I hope, sir, my behaviour has not occasioned this question.

THOMAS: Oh, no, my dear. It naturally took its rise from the subject. Has your cousin lately been here?

SOPHY: Sir!

THOMAS: Tom Oldham, my son?

SOPHY: We generally see him, sir, every day.

THOMAS: I am glad to hear that. I was afraid some improper attachment had drawn him from the City so often of late.

SOPHY: Improper! I dare say, sir, you will have nothing of that kind to fear from my cousin.

THOMAS: I hope not. And yet I have had my suspicions, I own. But not unlikely you can remove them. Children rarely make confidants of their fathers.

SOPHY: Sir!

THOMAS: Similarity of sentiments, nearness of blood, and the same season of life, perhaps may have induced him to unbosom to you.

SOPHY: Do you suppose, sir, that he would discover to me what he chose to conceal from so affectionate a father?

THOMAS: Nay, prithee, Sophy, don't be grave! Why, now, do you imagine I should think his preferring your ear to mine, for a melting passionate tale, any violent breach of his duty?

SOPHY: You are merry, sir.

THOMAS: And who knows but you might repay the communication with a similar story? You blush, Sophy.

SOPHY: You are really pleased to be so very particular, that I scarce know what answer to make.

THOMAS: Come, my good niece, I will perplex you no longer. My son has concealed nothing from me, and did the completion of your wishes depend on my appro-bation alone, you would have but little to fear. But my lady's notions are so very peculiar, you know, and her principles so determined and fixed, that I can enter-tain but little hopes of a prosperous issue.

SOPHY: The merits of my cousin, which she herself is not slow to acknowledge, and time, might, I should hope, soften my mother.

THOMAS: Why, then, my dear niece, leave it to time, in most cases the ablest physician. But let your partiality for Tom be a secret! – I must now endeavour to learn when I can obtain an audience from Sir Matthew.

SOPHY: An audience!

THOMAS: Yes, child, these new gentlemen, who from the caprice of fortune, and a strange chain of events, have acquired immoderate wealth, and rose to uncon-trolled power abroad, find it difficult to descend from their dignity, and admit of any equal at home. Adieu, my dear niece! But keep up your spirits! I think I foresee an event that will produce some change in our favour. (*Exeunt.*)

SCENE 2.   SIR MATTHEW MITE's *hall.* JANUS *and* CONSERVE *discovered.*

CONSERVE: I own the place of a porter, if one can bear the confinement, is – ; and then, Sir Matthew has the character of – (*low tap at the door*) Use no ceremony, Mr Janus, with me. Mind your door, I beseech you.

JANUS: No hurry! Keep your seat, Mr Conserve. It's only the tap of a tradesman. I make those people stay till they collect in a body, and so let in eight or ten at a time. It saves trouble.

CONSERVE: And how do they brook it?

JANUS: Oh, wonderfully well, here with us. In my last place indeed, I thought myself bound to be civil, for, as all the poor devils could get was good words, it would have been hard to have been sparing of them.

CONSERVE: Very considerate!

CONSERVE: in the Larpent MS – 'CROCANT, Lord Levee's conserve'.
confinement: Weston, who originally played Janus, was a large man and would have been well 'confined' in the normal porter's chair, which was a sort of small sentry-box.

JANUS: But here we are rich, and as the fellows don't wait for their money, it is but fair they should wait for admittance.

CONSERVE: Or they would be apt to forget their condition.

JANUS: True.

CONSERVE: Upon the whole, then, you do not regret leaving my lord?

JANUS: No. Lord Levee's place had its sweets, I confess, perquisites pretty enough, but what could I do? They wanted to give me a rider.

CONSERVE: A rider?

JANUS: Yes. To quarter Monsieur Frissart, my lady's *valet de chambre*, upon me. So you know I could not but in honour resign.

CONSERVE: No, there was no bearing to be rid by a Frenchman. There was no staying in after that.

JANUS: It would have been quoted as a precedent against the whole corps.

CONSERVE: Yes. Pox on 'em! Our masters are damned fond of encroachments. Is your present duty severe?

JANUS: I drudge pretty much at the door, but that, you know, is mere bodily labour. But then, my mind is at ease, not obliged to rack my brain for invention.

CONSERVE: No?

JANUS: No. Not near the lying here, as in my last place.

CONSERVE: I suppose not, as your master is but newly in town. But you must expect that branch to increase.

JANUS: When it does, I shall insist the door be done by a deputy. (*two raps*)

CONSERVE: Hark! To your post!

JANUS: No. Sit still! That is some awkward body out of the City, one of our people from Leadenhall Street, perhaps a director. I shan't stir for him.

CONSERVE: Not for a director? I thought he was the commanding officer, the great captain's captain.

JANUS: No, no, quite the reverse. The tables are turned, Mr Conserve. In acknowledgement for appointing us their servants abroad, we are so obliging as to make them directors at home. (*a loud rapping*)

CONSERVE: That rap will rouse you, I think.

JANUS: Let me take a peep at the wicket. Oh, oh! Is it you, with a pox to you? How the deuce came your long legs to find the way hither? I shall be in no haste to open for you.

CONSERVE: Who is it?

JANUS: That eternal teaser, Sir Timothy Tallboys. When once he gets footing, there is no such thing as keeping him out.

CONSERVE: What, you know him then?

JANUS: Yes, rot him, I know him too well! He had like to have lost me the best place I ever had in my life.

CONSERVE: How so?

JANUS: Lord Lofty had given orders on no account to admit him. The first time, he got

---

director: the directors of the East India Company remained in London, and their instructions were often ignored by the factors and merchants in India.
Sir Timothy Tallboys: probably to be taken as Sir Thomas Robinson MP, of Rokeby Park, Yorkshire. He was very tall and thin and well known for his interminable speeches in parliament.

by me under the pretence of stroking Keeper, my house dog, the next, he nick'd me by desiring only just leave to scratch the poll of the parrot, 'Poll, Poll, Poll!' I thought the devil was in him if he deceived me a third, but he did, notwithstanding.

CONSERVE: Prithee, Janus, how?

JANUS: By begging to set his watch by Tompion's clock in the hall. I smoked his design, and laid hold of him here (*taking hold of his coat*). As sure as you are alive, he made but two strides from the stairs to the study, and left the skirt of his coat in my hand.

CONSERVE: You got rid of him, then?

JANUS: He made one attempt more, and for fear he should slip by me, for you know he is as thin as a slice of beef at Marybone Gardens, I slapped the door in his face, and told him the dog was mad, the parrot dead, and the clock stood, and, thank heaven, I have never set eyes on him since. (*knock louder*)

CONSERVE: But the door!

JANUS: Time enough. You had no particular commands, Master Conserve?

CONSERVE: Only to let you know that Betsy Robins has a rout and supper on Sunday next.

JANUS: Constant still, Mr Conserve, I see. I'm afraid I can't come to cards, but I shall be sure to attend the repast. A picnic, I suppose?

CONSERVE: Yes, yes. We all contribute as usual. The substantials from Alderman Sirloin's, Lord Frippery's cook finds fricassees and ragouts, Sir Robert Bumper's butler is to send in the wine, and I shall supply the dessert.

JANUS: There are a brace of birds and a hare, that I cribbed this morning out of a basket of game.

CONSERVE: They will be welcome. (*knock louder*) But the folks grow impatient!

JANUS: They must stay till I come. – At the old place, I suppose?

CONSERVE: No. I had like to have forgot! Betsy grew sick of St Paul's, so I have taken her a house amongst the new buildings. Both the air and the company is better.

JANUS: Right.

CONSERVE: To say truth, the situation was disagreeable on many accounts. Do you know, though I took care few people should behave better at Christmas, that, because he thought her a citizen, the housekeeper of Drury Lane Theatre, when his master mounted, refused her a side-box?

JANUS: No wonder Miss Betsy was bent on moving. What is the name of her street?

CONSERVE: Rebel Row. It was built by a messenger who made his market in the year forty-five. But shall Miss Robins send you a card?

JANUS: No, no. I shall easily find the place. (*knock*) Now let us see, who have we here? Sir Timothy has gone I believe. Gads my life, Mrs Match'em! My master's amorous agent. It is as much as my place is worth to let her wait for a minute. (*Opens the door. Exit* CONSERVE.)

St Paul's: the disreputable area of St Paul's church, Covent Garden, rather than that of the City cathedral.

year forty-five: land could be bought cheap at the time of the 1745 Rebellion.

(*Enter* MRS MATCH'EM, *some* TRADESPEOPLE, *who bow low to* JANUS, *and* THOMAS OLDHAM.)

MATCH'EM: So, sir! This is pretty treatment, for a woman like me to dangle at your gate, surrounded by a parcel of tradesfolk!

JANUS: I beg pardon, but madam . . .

MATCH'EM: Suppose any of my ladies had chanced to drive by; in a pretty situation they'd have seen me! I promise you I shall make my complaints to Sir Matthew.

JANUS: I was receiving some particular commands from my master.

MATCH'EM: I shall know that from him. Where is he? Let him know I must see him directly; my hands are so full I have not a moment to spare.

JANUS: At that door the groom of the chamber will take you in charge. I am sure you'll be admitted as soon as announced.

MATCH'EM: There is as much difficulty to get a sight of this signior as of a member when the parliament's dissolved! (*Exit.*)

JANUS: So! What, you have brought in your bills? Damned punctual, no doubt! The steward's room is below. – And, do you hear? When you are paid, be sure you don't sneak away without seeing of me.

ALL TRADESPEOPLE: We hope you have a better opinion . . .

JANUS: Well, well, march along! (*Exeunt* TRADESPEOPLE.) So, friend, what is your business, pray?

THOMAS: I have a message to deliver to Sir Matthew.

JANUS: You have – and pray what is the purport?

THOMAS: That is for his ear alone.

JANUS: You will find yourself mistaken in that.

THOMAS: How?

JANUS: It must make its way to his, by passing through mine.

THOMAS: Is that the rule of the house?

JANUS: Ay, and the best way to avoid idle and impertinent prattlers.

THOMAS: And of that you are to judge?

JANUS: Or I should not be fit for my post. But you are very importunate. Who are you? I suppose a Jew broker, come to bring my master the price of stocks.

THOMAS: No.

JANUS: Or some country cousin, perhaps.

THOMAS: Nor that either.

JANUS: Or a voter from our borough below – we never admit them but against an election.

THOMAS: Still wide of the mark. (*aside*) There is but one way of managing here. I must give the Cerberus a sop, I perceive. – Sir, I have really business with Sir Matthew, of the utmost importance, and if you can obtain me an interview, I shall think myself extremely obliged. (*Gives money.*)

JANUS: As I see, sir, by your manner, that it is a matter of moment, we will try what can be done. But you must wait for his levee, there is no seeing him yet.

THOMAS: No?

JANUS: He is too busy at present. The waiter at Almack's has just brought him home

---

Almack's: a gaming club.

his macaroni dress for the hazard table, and is instructing him to throw the dice with a grace.

THOMAS: Then where can I wait?

JANUS: If you will step into that room, I will take care to call you in time. (*Exit* THOMAS.) Two guineas! A good sensible fellow! At first sight, how easily one may be mistaken in men! (*Exit.*)

ACT II

SCENE 1.   *A chamber.* SIR MATTHEW MITE *in his gaming dress, a* WAITER *instructing him in throwing the hazard dice.*

MITE: Main and chance?

WAITER: Five to nine, please your honour.

MITE: I am at all that is set. How must I proceed?

WAITER: With a tap, as the chances are equal. Then raise the box genteelly and gently, with the finger and thumb.

MITE: Thus? (*Throws the dice.*)

WAITER: Exactly, your honour. Cinque and quatre. You are out.

MITE: What is next to be done?

WAITER: Flirt the bones with an air of indifference, and pay the money that's set.

MITE: Will that do? (*Gathers the dice and pays his loss.*)

WAITER: With a little more experience, your honour.

MITE: Then pass the box to my neighbour.

WAITER: Yes, or you make a back hand, if you please.

MITE: Couldn't you give me some general rules? For then, you know, I might practise in private.

WAITER: By all means. Seven, sir, is better nicked by a stamp.

MITE: So? (*Stamps and throws.*)

WAITER: Yes. When you want to throw six and four, or two cinques, you must take the long gallery, and whirl the dice to the end of the table.

MITE: Thus? (*Throws.*)

WAITER: Pretty well, please your honour. When your chance is low, as tray, ace, or two douces, the best method is to dribble out the bones from the box.

MITE: Will that do? (*Throws.*)

WAITER: Your honour comes rapidly on.

MITE: So that, perhaps, in a couple of months, I shall be able to tap, flirt, stamp, dribble and whirl with any man in the club?

WAITER: As your honour has genius, you will make a wonderful progress, no doubt, but these nice matters are not got at in a moment, there must be parts, as well as practice, your honour.

MITE: What! Parts for the performance of this?

WAITER: This! Why there's Sir Christopher Clumsey, in the whole losing his fortune, and I believe he was near a twelvemonth about it, never once threw, paid, or received, with one atom of grace.

---

macaroni: a dandy.

MITE: He must have been a dull devil, indeed.

WAITER: A mere dunce – got no credit by losing his money; was ruined without the least reputation.

MITE: Perhaps so. Well, but, Dick, as to the oaths and phrases that are most in use at the club.

WAITER: I have brought them here in this paper. As soon as your honour has got them by heart, I will teach you when, and in what manner, to use them.

MITE: (*after looking at the paper*) How long do you apprehend before I may be fit to appear at the table?

WAITER: In a month or six weeks. I would advise your honour to begin in the Newmarket week, when the few people left do little better than piddle.

MITE: Right – so I shall gain confidence against the club's coming to town.
(*Enter* SERVANT.)

SERVANT: Mrs Crocus, from Brompton, your honour.

MITE: Has she brought me a bouquet?

SERVANT: Your honour?

MITE: Any nosegays, you blockhead!

SERVANT: She has a boy with a basket.

MITE: Show her in. (*Exit* SERVANT.) Well, Dick, you will go down to my steward, and teach him the best method of making a roleau. And, do you hear, let him give you one for your pains.

WAITER: Your honour's obedient! You'd have me attend every morning?

MITE: Without doubt. It would be madness to lose a minute, you know. (*Exit* WAITER. *Enter* MRS CROCUS.) Well, Mrs Crocus, let us see what you have brought me. Your last bouquet was as big as a broom, with a tulip strutting up like a magistrate's mace, and, besides, made me look like a devil.

CROCUS: I hope your honour could find no fault with the flowers. It is true, the polyanthuses were a little pinched by the easterly winds, but for pip, colour, and eye, I defy the whole parish of Fulham to match them.

MITE: Perhaps not, but it is not the flowers, but the mixture, I blame. Why, here now, Mrs Crocus, one should think you were out of your senses, to cram in this clump of jonquils!

CROCUS: I thought your honour was fond of their smell.

MITE: Damn their smell! It is their colour I talk of. You know my complexion has been tinged by the East, and you bring me here a blaze of yellow, that gives me the jaundice. Look! Do you see here, what a fine figure I cut? You might as well have tied me to a bundle of sun-flowers!

CROCUS: I beg pardon, your honour!

MITE: Pardon! There is no forgiving faults of this kind. Just so you served Harry Hectic. You stuck into his bosom a parcel of hyacinths, though the poor fellow's face is as pale as a primrose.

CROCUS: I did not know . . .

Newmarket week: when all the big gamblers will have gone to the race meeting.
roleau: a stack of coins made up in a roll of paper.

MITE: And there, at the opera, the poor creature sat in his side-box, looking like one of the figures in the glass-cases in Westminster Abbey, dead and dressed.

CROCUS: If gentlemen would but give directions, I would make it my study to suit them.

MITE: But that your cursed climate won't let you do. Have you any pinks or carnations in bloom?

CROCUS: They are not in season, your honour. Lilies of the valley . . .

MITE: I hate the whole tribe! What, you want to dress me up like a corpse! When shall you have any rose-buds?

CROCUS: The latter end of the month, please your honour.

MITE: At any time you may call.

CROCUS: Your honour has no further commands?

MITE: None. You may send nosegays for my chairmen, as usual. (*Exit* MRS CROCUS.) Piccard! Here, take that garland away. I believe the woman thought she was dressing a May-pole. Make a bouquet with the artificial flowers I brought from Milan.

      (*Enter* SERVANT.)

SERVANT: Would your honour please to see Madam Match'em?

MITE: Introduce her this instant. (*Enter* MRS MATCH'EM.) My dear Match'em! Well, what news from Cheapside?

MATCH'EM: Bad enough, very near a total defeat.

MITE: How so? you were furnished with ample materials.

MATCH'EM: But not of the right kind, please your honour. I have had but little intercourse with that part of the world, my business has chiefly lain on this side of the bar, and I was weak enough to think both cities alike.

MITE: And aren't they?

MATCH'EM: No two nations can differ so widely! Though money is supposed the idol of merchants, their wives don't agree in the worship.

MITE: In that article I thought the whole world was united.

MATCH'EM: No. They don't know what to do with their money. A Pantheon subscription or a masquerade ticket is more negotiable here than a note from the bank.

MITE: What think you of a bracelet, or a well-fancied aigret?

MATCH'EM: I should think they must make their way.

MITE: I have sent some rough diamonds to be polished in Holland. When they are returned, I will equip you, Match'em, with some of these toys.

MATCH'EM: Toys? How light he makes of these things! – Bless your noble and generous soul! I believe for a trifle more I could have obtained Lady Lurcher last night.

MITE: Indeed?

MATCH'EM: She has been pressed a good deal to discharge an old score, long due to a knight from the North, and play debts, your honour knows, there is no paying

---

Westminster Abbey: funeral effigies with wax death masks, including that of Charles II, were on view in the cloisters.

the bar: Temple Bar, the boundary between the City of London and Westminster.

Pantheon: concert rooms.

in part. She seemed deeply distressed, and I really believe another hundred would have made up the sum.

MITE: And how came you not to advance it?

MATCH'EM: I did not choose to exceed my commission. Your honour knows the bill was only for five.

MITE: Oh, you should have immediately made it up. You know I never stint myself in these matters.

MATCH'EM: Why, had I been in cash, I believe I should have ventured, your honour. If your honour approves, I have thought of a project that will save us both a good deal of trouble.

MITE: Communicate, good Mrs Match'em!

MATCH'EM: That I may not pester you with applications for every trifle I want, suppose you were to deposit a round sum in my hands.

MITE: What, Match'em, make you my banker for beauty? Ha, ha, ha!

MATCH'EM: Exactly, your honour. Ha, ha, ha!

MITE: Faith, Match'em, a very good conceit.

MATCH'EM: You may depend on my punctuality in paying your drafts.

MITE: I don't harbour the least doubt of your honour.

MATCH'EM: Would you have me proceed in Patty Parrington's business? She is expected from Bath in a week.

MITE: And what becomes of her aunt?

MATCH'EM: That Argus is to be left in the country.

MITE: You had better suspend your operations for a while. Do you know, Mrs Match'em, that I am going to be married?

MATCH'EM: Married? Your honour's pleased to be pleasant. That day I hope never to see.

MITE: The treaty wants nothing but her friends' ratification, and I think there is no danger of their withholding that, eh Match'em?

MATCH'EM: Nay, then, the matter is as good as concluded. I was always in dread of this fatal stroke.

MITE: But, Match'em, why should you be so averse to the measure?

MATCH'EM: Can it be thought, that with dry eyes I could bear the loss of such a friend as your honour? I don't know how it is, but I am sure I never took such a fancy to any man in my life.

MITE: Nay, Match'em!

MATCH'EM: Something so magnificent and princely in all you say or do, that a body has, as I may say, a pleasure in taking pains in your service.

MITE: Well, but, prithee, child . . .

MATCH'EM: And then, when one has brought matters to bear, no after-reproaches, no grumblings from parties, such general satisfaction on all sides! I am sure, since the death of my husband, as honest a man, except the trifling thing he died for . . .

MITE: How came that about, Mrs Match'em?

MATCH'EM: Why, Kit was rather apt to be careless, and put a neighbour's name to a note without stopping to ask his consent.

MITE: Was that all?

MATCH'EM: Nothing else. Since that day, I saw no mortal has caught my eye but your honour.

MITE: Really, Match'em?

MATCH'EM: I can't say, neither, it was the charms of your person – though they are such as any lady might like – but it was the beauties of your mind that made an impression upon me.

MITE: Nay, prithee, Match'em, dry up your tears! You distress me! Be persuaded you have nothing to fear.

MATCH'EM: How!

MOTE: Why, you don't suppose that I am prompted to this project by passion?

MATCH'EM: No?

MITE: Pho! No, I only wanted a wife to complete my establishment, just to adorn the head of my table.

MATCH'EM: To stick up in your room, like any other fine piece of furniture?

MITE: Nothing else. As an antique bust or a picture.

MATCH'EM: That alters the case.

MITE: Perhaps, I shall be confined a little at first, for, when you take or bury a wife, decency requires that you should keep your house for a week. After that time, you will find me, dear Match'em, all that you can wish.

MATCH'EM: Ah! That is more than your honour can tell. I have known some of my gentlemen, before marriage, make as firm and good resolutions not to have the least love or regard for their wives, but they have been seduced after all, and turned out the poorest tame family fools!

MITE: Indeed?

MATCH'EM: Good for nothing at all.

MITE: That shall not be my case.

(*Enter* SERVANT.)

SERVANT: Your honour's levee is crowded.

MITE: I come. Piccard, give me my coat. I have had some thoughts, Match'em, of founding in this town a seraglio. They are of singular use in the Indies. Do you think I could bring it to bear?

MATCH'EM: Why, a customer of mine did formerly make an attempt, but he pursued too violent measures at first, wanted to confine the ladies against their consent, and that, too, in a country of freedom.

MITE: Oh, fy! How the best institutions may fail, for want of a man proper to manage!

MATCH'EM: But your honour has had great experience. If you would bestow the direction on me . . .

MITE: Impossible, Match'em! In the East we never confide that office to your sex or complexion. I had some thoughts of importing three blacks from Bengal, who have been properly prepared for the service, but I shan't venture till the point is determined, whether those creatures are to be considered as mere chattles or men. (*Exeunt.*)

SCENE 2.   *A saloon. Enter* MAYOR, TOUCHIT, NATHAN, MOSES *etc.*

SERVANT: Walk in, gentlemen! His honour will be presently here.

---

chattles or men: the Somersett case of 1772 had ruled that slavery was illegal in Britain, and that a slave was automatically free as soon as he stepped ashore.
TOUCHIT: In the Larpent MS 'Touch'em'.

TOUCHIT: Do you see, Mr Mayor? Look about you! Here are noble apartments!

MAYOR: Very fine, very curious, indeed! But, after all, Master Touchit, I am not so over-fond of these Nabobs. For my part, I had rather sell myself to somebody else.

TOUCHIT: And why so, Mr Mayor?

MAYOR: I don't know – they do a mortal deal of harm in the country. Why, wherever any of them settles, it raises the price of provisions for thirty miles round. People rail at seasons and crops; in my opinion, it is all along with them there folks that things are so scarce.

TOUCHIT: Why, Mr Mayor, you talk like a fool! Suppose they have mounted the beef and mutton a trifle, aren't we obliged to them too for raising the value of boroughs? You should always set one against t'other.

MAYOR: That, indeed, is nothing but fair. But how comes it about? And where do these here people get all their wealth?

TOUCHIT: The way is plain enough, from our settlements and possessions abroad.

MAYOR: Oh, maybe so. I've been often minded to ask you what sort of things them there settlements are, because, why as you know, I have never been beyond sea.

TOUCHIT: Oh, Mr Mayor, I will explain that in a moment. Why, here are a body of merchants that beg to be admitted as friends, and take possession of a small spot in a country, and carry on a beneficial commerce with the inoffensive and innocent people, to which their chiefs kindly gave their consent.

MAYOR: Don't you think now, that is very civil of them?

TOUCHIT: Doubtless. Upon which, Mr Mayor, we cunningly encroach, and fortify by little and by little, till at length, growing too strong for the natives, we turn them out of their lands and take possession of their money and jewels.

MAYOR: And don't you think, Master Touchit, that is a little uncivil in us?

TOUCHIT: Oh, nothing at all. These people are but a little better than Tartars or Turks.

MAYOR: No, no, Master Touchit, just the reverse: it is they have caught the Tartar in us.

TOUCHIT: Ha, ha, ha! Well said, Mr Mayor. But hush! Here comes his honour. Fall back!

(*Enter* SIR MATTHEW MITE.)

MITE: Oh, Nathan! Are you there? You have split the stock as I bid you?

NATHAN: I vas punctually obey your directions.

MITE: And I shall be in no danger of losing my list?

NATHAN: Dat is safe, your honour. We have nothing to fear.

MITE: Moses Mendoza! You will take care to qualify Peter Pratewell and Counsellor Quibble? I shall want some speakers at the next General Court.

MOSES: Please you honour, I shall be careful of dat.

MITE: How is the stock?

MOSES: It vas got up the end of the week.

MITE: Then sell out till you sink it two and a half. Has my advice been followed for burning the tea?

MOSES: As to dat matter, I vas not inquire dat. I believe not.

MITE: So, that commodity will soon be a drug. The English are too proud to profit by the practice of others. What would become of the spice trade, if the Dutch brought their whole growth to market?

MOSES: Dat is very true. Your honour has no farder commands?

MITE: None at present, Master Mendoza. (*Exit* MOSES.)

NATHAN: For de next settlement, would your honour be de bull or de bear?

MITE: I shall send you my orders to Jonathon's. Oh, Nathan! Did you tell that man in Berkshire I would buy his estate?

NATHAN: Yes, but he say he has no mind, no occasion to sell it. Dat de estate belong to great many faders before him.

MITE: Why, the man must be mad. Did you tell him I had taken a fancy to the spot when I was but a boy?

NATHAN: I vas tell him as much.

MITE: And that all the time I was in India my mind was bent upon the purchase?

NATHAN: I vas say so.

MITE: And now I'm come home, am determined to buy it?

NATHAN: I make use of de very words.

MITE: Well then! What would the booby be at?

NATHAN: I don't know.

MITE: Give the fellow four times the value, and bid him turn out in a month. (*to* TOUCHIT) May I presume, sir, to ask who you are, and what your business may be?

TOUCHIT: My name, sir, is Touchit, and these gentlemen some friends and neighbours of mine. We are ordered by the Christian Club, of the borough of Bribe'em, to wait upon your honour, with a tender of the nomination of our two members at the ensuing election.

MITE: Sir, I accept their offer with pleasure, and am happy to find, notwithstanding all that has been said, that the union still subsists between Bengal and the ancient corporation of Bribe'em.

TOUCHIT: And if they are ever severed, I can assure your honour the Christian Club will not be to blame. Your honour understands me I hope?

MITE: Perfectly. Nor shall it, I promise you, be my fault, good Mr Touchit. But, you will forgive my curiosity, sir, the name your club has adopted, has at first a whimsical sound, but you had your reasons, no doubt.

TOUCHIT: The very best in the world, please your honour; from our strict union and brotherly kindness, we hang together. Like the primitive Christians too, we have all things in common.

MITE: In common! I don't apprehend you.

TOUCHIT: Why, please your honour, when the bargain is struck, and the deposit is made, as proof that we love our neighbours as well as ourselves, we submit to an equal partition, no man has a larger share than another.

MITE: A most Christian-like dispensation!

TOUCHIT: Yes, in our borough all is unanimity now. Formerly, we had nothing but

---

Jonathon's: a stock-broking coffee-house in the City.

Christian Club: 'humorously and satirically exposing the late proceedings of the Christian Club of Shoreham' (*Town and Country*, vol. IV, p. 374).

discontents and heart-burnings amongst us, each man jealous and afraid that his neighbour got more and did better than himself.

MITE: Indeed!

TOUCHIT: Ay, and with reason sometimes. Why, I remember, at the election some time ago, when I took up my freedom, I could get but thirty guineas for a new pair of jack-boots, whilst Tom Ramskin over the way had a fifty-pound note for a pair of wash-leather breeches.

MITE: Very partial indeed!

TOUCHIT: So, upon the whole, we thought it best to unite.

MITE: Oh, much the best. Well, sir, you may assure your principals that I shall take care properly to acknowledge the service they do me.

TOUCHIT: No doubt, no doubt. But – will your honour step a little this way? Though no question can be made of your honour's keeping your word, yet it has always been the rule with our club to receive the proper acknowledgement before the service is done.

MITE: Ay, but, Mr Touchit, suppose the service should never be done?

TOUCHIT: What then must become of our consciences? We are Christians, your honour.

MITE: True; but, Mr Touchit, you remember the proverb?

TOUCHIT: What proverb, your honour?

MITE: There are two bad paymasters; those who pay before, and those who pay never.

TOUCHIT: True, your honour, but our club has always found that those who don't pay before are sure never to pay.

MITE: How! Impossible! The man who breaks his word with such faithful and honest adherents, deserves richly a halter. Gentlemen, in my opinion, he deserves to be hanged.

TOUCHIT: Hush! Have a care what you say.

MITE: What is the matter?

TOUCHIT: You see the fat man that is behind? He is to be the returning officer at the election.

MITE: What then?

TOUCHIT: On a gibbet, at the end of our town, there hangs a smuggler, for robbing the custom-house.

MITE: Well?

TOUCHIT: The mayor's own brother, your honour. Now, perhaps he may be jealous that you meant to throw some reflection on him or his family.

MITE: Not unlikely. I say, gentlemen, whoever violates his promise to such faithful friends as you are, in my poor opinion, deserves to be damned!

TOUCHIT: That's right! Stick to that! For though the Christian Club may have some fears of the gallows, they don't value damnation of a farthing.

MITE: Why should they, as it may be so long before anything of that kind may happen, you know?

TOUCHIT: Good! Good again! Your honour takes us rightly, I see. I make no doubt it won't be long before we come to a good understanding.

---

jack-boots . . . breeches: indirect bribery often took the form of paying excessively for the voters' products.

MITE: The sooner the better, good Master Touchit, and, therefore, in one word, pray what are your terms?

TOUCHIT: Do you mean for one, or would your honour bargain for both?

MITE: Both, both.

TOUCHIT: Why, we could not have afforded you one under three thousand at least, but as your honour, as I may say, has a mind to deal in the gross, we shall charge you but five for both.

MITE: Oh fie! Above the market, good Mr Touchit!

TOUCHIT: Dog-cheap; neck-beef; a penny-loaf for a halfpenny! Why, we had partly agreed to bring in Sir Christopher Quinze and Major Match'em for the very same money, but the major has been a little unlucky at Almack's, and at present can't deposit the needful; but he says, however, if he should be successful at the next Newmarket meeting, he will faithfully abide by the bargain. But the turf, your honour knows, is but an uncertain estate, and so we can't depend upon him.

MITE: True. Well, sir, as I may soon have occasion for all the friends I can make, I shall haggle no longer. I accept your proposals. In the next room we will settle terms.

TOUCHIT: Your honour will always find the Christians steady and firm. But won't your honour introduce us to his worship whilst we are here?

MITE: To his worship? To whom?

TOUCHIT: To the gentleman in black.

MITE: Worship! You are mad, Mr Touchit! That is a slave I brought from the Indies.

TOUCHIT: Good lack! May be so! I did not know but the gentleman might belong to the tribe, who, we are told by the papers, conferred those splendid titles upon your honour in India.

MITE: Well, Master Touchit, what then?

TOUCHIT: I thought it not unlikely, but, in return to that compliment, your honour might choose to make one of the family member for the corporation of Bribe'em.

MITE: Why, you would not submit to accept a negro?

TOUCHIT: Our present members, for aught we know, may be of the same complexion, your honour, for we have never set eyes on them yet.

MITE: That's strange! But, after all, you could not think of electing a black?

TOUCHIT: That makes no difference to us. The Christian Club has ever been peresuaded that a good candidate, like a good horse, can't be of a bad colour. (*Exit with friends.*)

(*Enter* THOMAS OLDHAM *and others.*)

MITE: (*to* THOMAS OLDHAM) What is your business and name?

THOMAS: Oldham.

MITE: The brother of Sir John? I have heard of you. You are, if I mistake not, a merchant?

THOMAS: I have that honour, Sir Matthew.

MITE: Humph! Honour! Well, sir, and what are your commands?

THOMAS: I wait on you in the name of my brother, with . . .

MITE: An answer to the message I sent him. When do we meet to finish the matter? It must be tomorrow or Sunday, for I shall be busy next week.

THOMAS: Tomorrow?

---

both: many boroughs returned two members to parliament.

MITE: Ay, it is not like me to dangle and court, Mr Oldham.

THOMAS: Why, to be plain, Sir Matthew, it would, I am afraid, be but losing your time.

MITE: Sir?

THOMAS: As there is not one in the family that seems the least inclined to favour your wish.

MITE: No? Ha, ha, ha! That's pleasant enough! Ha, ha, ha! And why not?

THOMAS: They are, Sir Matthew, no strangers to your great power and wealth, but corrupt as you may conceive this country to be, there are superior spirits living who would disdain an alliance with grandeur obtained at the expense of honour and virtue.

MITE: And what relation has this sentimental declaration to me?

THOMAS: My intention, Sir Matthew, was not to offend. I was desired to wait on you with a civil denial.

MITE: And you have faithfully discharged your commission.

THOMAS: Why, I am a man of plain manners, Sir Matthew; a supercilious air, or a sneer, will not prevent me from speaking my thoughts.

MITE: Perfectly right, and prodigiously prudent! – Well, sir, I hope it won't be thought too presuming, if I desire to hear my sentence proceed from the mouth of the father and daughter.

THOMAS: By all means. I will wait on you thither.

MITE: That is not so convenient at present. I have brought from Italy antiques, some curious remains, which are to be deposited in the archives of this country. The Antiquarian Society have, in consequence, chosen me one of their body, and this is the hour of reception.

THOMAS: We shall see you in the course of the day?

MITE: At the close of the ceremony. Perhaps I shall have something to urge that may procure me some favour from your very respectable family. – Piccard, attend Mr A–a–a to the door.

THOMAS: I guess your design. (*Exit.*)

MITE: Who waits there? (*Enter* SERVANT.) Step to my attorney directly. Bid him attend me within an hour at Oldham's, armed with all the powers I gave him. (*Exit* SERVANT.) I will see if I can't bend to my will this sturdy race of insolent beggars! – After all, riches to a man who knows how to employ them are as useful in England as in any part of the East. There they gain us those ends in spite and defiance of law, which, with a proper agent, may here be obtained under the pretence and colour of law. (*Exit.*)

ACT III

SCENE 1.   *The Antiquarian Society. Discovered* ANTIQUARIANS *and* SECRETARY *to the Society.*

SECRETARY: Sir Matthew Mite, preceded by his presents, will attend this honourable Society this morning.

1st ANTIQUARIAN: Is he apprised that an inauguration speech is required, in which he is to express his love of *virtù*, and produce proofs of his antique erudition?

SECRETARY: He has been apprised, and is rightly prepared.

2nd ANTIQUARIAN: Are the minutes of our last meeting fairly recorded and entered?

SECRETARY: They are.

1st ANTIQUARIAN: And the valuable antiques which have happily escaped the depredations of time ranged and registered rightly?

SECRETARY: All in order.

2nd ANTIQUARIAN: As there are acquisitions to the Society's stock, I think it right that the members should be instructed in their several natures and names.

1st ANTIQUARIAN: By all means. Read the list!

SECRETARY: '*Imprimis*, In a large glass-case, and fine preservation, the toe of the slipper of Cardinal Pandulpho, with which he kicked the breech of King John, at Swinstead Abbey, when he gave him absolution and penance.'

2nd ANTIQUARIAN: A most noble remains!

1st ANTIQUARIAN: An excellent antidote against the progress of Popery, as it proves the Pontiff's insolent abuse of his power! – Proceed.

SECRETARY: 'A pair of nut-crackers presented by Harry the Eighth to Anna Bullen on the eve of their nuptials; the wood supposed to be walnut.'

1st ANTIQUARIAN: Which proves that before the Reformation walnut trees were planted in England.

SECRETARY: 'The cape of Queen Elizabeth's riding-hood, which she wore on a solemn festival, when carried behind Burleigh to Paul's; the cloth undoubtedly Kidderminster.'

2ns ANTIQUARIAN: A most instructive lesson to us, as it proves that patriotic princess wore nothing but the manufactures of England!

SECRETARY: 'A cork-screw presented by Sir John Falstaff to Harry the Fifth; with a tobacco-stopper of Sir Walter Raleigh's, made of the stern of the ship in which he first compassed the globe; given to the Society by a clergyman from the North Riding of Yorkshire.'

1st ANTIQUARIAN: A rare instance of generosity, as they must have both been of singular use to the reverend donor himself!

SECRETARY: 'A curious collection, in regular and undoubted succession, of all the tickets of Islington turnpike, from its first institution to the twentieth of May.'

2nd ANTIQUARIAN: Preserve them with care, as they may hereafter serve to illustrate that part of the English history.

SECRETARY: 'A wooden medal of Shakespeare, made from the mulberry tree planted by himself; with a Queen Anne's farthing; from the manager of Drury Lane playhouse.'

1st ANTIQUARIAN: Has he received the Society's thanks?

SECRETARY: They are sent.

(*Enter* BEADLE.)

BEADLE: Sir Matthew Mite attends at the door.

1st ANTIQUARIAN: Let him be admitted directly.

(*Enter* SIR MATTHEW MITE, *preceded by four Blacks; first Black*

---

manager of Drury Lane: David Garrick wore this wooden medallion as Steward of the Stratford Jubilee, 1769. His treasuring a Queen Anne farthing is a dig at his reputed parsimony.

bearing a large book; second, a green chamber-pot; third, some lava from the Mountain Vesuvius; fourth, a box. SIR MATTHEW *takes his seat.* SECRETARY *receives the first present, and reads the label.*)

SECRETARY: 'Purchased of the Abbé Montini at Naples, for five hundred pounds, an illegible manuscript in Latin, containing the twelve books of Livy, supposed to be lost.'

MITE: This invaluable treasure was very near falling into the hands of the Pope, who designed to deposit it in the Vatican Library, and I rescued it from idolatrous hands.

1st ANTIQUARIAN: A pious, learned and laudable purchase!

SECRETARY: (*Receives the second present, and reads the label.*) 'A sarcophagus, or Roman urn, dug from the temple of Concord.'

MITE: Supposed to have held the dust of Mark Antony's coachman.

SECRETARY: (*Receives the third present, and reads the label.*) 'A large piece of the lava thrown from the Vesuvian volcano at the last great eruption.'

MITE: By a chemical analysis, it will be easy to discover the constituent parts of this mass, which, by properly preparing it, will make it no difficult task to propagate burning mountains in England.

2nd ANTIQUARIAN: If the propagation be encouraged by premiums.

1st ANTIQUARIAN: Which it will, no doubt.

MITE: Gentlemen! Not contented with collecting, for the use of my country, these inestimable relics, with a large catalogue of petrifactions, bones, beetles, and butterflies, contained in that box (*pointing to the present borne by the fourth Black*), I have likewise laboured for the advancement of national knowledge, for which end permit me to clear up some doubts relative to a material and interesting point in the English history. Let others toil to illumine the dark annals of Greece or of Rome, my searches are sacred only to the service of Britain! – The point I mean to clear up is an error crept into the life of that illustrious magistrate, the great Whittington, and his no less eminent cat, and in this disquisition four material points are in question.

1st. Did Whittington ever exist?

2nd. Was Whittington Lord Mayor of London?

3rd. Was he really possessed of a cat?

4th. Was that cat the source of his wealth?

That Whittington lived no doubt can be made; that he was Lord Mayor of London is equally true; but as to his cat, that, gentlemen, is the gordian knot to untie. And here, gentlemen, be it permitted me to define what a cat is. A cat is a domestic, whiskered, four-footed animal, whose employment is catching mice. But let puss have been ever so subtle, let puss have been ever so successful, to what could puss's captures amount? No tanner can curry the skin of a mouse, no family make a meal of the meat, consequently, no cat could give Whittington his wealth. From whence, then, does this error proceed? Be that my care to point out!

The commerce this worthy merchant carried on was chiefly confined to our

---

Whittington: Sir Samuel Pegge delivered a dissertation on Whittington and his cat to the Society of Antiquaries in December 1771 (John Nichols, *Literary Anecdotes*, vol. VIII, p. 575, London, 1812–16).

coasts. For this purpose he constructed a vessel, which, from its agility and
lightness, he aptly christened a cat. Nay, to this day, gentlemen, all our coals from
Newcastle are imported in nothing but cats. From thence it appears that it was not
the whiskered, four-footed, mouse-killing cat that was the source of the magistrate's wealth, but the coasting, sailing, coal-carrying cat. That, gentlemen, was
Whittington's cat.

1st ANTIQUARIAN: What a fund of learning!

2nd ANTIQUARIAN: Amazing acuteness of erudition!

1st ANTIQUARIAN: Let this discovery be made public directly.

2nd ANTIQUARIAN: And the author mentioned with honour.

1st ANTIQUARIAN: I make no doubt but the City of London will desire him to sit for
his picture, or send him his freedom in a fifty-pound box.

2nd ANTIQUARIAN: The honour done their first magistrate richly deserves it.

1st ANTIQUARIAN: Break we up this assembly, with a loud declaration that Sir
Matthew Mite is equally skilled in arts as well as in arms.

2nd ANTIQUARIAN: *Tam mercurio quam marti.* (*Exeunt* ANTIQUARIANS.)

MITE: Having thus discharged my debt to the public, I must attend to my private
affairs. Will Rapine, my attorney, attend as I bid him?

SERVANT: He will be punctual, your honour.

MITE: Then drive to Hanover Square.

PUTTY: (*without*) I will come in!
                        (*Enter* SERVANT.)

SERVANT: There's a little shabby fellow without that insists on seeing your honour.

MITE: Why, who and what can he be?

SERVANT: He calls himself Putty, and says he went to school with your honour.

SERVANT: (*without*) His honour don't know you!

PUTTY: (*without*) I will come in! Not know me, you oaf! What should ail him? Why, I
tell you we were bred up together from boys. Stand by, or I'll – (*Enter* PUTTY.)
Hey! Yes, it is – no, it an't – yes, it is Matthew Mite. Lord love your queer face!
What a figure you cut! How you are altered! Well, had I met you by chance, I
don't think I should ever have known you. I had a deuced deal of work to get at
you.

MITE: This is a lucky encounter!

PUTTY: There is a little fat fellow that opens the door at your house, was pert as a
'prentice just out of his time, he would not give me the least inkling about you!
And I should have returned to Shoreditch as wise as I came, if some folks who are
gazing at the fine gilt coach in the street hadn't told me 'twas yours. Well, Master
Mite, things are mainly changed since we were boys at the Blue-coat. Who could
have thought that you would have got so up in the world? For you know you were
reckoned a dull one at school.

SERVANT: Friend, do you know who you talk to?

PUTTY: Yes, friend, much better than you do. I am told he is become a knight and a
nabob – and what of all that? For your nabobs, they are but a kind of outlandish
creatures that won't pass current with us, and as to knights, we have a few of them

---

little fat fellow: Weston played both parts of Janus and Putty.
Blue-coat: Christ's Hospital School, so called after the pupils' choir-boy cassocks.

in the city whom I dare speak to without doffing my hat. So, Mr Scrapetrencher,
let's have no more of your jaw. – I say, Mat, doesn't remember one Easter
Tuesday, how you tipped the barrow-woman into Fleet-ditch, as we were going
about with the hymns?

MITE: An anecdote that does me infinite honour!

PUTTY: How all the folks laughed to see how bolt upright she stood on her head in the
mud! Ha, ha, ha! And one fifth of November, I shall never forget, how you
frightened a preaching Methodist tailor by throwing a cracker into the pulpit!

MITE: Another pretty exploit!

PUTTY: At every bounce, how poor Stitch capered and jumped! Ah! Many's the merry
freak we have had. For this I must say, though Mat was but bad at his book, for
mischiefful matters there wasn't a more ingenious, cuter lad in the school.

MITE: Yes, I have got a fine reputation, I see.

PUTTY: Well, but Mat! What, be'st dumb? Why doesn't speak to a school-fellow?

MITE: That at present is more than I'll own. – I fancy, Mr A–a–a, you have made some
mistake.

PUTTY: Some mistake!

MITE: I don't recollect that I ever had the honour to know you.

PUTTY: What, don't you remember Phil Putty?

MITE: No.

PUTTY: That was 'prentice to Master Gibon, the glazier, in Shoreditch?

MITE: No.

PUTTY: That, at the Blue-coat Hospital, has often saved your bacon by owning your
pranks?

MITE: No.

PUTTY: No! What, then, maybe you ben't Mat Mite, son of old John and Margery
Mite, at the Sow and Sausage in St Mary Axe, that took the tarts from the man in
Pie Corner, and was sent beyond the sea, for fear worse should come on it?

MITE: You see, Mr Putty, the glazier, if that is your name and profession, you are
entirely out in this matter, so you need not repeat your visits to me. (*Exit.*)

PUTTY: Now, here's a pretty purse-proud son of a —, who, forsooth, because he is
grown great by robbing the heathens, won't own a friend and acquaintance, and
one, too, of the livery beside! Damme, the great Turk himself need not be
ashamed to shake hands with a citizen! 'Mr Putty, the glazier!' Well, what a pox
am I the better for you? I'll be sworn our company has made more money by a
single election at Brentford, than by all his exploits put together. (*Exit.*)

SCENE 2.   SIR JOHN OLDHAM's *house. Enter* MR THOMAS OLDHAM,
        followed by a SERVANT.

THOMAS: Sir Matthew Mite is not come?

SERVANT: No, sir.

THOMAS: Is Tom here?

SERVANT: Mr Oldham is, I believe, with miss, in the parlour.

THOMAS: Let him know I would see him. (*Exit* SERVANT.) Poor boy! Nay, I

---

election at Brentford: a great occasion for breaking windows.

sincerely grieve for them both! This disappointment, like an untimely frost, will hang heavy on their tender years. To conquer the first and finest feelings of nature is an arduous task. (*Enter* YOUNG OLDHAM.) So, Tom, still attached to this spot, I perceive.

YOUNG OLDHAM: Sir, I arrived but the instant before you.

THOMAS: Nay, child, I don't blame you. You are no stranger to the almost invincible bars that oppose your views regarding my niece. It would be therefore prudent, instead of indulging, to wean yourself by degrees.

YOUNG OLDHAM: Are there no hopes, then, sir, of subduing my aunt?

THOMAS: I see none. Nay, perhaps, as matters now stand, compliance may be out of her power.

YOUNG OLDHAM: How is that possible, sir? Out of her power!

THOMAS: I won't anticipate. Misfortunes come too soon of themselves. A short time will explain what I mean.

YOUNG OLDHAM: You alarm me! Would you condescend to instruct me. I hope, sir, I shall have discretion enough . . .

THOMAS: It would answer no end. I would have you both prepare for the worse. See your cousin again, and remember, this, perhaps, may be the last time of your meeting.

YOUNG OLDHAM: The last of our . . .

THOMAS: But Sophy is here. I must go in to Sir John. (THOMAS OLDHAM *bows low to* SOPHY, *and retires.*)
>   (*Enter* SOPHY.)

SOPHY: Sir, what can be the meaning of this? My uncle Oldham avoids me! You seem shocked! No additional misfortune, I hope.

YOUNG OLDHAM: My father has threatened me, in obscure terms, with the worst that can happen.

SOPHY: How!

YOUNG OLDHAM: The total, nay, perhaps, immediate loss of my Sophy.

SOPHY: From what cause?

YOUNG OLDHAM: That, in tenderness, he chose to conceal.

SOPHY: But why make it a mystery? Have you no guess?

YOUNG OLDHAM: Not the most distant conception. My lady's dislike would hardly prompt her to such violent measures. I can't comprehend how this can possibly be; but yet my father has too firm, too manly a mind, to encourage or harbour vain fears.

SOPHY: Here they come. I suppose the riddle will soon be explained.
>   (*Enter* SIR JOHN, LADY *and* THOMAS OLDHAM.)

LADY OLDHAM: But what motive could he have for demanding this whimsical interview? He could not doubt your credentials, or think his presence could be grateful to us?

THOMAS: I have delivered my message.

LADY OLDHAM: Perhaps he depends on his rhetorical powers, I hear he has a good opinion of them. Stay, Sophy! Sir Matthew Mite, distrusting the message we begged your uncle to carry, desires to have it confirmed by ourselves. I fancy, child, you will do yourself no violence in rejecting this lover. He is an amiable swain, I confess!

SOPHY: I shall be always happy in obeying your ladyship's orders.

LADY OLDHAM: Are you sure of that Sophy? A time may soon come for the trial.

SIR JOHN: Well, in the main, I am glad of this meeting. It will not only put a final end to this business, but give us an opportunity of discussing other matters, my dear.

LADY OLDHAM: Is that your opinion, Sir John? I fancy he will not be very fond of prolonging his visit.

(*Enter* SERVANT.)

SERVANT: Sir Matthew Mite.

LADY OLDHAM: Show him in! – Now, Sir John, be on your guard; support this scene with a dignity that becomes one of your birth and . . .

SIR JOHN: Never fear my dignity, love. I warrant you I'll give him as good as he brings.

(*Enter* SIR MATTHEW MITE.)

MITE: I find the whole tribe is convened. – I hope I am not an intruder, but I confess the extraordinary answer I received from the mouth of this worthy citizen, to a message conveyed by my secretary, induced me to question its authenticity, unless confirmed by yourselves.

LADY OLDHAM: And why should you think our reply so very extraordinary?

MITE: You must give me leave to smile at that question.

LADY OLDHAM: A very decisive answer, I own!

MITE: You are, Lady Oldham, a woman of the world, and supposed not to be wanting in sense.

LADY OLDHAM: Which this conduct of mine inclines you to doubt?

MITE: Why, to be plain, my condition and your own station considered, prudence might have dictated a different reply.

LADY OLDHAM: And yet, Sir Matthew, upon the maturest deliberation, all the parties, you see, persist in giving no other.

MITE: Is it so? You will permit me, Lady Oldham, to desire one of those reasons which influenced this august assembly upon the occasion?

LADY OLDHAM: They will, I dare say, appear but trifling to you.

MITE: Let us have them, however.

LADY OLDHAM: First, we think it right to have a little regard to her happiness, as she is indebted for her existence to us.

MITE: Which you think she risks in an union with me? (LADY OLDHAM *bows.*) And why so? I have the means to procure her, madam, those enjoyments with which your sex is chiefly delighted.

LADY OLDHAM: You will, Sir Matthew, pardon my weakness, but I would much rather see my child reduced to an indigent state, than voluptuously rioting in pleasures that derive their source from the ruin of others.

MITE: Ruin! What, you, I find, adopt the popular prejudice, and conclude that every man that is rich is a villain!

LADY OLDHAM: I only echo the voice of the public. Besides, I would wish my daughter a more solid establishment. The possessions arising from plunder very rarely are permanent. We every day see what has been treacherously and rapaciously gained, as profusely and full as rapidly squandered.

MITE: I am sorry, madam, to see one of your fashion concur in the common cry of the times, but such is the gratitude of this country to those who have given it dominion and wealth.

THOMAS: I could wish even that fact was well founded, Sir Matthew. Your riches, which perhaps, too, are only ideal, by introducing a general spirit of dissipation, have extinguished labour and industry, the slow, but sure source of national wealth.

MITE: To these refinements I have no time to reply. By one of your ladyship's hints I shall profit at least: I shall be a little more careful of the plunder I have made. Sir John Oldham, you recollect a small sum borrowed by you?

SIR JOHN: I do.

MITE: The obligations for which are in my possession at present.

SIR JOHN: I understand as much by your letter.

MITE: As I find there is an end of our treaty, it would be right, I think, to discharge them directly.

SIR JOHN: I cannot say that is quite so convenient. Besides, I understood the party was to wait till the time that Jack comes of age.

MITE: I am told the law does not understand what is not clearly expressed. Besides, the probable event of your death, or the young gentleman's shyness to fulfil the agreement, are enough to put a man on his guard.

THOMAS: Now comes on the storm.

MITE: And, that my prudence may not suffer in that lady's opinion, I have taken some precautions which my attorney will more clearly unfold. Mr Rapine! (*Enter* RAPINE.) You will explain this affair to Sir John. I am a military man, and quite a stranger to your legal manoeuvres.

RAPINE: By command of my client, Sir Matthew, I have issued here a couple of writs.

LADY OLDHAM: Sir John!

SIR JOHN: What?

RAPINE: By one of which, the plaintiff possesses the person, by the other, the goods and chattels, of Sir John, the defendant.

MITE: A definition very clear and concise!

LADY OLDHAM: Goods, sir! What, must I be turned out of my house?

RAPINE: No, madam. You may stay here till we sell, which perhaps mayn't happen these two days. We must, indeed, leave a few of our people, just to take care that there is nothing embezzled.

LADY OLDHAM: A short respite, indeed! For a little time, I dare say, my brother Oldham will afford us protection. Come, Sir John, nor let us indulge that monster's malice with a longer sight of our misery.

RAPINE: You, madam, are a wife, and may go where you please, but as to Sir John . . .

LADY OLDHAM: Well?

RAPINE: He must not stir. We are answerable for the possession of him.

LADY OLDHAM: Of him? A prisoner? Then, indeed, is our ruin complete!

SOPHY: Oh, uncle! – You have been pleased, sir, to express an affection for me; is it possible, sir, you can be so cruel, so unkind to my parents . . .

MITE: They are unkind to themselves.

SOPHY: Let me plead for mercy! Suspend but a little! – My uncle, you, sir, are wealthy too! – Indeed we are honest! You will not run the least risk.

MITE: There is a condition, miss, in which you have a right to command.

SOPHY: Sir!

MITE: It is in your power, and that of your parents, to establish one common interest among us.

LADY OLDHAM: Never! After rejecting, with the contempt they deserve, the first arrogant offers you made, do you suppose this fresh insult will gain us?

MITE: I am answered. – I presume, Mr Rapine, there is no longer occasion for me?

SOPHY: Stop, sir! Mr Oldham teaches me what I should do. Can I see their distress? Heaven knows with what eagerness I would sacrifice my own peace, my own happiness, to procure them relief! (*Kneels to* SIR MATTHEW.)

THOMAS: Rise, niece! Nor hope to soften that breast, already made too callous by crime! I have long seen, sir, what your malice intended, and prepared myself to baffle its purpose. I am instructed, sir, in the amount of this man's demands on my brother. You will find there a sum more than sufficient to pay it. – And now, my dear sister, I hope you will please to allow a citizen may be useful sometimes.

MITE: Mr Rapine, is this manoeuvre according to law?

RAPINE: The law, Sir Matthew, always sleeps when satisfaction is made.

MITE: Does it? Our practice is different in the Mayor's Court at Calcutta. – I shall now make my bow, and leave this family, whom I wished to make happy in spite of themselves, soon to regret the fatal loss sustained by their obstinate folly.

THOMAS: Nor can it be long before the wisdom of their choice will appear, as, by partaking of the spoil, they might have been involved in that vengeance, which, soon or late, cannot fail to fall on the head of the author; and, sir, notwithstanding your seeming security, perhaps the hour of retribution is near!

MITE: You must, Master Oldham, give me leave to laugh at your prophetic effusion. This is not Sparta, nor are these the chaste times of the Roman republic. Nowadays, riches possess, at least, one magical power, that, being rightly dispensed, they closely conceal the source from whence they proceeded. That wisdom, I hope never to want. – I am the obsequious servant of this respectable family! Adieu! (*Exit with* RAPINE.)

LADY OLDHAM: Brother, what words can I use, or how can we thank you as we ought? Sir John! Sophy!

THOMAS: I am doubly paid, Lady Oldham, in supplying the wants of my friends, and defeating the designs of a villain. As to the mere money, we citizens, indeed, are odd kind of folks, and always expect good security for what we advance.

LADY OLDHAM: Sir John's person, his fortune, every . . .

THOMAS: Nay, nay, nay, upon this occasion we will not be troubled with land. If you, sister, will place as a pledge my fair cousin in the hands of my son . . .

LADY OLDHAM: I freely resign her disposal to you.

SIR JOHN: And I too.

THOMAS: Then be happy, my children! And as to my young cousins within, I hope we shall be able to settle them without Sir Matthew's assistance, for, however praiseworthy the spirit of adventure may be, whoever keeps his post, and does his duty at home, will be found to render his country best service at last! (*Exeunt.*)

2 *The Citizen*, act II, scene 1, at Drury Lane, 1761.
From *Parson's Minor Theatre*

THE CITIZEN

A farce

by ARTHUR MURPHY

Aeque neglectum pueris senibusque nocebit. HOR.

First performed in a three-act version at Drury Lane, on 2 July 1761; performed in a two-act version at the Theatre Royal, Covent Garden, with the following cast:

OLD PHILPOT	Mr Shuter
YOUNG PHILPOT	Mr Woodward
SIR JASPER WILDING	Mr Dunstall
YOUNG WILDING	Mr Dyer
BEAUFORT	Mr Young
DAPPER	Mr Costollo
QUILLDRIVE	Mr Perry
MARIA	Miss Elliott
CORINNA	Miss Davies
SERVANTS etc.	

Aeque neglectum: 'If neglected it will be harmful to young and old alike'. Horace, *Epistles*, I, i, 26.
three-act version: the cast included Old Philpot -- Yates; Young Philpot – Foote; Sir Jasper – Baddeley; Wilding – O'Brien; and Maria – Ann Elliott.

3 *The Citizen*, act II, scene 1, at Covent Garden, 1761. From *The London Theatres*

DEDICATION

Lincoln's Inn, 25 January 1763

The Author's compliments to Miss ELLIOTT, and he desires to inscribe to her the following scenes. She need not be alarmed at a dedication, the propriety of which will strike every reader, who remembers that Miss ELLIOT and the CITIZEN made their first appearance on the stage together, and that her uncommon talents gave the piece the best and most effectual protection. Elegance of figure, a voice of pleasing variety, a strong expression of humour, not impaired, but rendered exquisite by delicacy; these were circumstances that secured the farce at first, and have since brought it into favour. No author ever met with a better patronage; and though the CITIZEN, like other *things of this kind*, has many faults, yet it has this peculiar merit, that it produced, in the character of MARIA, a genuine comic genius. The CITIZEN claims another praise. When all the arts of theatrical malice were conspiring against her, it recommended Miss ELLIOTT to the notice of Mr BEARD, and obtained for her that generous treatment, which *that manager* seemed determined to extend to real merit. The author therefore desires Miss ELLIOTT's acceptance of this farce, for the defects of which he makes no apology, because, should the most severe judge in this kind resolve to arm himself with criticisms, let him but look at the acting of MARIA, *and he will forget them all*.

Miss ELLIOTT: Ann Elliott had joined the Foote/Murphy summer season in 1761. She became, or maybe was already, Murphy's mistress, to whom he was faithful until her early death in 1769. Although she had been taken up by the King's brother, Henry, Duke of Cumberland in 1766, in that year Murphy specifically wrote *The School for Guardians* for her. It was based on *The Country Wife*, and Garrick forestalled it with his own *The Country Girl*, see Introduction, p. 23 above. *theatrical malice*: even before 1766, Garrick had moved against Murphy and Elliott, though whether he was antagonistic to the author or the actress is unclear. She was not employed at Drury Lane in the autumn of 1761, and *The Citizen* was rejected by Garrick, although he took up the other plays that Murphy had presented in the summer season. However, both the farce and the actress were welcomed by the Covent Garden manager, John Beard, and Ann Elliott appeared in the play there on 15 November 1762.

ACT I

SCENE 1.   *A room in* SIR JASPER WILDING's *house. Enter* YOUNG
      WILDING, BEAUFORT, *and* WILL *following.*

WILDING: Ha, ha! My dear Beaufort! A fiery young fellow like you, melted down into
      a sighing, love-sick dangler after a high heel, a well-turned ankle, and a short
      petticoat!

BEAUFORT: Prithee, Wilding, don't laugh at me. Maria's charms . . .

WILDING: Maria's charms! And so now you would fain grow wanton in her praise, and
      have me listen to your raptures about my own sister? Poor Beaufort! Is my sister
      at home, Will?

WILL: She is, sir.

WILDING: How long has my father been gone out?

WILL: This hour, sir.

WILDING: Very well. Pray, give Mr Beaufort's compliments to my sister, and he is
      come to wait on her. (*Exit* WILL.) You will be glad to see her, I suppose, Charles?

BEAUFORT: I live but in her presence!

WILDING: Live but in her presence! How the devil could the young baggage raise this
      riot in your heart? It's more than her brother could ever do with any of her sex.

BEAUFORT: Nay, you have no reason to complain. You are come up to town, post-
      haste, to marry a wealthy citizen's daughter, who only saw you last season at
      Tunbridge, and has been languishing for you ever since.

WILDING: It's more than I do for her, and, to tell you the truth, more than I believe
      she does for me. This is a match of prudence, man – bargain and sale! My reverend
      dad and the old put of a citizen finished the business at Lloyd's coffee-house by
      inch of candle – a mere transferring of property! 'Give your son to my daughter,
      and I will give my daughter to your son.' That's the whole affair; and so I am just
      arrived to consummate the nuptials.

BEAUFORT: Thou art the happiest fellow . . .

WILDING: Happy! So I am. What should I be otherwise for? If Miss Sally – upon my
      soul, I forget her name.

BEAUFORT: Well! That is so like you – Miss Sally Philpot.

WILDING: Ay, very true – Miss Sally Philpot – she will bring fortune sufficient to pay
      off an old incumbrance upon the family estate, and my father is to settle hand-
      somely upon me. And so I have reason to be contented, have not I?

BEAUFORT: And you are willing to marry her without having one spark of love for
      her?

WILDING: Love! Why, I make myself ridiculous enough by marrying, don't I, without
      being in love into the bargain? What, am I to pine for a girl that is willing to go to
      bed with me? Love of all things! My dear Beaufort, one sees so many breathing
      raptures about each other before marriage, and dinning their insipidity into the
      ears of all their acquaintance: 'My dear madam, don't you think him a sweet
      man? A charminger creature never was!' Then he on his side: 'My life, my angel!
      Oh! She's a paradise of ever-blooming sweets!' And then in a month's time: 'He's

---

by inch of candle: an auction in which the bidding continued until a small candle burnt out.

a perfidious wretch! I wish I had never seen his face – the devil was in me when I had anything to say to him.' – 'Oh! damn her for an unanimated piece – I wish she'd poison herself, with all my heart.' That is ever the way. And so you see love is all nonsense; well enough to furnish romances for boys and girls at circulating libraries. That is all, take my word for it.

BEAUFORT: Po! That is idle talk. And in the mean time, I am ruined.

WILDING: How so?

BEAUFORT: Why, you know the old couple have bargained your sister away.

WILDING: Bargained her away! And will you pretend you are in love? Can you look tamely on, and see her bartered away at Garraway's like logwood, cochineal or indigo? Marry her privately, man, and keep it secret till my affair is over.

BEAUFORT: My dear Wilding, will you propose it to her?

WILDING: With all my heart – she is a very long time acoming – I'll tell you what, if she has a fancy for you, carry her off at once. But, perhaps, she has a mind to this cub of a citizen, Miss Sally's brother . . .

BEAUFORT: Oh, no! He's her aversion.

WILDING: I have never seen any of the family, but my wife that is to be – my father-in-law and my brother-in-law, I know nothing of them. What sort of fellow is the son?

BEAUFORT: Oh, a diamond of the first water! A buck, sir! A blood! Every night at this end of the town; at twelve next day he sneaks about the 'Change, in a little bit of a frock and a bob-wig, and looks like a sedate book-keeper in the eyes of all who behold him.

WILDING: Upon my soul, a gentleman of spirit!

BEAUFORT: Spirit! He drives a phaeton two stories high, keeps his girl at this end of the town, and is the gay George Philpot all round Covent Garden.

WILDING: Oh, brave! And the father . . .

BEAUFORT: The father, sir . . . But here comes Maria. Take the picture from her. (MARIA *is heard singing within.*)

WILDING: Hey! She is musical this morning. She holds her usual spirits, I find.

BEAUFORT: Yes, yes, the spirit of eighteen, with the idea of love in her head.

WILDING: Ay, and such a lover as you too! Though still in her teens, she can play on all your foibles as she does her monkey – tickle you, torment you, enrage you, soothe you, exalt you, depress you, pity you, laugh at you – *Ecce signum!* (*Enter* MARIA, *singing.*) The same giddy girl! Sister! Come my dear . . .

MARIA: Have done, brother. Let me have my own way. I will go through my song.

WILDING: I have not seen you this age. Ask me how I do.

MARIA: I won't ask you how you do. I won't take any notice of you. I don't know you.

WILDING: Do you know this gentleman, then? Will you speak to him?

MARIA: No, I won't speak to him. I'll sing to him. It's my humour to sing. (*Sings.*)

BEAUFORT: Be serious but for a moment, Maria! My all depends upon it.

MARIA: Oh, sweet sir! You are dying, are you? Then, positively, I will sing the song, for it is a description of yourself. Mind it, Mr Beaufort, mind it – Brother! How do you do? (*Kisses him.*) Say nothing. Don't interrupt me. (*Sings.*)

Garraway's: a commercial coffee-house, like Lloyd's.
phaeton: a two-horse, four-wheeled open carriage.

WILDING: Have you seen your city lover yet?

MARIA: No, but I long to see him. I fancy he is a curiosity!

BEAUFORT: Long to see him, Maria?

MARIA: Yes, long to see him! (BEAUFORT *fiddles with his lip, and looks thoughtful.*) Brother, brother! (*Goes to him softly, beckons him to look at* BEAUFORT.) Do you see that? (*Mimics him.*) Mind him. Ha, ha!

BEAUFORT: Make me ridiculous if you will, Maria, so you don't make me unhappy by marrying this citizen.

MARIA: And would you not have me marry, sir? What, must I lead a single life to please you, must I? Upon my word, you are a pretty gentleman to make up laws for me. (*Sings.*)

> Can it be, or by law, or by equity said,
> That a comely young girl ought to die an old maid?

WILDING: Come, come, Miss Pert, compose yourself a little. This will never do.

MARIA: My cross, ill-natured brother! But it will do – Lord! What, do you both call me hither to plague me? I won't stay among ye – *à l'honneur, à l'honneur,* (*running away*) *à l'honneur.*

WILDING: Hey, hey, Miss Notable! Come back! Pray, madam, come back. (*Forces her back.*)

MARIA: Lord of heaven! What do you want?

WILDING: Come, come, truce with your frolics, Miss Hoyden, and behave like a sensible girl. We have serious business with you.

MARIA: Have you? Well, come, I will be sensible. There, I blow all my folly away – 'tis gone, 'tis gone – and now I'll talk sense. Come, is that a sensible face?

WILDING: Poh, poh! Be quiet, and hear what we have to say to you.

MARIA: I will. I am quiet – It's charming weather; it will be good for the country, this will.

WILDING: Poh, ridiculous! How can you be so silly?

MARIA: Bless me! I never saw anything like you. There's no such thing as satisfying you. I am sure it was very good sense, what I said. Papa talks in that manner – Well, well, I'll be silent, then – I won't speak at all. Will that satisfy you? (*Looks sullen.*)

WILDING: Come, come, no more of this folly, but mind what is said to you. You have not seen your city lover, you say? (MARIA *shrugs her shoulders, and shakes her head.*) Why don't you answer?

BEAUFORT: My dear Maria, put me out of pain. (MARIA *shrugs her shoulders again.*)

WILDING: Poh, don't be so childish, but give a rational answer.

MARIA: Why, no, then; no – no, no, no, no, no, – I tell you no, no, no!

WILDING: Come, come, my giddy little sister, you must not be so flighty. Behave sedately, and don't be a girl always.

MARIA: Why, don't I tell you I have not seen him – but I am to see him this very day.

BEAUFORT: To see him this day, Maria!

MARIA: Ha, ha! Look there, brother. He is beginning again. But don't fright yourself, and I'll tell you all about it. My papa comes to me this morning – by the by, he makes a fright of himself with this strange dress. Why doesn't he dress as other gentlemen do, brother?

WILDING: He dresses like his brother fox-hunters in Wiltshire.

MARIA: But when he comes to town, I wish he would do as other gentlemen do here. I am almost ashamed of him. But he comes to me this morning: 'Hoic, hoic! our Moll. Where is the sly puss? Tally ho!' 'Did you want me, papa?' 'Come hither, Moll, I'll *gee* you a husband, my girl; one that has mettle enow; he'll take cover, I warrant un – Blood to the bone!'

BEAUFORT: There now, Wilding, didn't I tell you this?

WILDING: Where are you to see the young citizen?

MARIA: Why, papa will be at home in an hour, and then he intends to drag me to the City with him, and there the sweet creature is to be introduced to me. The old gentleman his father is delighted with me – but I hate him, an ugly old thing.

WILDING: Give us a description of him. I want to know him.

MARIA: Why, he looks like the picture of Avarice, sitting with pleasure upon a bag of money, and trembling for fear anybody should come and take it away. He has got square-toed shoes, and little tiny buckles, a brown coat, with small round brass buttons, that looks as if it was new in my great grandmother's time, and his face all shrivelled and pinched with care, and he shakes his head like a Mandarin upon a chimney-piece. 'Ay, ay, Sir Jasper, you are right.' – And then he grins at me – 'I profess she is a very pretty bale of goods. Ay, ay!' 'And my son Bob is a very sensible lad.' 'Ay, ay, and I will underwrite their happiness for one and a half per cent.'

WILDING: Thank you, my dear girl! Thank you for this account of my relations.

BEAUFORT: Destruction to my hopes! Surely, my dear little angel, if you have any regard for me . . .

MARIA: There, there! There he is frightened again. (*Sings 'Dearest creature', etc.*)

WILDING: Psha! Give over these airs. Listen to me, and I'll instruct you how to manage them all . . .

MARIA: Oh, my dear brother, you are very good, but don't mistake yourself. Though just come from a boarding-school, give me leave to manage for myself. There is in this case a man I like, and a man I don't like. (*to* BEAUFORT) It is not you I like. No, no. I hate you. But let this little head alone! I know what to do. I shall know how to prefer one, and get rid of the other.

BEAUFORT: What will you do, Maria?

MARIA: Ha, ha! I can't help laughing at you. (*Sings.*)
> Do not grieve me,
> Oh, relieve me, etc.

WILDING: Come, come, be serious, Miss Pert, and I'll instruct you what to do. The old cit, you say, admires you for your understanding, and his son would not marry you, unless he found you a girl of sense and spirit.

MARIA: Even so – this is the character of your giddy sister.

WILDING: Why then, I'll tell you. You shall make him hate you for a fool, and so let the refusal come from himself.

MARIA: But how? How, my dear brother, tell me how?

Mandarin: a china figure, its nodding head generally considered to be rather tasteless.

WILDING: Why, you have seen a play, with me, where a man pretends to be a down-right country oaf, in order to rule a wife and have a wife?

MARIA: Very well. What then? What then? – Oh! I have it; I understand you; say no more; it's charming! I like it of all things! I'll do it, I will, and I will so plague him that he won't know what to make of me. He shall be a very toad-eater to me! The sour, the sweet, the bitter, he shall swallow all, and all shall work upon him alike for my diversion. Say nothing of it; it's all among ourselves. But I won't be cruel. I hate ill-nature. And, then, who knows but I may like him?

BEAUFORT: My dear Maria, don't talk of liking him.

MARIA: Oh, now you are beginning again. (*Sings 'Voi Amanti' etc. and exit.*)

BEAUFORT: 'Sdeath, Wilding, I shall never be your brother-in-law at this rate!

WILDING: Psha, follow me: don't be apprehensive. I'll give her further instructions, and she will execute them, I warrant you. The old fellow's daughter shall be mine, and the son may go shift for himself elsewhere. (*Exeunt.*)

SCENE 2.   *A room in* OLD PHILPOT'*s house. Enter* OLD PHILPOT, DAPPER, *and* QUILLDRIVE.

OLD PHILPOT: Quilldrive, have those dollars been sent to the bank, as I ordered?

QUILLDRIVE: They have, sir.

OLD PHILPOT: Very well. Mr Dapper, I am not fond of writing anything of late, but at your request . . .

DAPPER: You know I would r.ot offer you a bad policy.

OLD PHILPOT: I believe it. Well, step with me to my closet, and I will look at your policy. How much do you want upon it?

DAPPER: Three thousand. You had better take the whole, there are very good names on it.

OLD PHILPOT: Well, well, step with me, and I'll talk with you. Quilldrive, step with those bills for acceptance. This way, Mr Dapper, this way. (*Exeunt.*)

QUILLDRIVE: A miserly old rascal! Digging, digging money out of the very hearts of mankind; constantly, constantly scraping together, and yet trembling for fear of coming to want. A canting old hypocrite! And yet under his veil of sanctity he has a liquorish tooth left – running to the other end of town slyly every evening, and there he has his solitary pleasures in holes and corners.

(GEORGE PHILPOT, *peeping in.*)

GEORGE: Hist, hist! Quilldrive!

QUILLDRIVE: Ha, Mr George!

GEORGE: Is Square Toes at home?

QUILLDRIVE: He is.

GEORGE: Has he asked for me?

QUILLDRIVE: He has.

GEORGE: (*Walks in on tip-toe.*) Does he know I did not lie at home?

QUILLDRIVE: No. I sunk that upon him.

---

rule a wife and have a wife: the play of that title was by Beaumont and Fletcher, adapted by Garrick for his first appearance in it in 1756.

policy: Dapper, as a broker, is asking Old Philpot to underwrite the insurance of a ship. Individual merchants acted as underwriters and their business was usually transacted at Lloyd's coffee-house.

GEORGE: Well done! I'll give you a choice gelding to carry you to Dulwich of a Sunday. Damnation! Up all night, stripped of nine hundred pounds. Pretty well for one night! Piqued, repiqued, flammed, and capotted every deal! Old Drybeard shall pay all! – is forty-seven good? No – fifty good? No, no – to the end of the chapter. Cruel luck! Damn me, it is life though – this is life! 'Sdeath, I hear him coming! (*Runs off, and peeps.*) No, all's safe. I must not be caught in these clothes, Quilldrive.

QUILLDRIVE: How came you did not leave them at Madam Corinna's as you generally do?

GEORGE: I was afraid of being too late for old Square Toes, and so I whipped into a hackney-coach, and drove with the windows up, as if I was afraid of a bum-bailiff. Pretty clothes, an't they?

QUILLDRIVE: Ah! sir . . .

GEORGE: Reach me one of my mechanic city frocks – no – stay – it's in the next room, an't it?

QUILLDRIVE: Yes, sir.

GEORGE: I'll run and slip it on in a twinkle. (*Exit.*)

QUILLDRIVE: Mercy on us! What a life does he lead! Old Codger within here will scrape together for him, and the moment young master comes to possession, 'Ill got, ill gone', I warrant me. A hard card I have to play between them both, drudging for the old man, and pimping for the young one. The father is a reservoir of riches, and the son is a fountain to play it all away in vanity and folly!
(*Re-enter* GEORGE PHILPOT.)

GEORGE: Now I'm equipped for the City. Damn the City! I wish the papishes would set fire to it again. I hate to be beating the hoof here among them. Here comes father – no, it's Dapper. Quilldrive, I'll give you the gelding.

QUILLDRIVE: Thank you, sir. (*Exit.*)
(*Enter* DAPPER.)

DAPPER: Why, you look like a devil, George.

GEORGE: Yes, I have been up all night, lost all my money, and I'm afraid I must smash for it.

DAPPER: Smash for it – What have I let you into the secret for? Have not I advised you to trade upon your own account? And you feel the sweets of it. How much do you owe in the City?

GEORGE: At least twenty thousand.

DAPPER: Poh, that's nothing! Bring it up to fifty or sixty thousand, and then give them a good crash at once. I have insured the ship for you.

GEORGE: Have you?

DAPPER: The policy's full; I have just touched your father for the last three thousand.

GEORGE: Excellent! Are the goods re-landed?

DAPPER: Every bale. I have had them up to town, and sold them all to a packer for you.

GEORGE: Bravo! And the ship is loaded with rubbish, I suppose?

DAPPER: Yes, and is now proceeding on the voyage.

---

piqued . . . capotted: in Piquet, to be capotted was to loose all the tricks.
smash: be declared bankrupt.

GEORGE: Very well! And tomorrow, or next day, we shall hear of her being lost upon the Goodwin Sands, or sunk between the Needles?

DAPPER: Certainly.

GEORGE: Admirable! And then we shall come upon the underwriters?

DAPPER: Directly.

GEORGE: My dear Dapper! (*Embraces him.*)

DAPPER: Yes, I do a dozen every year. How do you think I can live as I do, otherwise?

GEORGE: Very true. Shall you be at the club after 'Change?

DAPPER: Without fail.

GEORGE: That's right! It will be a full meeting. We shall have Nat Pigtail the dry-salter there, and Bob Reptile the change-broker, and Sobersides the banker – we shall all be there. We shall have deep doings.

DAPPER: Yes, yes. Well, a good morning. I must go now, and fill up a policy for a ship that has been lost these three days.

GEORGE: My dear Dapper, thou art the best of friends.

DAPPER: Ay, I'll stand by you. It will be time enough for you to break, when you see your father near his end. Then give them a smash, and put yourself at the head of his fortune, and begin the world again. Good morning. (*Exit.*)

GEORGE: Dapper, adieu! Who now in my situation would envy any of your great folk at the court-end? A lord has nothing to depend on but his estate. He can't spend you a hundred thousand pounds of other people's money – no, no – I had rather be a little bob-wig citizen in good credit than a commissioner of the customs – Commissioner! – The King has not so good a thing in his gift as a commissioner of bankruptcy. Don't we see them all with their country-seats at Hogsdon, and at Kentish Town, and at Newingtonbutts, and at Islington? With their little flying Mercurys, tipped on the top of the house, their Apollos, their Venuses and their leaden Herculeses in the garden, and themselves sitting before the door, with pipes in their mouths, waiting for a good digestion – Zoons! here comes old Muckworm. Now for a few dry maxims of left-handed wisdom, to prove myself a scoundrel in sentiment, and pass in his eyes for a hopeful young man, likely to do well in the world.

(*Enter* OLD PHILPOT.)

OLD PHILPOT: Twelve times twelve is a hundred and forty-four . . .

GEORGE: I'll attack him in his own way – Commission at two and a half per cent . . .

OLD PHILPOT: There he is, intent upon business! What, plodding, George?

GEORGE: Thinking a little of the main chance, sir.

OLD PHILPOT: That's right: it is a wide world, George.

GEORGE: Yes, sir, but you instructed me early in the rudiments of trade.

OLD PHILPOT: Ay, ay, I instilled good principles into thee.

GEORGE: So you did, sir. (*aside*) Principal and interest is all I ever heard from him – I shall never forget the story you recommended to my earliest notice, sir.

OLD PHILPOT: What was that, George? It is quite out of my head.

GEORGE: It intimated, sir, how Mr Thomas Inkle of London, merchant, was cast

---

Mr Thomas Inkle: the story of Inkle and Yariko was to be found in Steele's *Spectator*, no. 11 (13 March 1711). It also furnished the plot for the comic opera *Inkle and Yariko* by George Colman the Younger (1787).

away, and was afterwards protected by a young lady, who grew in love with him, and how he afterwards bargained with a planter to sell her for a slave.

OLD PHILPOT: Ay, ay! (*Laughs.*) I recollect it now.

GEORGE: And when she pleaded being with child by him, he was no otherwise moved than to raise his price, and make her turn to better account.

OLD PHILPOT: (*Bursts into a laugh.*) I remember it – ha, ha! There was the very spirit of trade! Ay, ay! Ha, ha!

GEORGE: That was calculation for you . . .

OLD PHILPOT: Ay, ay!

GEORGE: The Rule of Three – If one gives me so much, what will two give me?

OLD PHILPOT: (*Laughs.*) Ay, ay!

GEORGE: That was a hit, sir!

OLD PHILPOT: Ay, ay!

GEORGE: That was having his wits about him!

OLD PHILPOT: Ay, ay! It is a lesson for all young men. It was a hit indeed, ha, ha! (*Both laugh.*)

GEORGE: (*aside*) What an old negro it is!

OLD PHILPOT: Thou art a son after my own heart, George.

GEORGE: Trade must be minded. A penny saved, is a penny got . . .

OLD PHILPOT: Ay, ay! (*Shakes his head, and looks cunning.*)

GEORGE: He that hath money in his purse, won't want a head on his shoulders.

OLD PHILPOT: Ay, ay!

GEORGE: Rome was not built in a day – Fortunes are made by degrees – Pains to get, care to keep, and fear to lose.

OLD PHILPOT: Ay, ay!

GEORGE: He that lies in bed, his estate feels it.

OLD PHILPOT: Ay, ay! The good boy!

GEORGE: (*aside*) The old curmudgeon thinks nothing mean that brings in an honest penny.

OLD PHILPOT: The good boy! George, I have great hopes of thee.

GEORGE: Thanks to your example; you have taught me to be cautious in this wide world – Love your neighbour, but don't pull down your hedge!

OLD PHILPOT: I profess it is a wise saying. I never heard it before. It is a wise saying, and shows how cautious we should be of too much confidence in friendship.

GEORGE: Very true.

OLD PHILPOT: Friendship has nothing to do with trade.

GEORGE: It only draws a man into lending money.

OLD PHILPOT: Ay, ay.

GEORGE: There was your neighbour's son, Dick Worthy, who was always cramming his head with Greek and Latin at school. He wanted to borrow of me the other day, but I was too cunning.

OLD PHILPOT: Ay, ay. Let him draw bills of exchange in Greek and Latin, and see where he will get a pound sterling for them.

GEORGE: So I told him. I went to him to his garret in the Minories, and there I found him in all his misery! And a fine scene it was – there was his wife in a corner of the room, at a washing tub, up to the elbows in suds; a solitary pork-steak was dangling by a pack-string before a melancholy fire; himself seated at a three-legged table, writing a pamphlet against the German war; a child on his left knee, his right leg employed in rocking a cradle with a bratling in it. And so there was business enough for them all – his wife rubbing away (*Mimics a washerwoman.*) and he writing on. 'The King of Prussia shall have no more subsidies – Saxony shall be indemnified – He shan't have a foot in Silesia.' 'There is a sweet little baby!' (*to the child on his knee*) Then he rocked the cradle, 'Hush ho! hush ho!' Then twisted the griskin. (*Snaps his fingers.*) 'Hush ho!' 'The Russians shall have Prussia.' (*Writes.*) The wife – (*Washes and sings.*) He – 'There's a dear.' Round goes the griskin again – (*Snaps his fingers.*) 'and Canada must be restored'. (*Writes.*) – And so you have a picture of the whole family.

OLD PHILPOT: Ha, ha! What becomes of his Greek and Latin now? Fine words butter no parsnips. – He had no money from you, I suppose, George?

GEORGE: Oh, no! Charity begins at home, says I.

OLD PHILPOT: And it was wisely said. I have an excellent saying, when any man wants to borrow from me – I am ready with my joke – 'A fool and his money are soon parted.' – Ha, ha, ha!

GEORGE: Ha, ha! (*aside*) An old skin-flint!

OLD PHILPOT: Ay, ay – a fool and his money are soon parted – ha, ha, ha!

GEORGE: (*aside*) Now, if I can wring a handsome sum out of him, it will prove the truth of what he says. – And yet trade has its inconveniences – great houses stopping payment!

OLD PHILPOT: Hey, what! You look chagrined. Nothing of that sort has happened to thee, I hope?

GEORGE: A great house at Cadiz, Don John de Alvarada. The Spanish galleons not making quick returns – and so my bills are come back.

OLD PHILPOT: Ay! (*Shakes his head.*)

GEORGE: I have, indeed, a remittance from Messina. That voyage yields me thirty per cent profit – but this blow coming upon me –

OLD PHILPOT: Why, this is unlucky. How much money?

GEORGE: Three-and-twenty hundred.

OLD PHILPOT: George, too many eggs in one basket! I'll tell thee, George; I expect Sir Jasper Wilding here presently to conclude the treaty of marriage I have on foot for thee: then hush this up; say nothing of it; and in a day or two you pay these bills with his daughter's portion.

GEORGE: (*aside*) The old rogue! – That will never do. I shall be blown on the 'Change. Alvarada will pay in time . . . He has opened his affairs . . . He appears a good man.

OLD PHILPOT: Does he?

GEORGE: A great fortune left behind . . . will pay in time, but I must crack before that.

OLD PHILPOT: It is unlucky . . . A good man you say he is?

GEORGE: Nobody better.

OLD PHILPOT: Let me see . . . Suppose I lend this money?

German War: the Seven Years' War had started in 1755. From Murphy's own political writing since 1756, it is clear that he shared Dick Worthy's distrust of England's German ally Frederick the Great of Prussia.
griskin: loin of pork.

GEORGE: Ah, sir!

OLD PHILPOT: How much is your remittance from Messina?

GEORGE: Seven hundred and fifty.

OLD PHILPOT: Then you want fifteen hundred and fifty?

GEORGE: Exactly.

OLD PHILPOT: Don Alvarada is a good man, you say?

GEORGE: Yes, sir.

OLD PHILPOT: I will venture to lend the money. You must allow me commission on those bills, for taking them up for honour of the drawer?

GEORGE: Agreed.

OLD PHILPOT: Lawful interest, while I am out of my money?

GEORGE: I subscribe.

PHILPOT: A power of attorney to receive the monies from Alvarada, when he makes a payment?

GEORGE: You shall have it.

OLD PHILPOT: Your own bond?

GEORGE: To be sure.

OLD PHILPOT: Go and get me a cheque – You shall have a draught on the bank.

GEORGE: Yes, sir. (*going*)

OLD PHILPOT: But stay – I had forgot – I must sell out for this. Stocks are under *par* – you must pay the difference.

GEORGE: (*aside*) Was there ever such a leech! – By all means sir.

OLD PHILPOT: Step and get me a cheque.

GEORGE: (*aside*) A fool and his money are soon parted. (*Exit.*)

OLD PHILPOT: What with commission, lawful interest, and his paying the difference of the stocks – which are higher now than when I bought in – this will be no bad morning's work. And then, in the evening, I shall be in the rarest spirits for this new adventure I am recommended to – let me see – what is the lady's name? (*Takes a letter out.*) Corinna! Ay, ay, by the description, she is a bale of goods. I shall be in rare spirits. Ay, this is the way, to indulge one's passions and yet conceal them, and to mind one's business in the City here, as if one had no passions at all. I long for the evening. Methinks – body o' me – I am a young man still!

(*Enter* QUILLDRIVE.)

QUILLDRIVE: Sir Jasper Wilding, sir, and his daughter.

OLD PHILPOT: I am at home.

(*Enter* SIR JASPER *and* MARIA. SIR JASPER, *dressed as a fox-hunter, and singing.*)

OLD PHILPOT: Sir Jasper, your very humble servant.

SIR JASPER: Master Philpot, I be glad to zee ye, I am indeed.

OLD PHILPOT: The like compliment to you, Sir Jasper. Miss Maria, I kiss your fair hand.

MARIA: Sir, your most obedient.

SIR JASPER: Ay, ay, I ha' brought un to zee you – There's my girl. I ben't ashamed of my girl.

MARIA: (*aside*) That's more than I can say of my father. Luckily, these people are as much strangers to decorum as my old gentleman, otherwise this visit from a lady to meet her lover would have an odd appearance. – Though but late a boarding-school girl, I know enough of the world for that.

OLD PHILPOT: Truely, she is a blooming young lady, Sir Jasper, and I verily shall like to take an interest in her.

SIR JASPER: I ha' brought her to zee ye, and zo your zon may ha' her as soon as he will.

OLD PHILPOT: Why, she looks three and a half per cent better than when I saw her last.

MARIA: (*aside*) Then, there are hopes in that, in a little time, I shall be above *par*. – He rates me like a lottery ticket!

OLD PHILPOT: Ay, ay, I doubt not, Sir Jasper, miss has the appearance of a very sensible, discreet young lady, and, to deal freely, without that, she would not do for my son. – George is a shrewd lad, and I have often heard him declare no consideration should ever prevail on him to marry a fool.

MARIA: (*aside*) Ay, you have told me so before, old gentleman, and I have my cue from my brother, and if I don't give master George a surfeit of me, why, then, I am not a notable girl.

(Enter GEORGE PHILPOT.)

GEORGE: (*aside*) A good, clever old cuff this, after my own heart. I think I will have his daughter, if it's only for the pleasure of hunting with him.

SIR JASPER: Zon-in-law, gee us your hand – what say you? Are you ready for my girl?

GEORGE: Say grace as soon as you will, sir, I'll fall to.

SIR JASPER: Well zaid; I like you; I like un, master Philpot; I like un; I tell you what, let un talk to her now.

OLD PHILPOT: And so he shall. George, she is a bale of goods. Speak her fair now, and then you'll be in cash.

GEORGE: I think I had rather not speak to her now – I hate speaking to these modest women, sir – sir, a word in your ear: had not I better break my mind, by advertising for her in a newspaper?

OLD PHILPOT: Talk sense to her, George. She is a notable girl – and I'll give you the draft upon the bank presently.

SIR JASPER: Come along, master Philpot, come along. I ben't afraid of my girl – come along. (*Exeunt* SIR JASPER *and* OLD PHILPOT.)

MARIA: (*aside*) A pretty sort of a lover they have found for me.

GEORGE: (*aside*) How shall I speak my mind to her? She is almost a stranger to me.

MARIA: (*aside*) Now, I'll make the hideous thing hate me, if I can.

GEORGE: (*aside*) Ay, she is as sharp as a needle, I warrant her.

MARIA: (*aside*) When will he begin? Ah, you fright! You rival Mr Beaufort! I'll give him an aversion to me, that's what I will, and so let him have the trouble of breaking off the match. Not a word yet – he is in a fine confusion. (*Looks foolish.*) I think I may as well sit down, sir.

GEORGE: Madam – I – I – I – I (*frightened*) I'll hand you a chair, madam – there madam! (*Bows awkwardly.*)

MARIA: Sir, I thank you.

GEORGE: (*in confusion*) I'll sit down, too.

MARIA: Heigho!

GEORGE: Madam!

MARIA: Sir!

GEORGE: I thought – I – I – did not you say something, madam?

MARIA: No, sir. Nothing.

GEORGE: I beg your pardon, madam.

MARIA: (*aside*) Oh you are a sweet creature!

GEORGE: (*aside*) The ice is broke now. I have begun, and so I'll go on. (*Sits silent, looks foolish, and steals a look at her.*)

MARIA: (*aside*) An agreeable interview this!

GEORGE: Pray, madam, do you ever go to concerts?

MARIA: Concerts! What's that, sir?

GEORGE: A music meeting.

MARIA: I have been at a Quaker's meeting, but never at a music meeting.

GEORGE: Lord, madam, all the gay world goes to concerts. (*aside*) She's notable! I'll take courage, she's nobody. – Will you give me leave to present you a ticket for the Crown and Anchor, madam?

MARIA: (*looking simple and awkward*) A ticket! What is a ticket?

GEORGE: There, madam, at your service.

MARIA: (*Curtsies awkwardly.*) I long to see what a ticket is.

GEORGE: (*aside*) What a curtsey there is for St James's end of the town! I hate her; she seems to be an idiot.

MARIA: (*aside*) Here's a charming ticket he has given me. – And is this a ticket, sir?

GEORGE: Yes, madam. (*Mimics her; aside*) And is this a ticket?

MARIA: (*Reads.*) 'For sale, by the candle, the following goods: thirty chests, straw-hats; fifty tubs, chip-hats; pepper, sago, borax.' Ha, ha! Such a ticket!

GEORGE: I – I – I have made a mistake, madam . . . Here – here is the right one.

MARIA: You need not mind it, sir. I never go to such places.

GEORGE: No, madam? (*aside*) I don't know what to make of her. – Was you ever at White Conduit House?

MARIA: (*aside*) There's a question! – Is that a nobleman's seat?

GEORGE: (*Laughs.*) Simpleton! – No, miss, it is not a nobleman's seat. Lord! It's at Islington.

MARIA: Lord Islington! I don't know my Lord Islington.

GEORGE: The town of Islington.

MARIA: I have not the honour of knowing his lordship.

GEORGE: Islington is a town, madam.

MARIA: Oh! It's a town?

GEORGE: Yes, madam.

MARIA: I am glad of it.

GEORGE: (*aside*) What is she glad of?

MARIA: (*aside*) A pretty husband my papa has chose for me!

GEORGE: (*aside*) What shall I say to her next? – Have you been to the burletta, madam?

MARIA: Where?

GEORGE: The burletta.

Crown and Anchor: a tavern with facilities for illegitimate theatre.
White Conduit House: a garden pleasure resort opened by Robert Bartholomew in 1745.

MARIA: Sir, I would have you know that I am no such person. I go to burlettas! I am not what you take me for.

GEORGE: Madam . . .

MARIA: I am come of good people, sir, and have been properly educated, as a young girl ought to be.

GEORGE: (*aside*) What a damned fool she is! – The burletta is an opera, madam.

MARIA: Opera, sir! I don't know what you mean by this usage – to affront me in this manner!

GEORGE: Affront! I mean quite the reverse, madam; I took you for a connoisseur.

MARIA: Who, me a connoisseur, sir! I desire you won't call me such names. I am sure I never so much as thought of such a thing. Sir, I won't be called a connoisseur–I won't – I won't – I won't. (*Bursts out crying.*)

GEORGE: Madam. I meant no offence. A connoisseur is a virtuoso.

MARIA: Don't virtuoso me! I am no virtuoso, sir! I would have you to know it, I am as virtuous a girl as any in England, and I will never be a virtuoso. (*Cries bitterly.*)

GEORGE: But, madam, you mistake me quite.

MARIA: (*in a passion, and choking her tears, and sobbing*) Sir, I am come of as virtuous people as any in England – My family was always remarkable for virtue – My mamma was as good a woman as ever was born, and my Aunt Bridget (*sobbing*) was a virtuous woman, too – and there's my sister Sophy makes as good and virtuous a wife as any at all. And so, sir, don't call me a virtuoso. I won't be brought here to be treated in this manner – I won't – I won't – I won't. (*Cries bitterly.*)

GEORGE: (*aside*) The girl's a natural – so much the better. I'll marry her, and lock her up. – Madam, upon my word, you misunderstand me.

MARIA: (*drying her tears*) Sir, I won't be called connoisseur by you or anybody. And I know I am no virtuoso – I would have you know that.

GEORGE: Madam, connoisseur and virtuoso are words for a person of taste.

MARIA: (*sobbing*) Taste!

GEORGE: Yes, madam.

MARIA: And did you mean to say as how I am a person of taste?

GEORGE: Undoubtedly.

MARIA: Sir, your most obedient humble servant. Oh, that's another thing. I have a taste, to be sure.

GEORGE: I know you have, madam. (*aside*) Oh you're a cursed ninny!

MARIA: Yes, I know I have. I can read tolerably, and I begin to write a little.

GEORGE: Upon my word you have made a great progress! (*aside*) What could old Square Toes mean by passing her upon me for a sensible girl? And what a fool I was to be afraid to speak to her! I'll talk to her openly at once. – Come, sit down, miss. Pray, madam, are you inclined to matrimony?

MARIA: Yes, sir.

GEORGE: Are you in love?

MARIA: Yes, sir.

GEORGE: (*aside*) These naturals are always amorous. – How should you like me?

MARIA: Of all things.

GEORGE: (*aside*) A girl without ceremony! – Do you love me?

MARIA: Yes, sir.

GEORGE: But you don't love anybody else?

MARIA: Yes, sir.

GEORGE: (*aside*) Frank and free! – But not so well as me?

MARIA: Yes, sir.

GEORGE: Better, may be?

MARIA: Yes, sir.

GEORGE: (*aside*) The devil you do! – And, perhaps, if I should marry you, I should have a chance to be made a —

MARIA: Yes, sir!

GEORGE: The case is clear. Miss Maria, your humble servant. You are not for my money, I promise you.

MARIA: Sir!

GEORGE: I have done, madam, that's all, and I take my leave.

MARIA: But you'll marry me?

GEORGE: No, madam, no; no such thing. You may provide yourself a husband elsewhere: I am your humble servant.

MARIA: Not marry me, Mr Philpot? But you must – my papa said you must – and I will have you.

GEORGE: (*aside*) There's another proof of her nonsense! – Make yourself easy, for I shall have nothing to do with you.

MARIA: Not marry me, Mr Philpot? (*Bursts out in tears.*) But I say you shall, and I will have a husband, or I'll know the reason why – You shall – you shall.

GEORGE: A pretty sort of a wife they intend for me here . . .

MARIA: I wonder you an't ashamed of yourself, to affront a young girl in this manner. I'll go and tell my papa – I will – I will – I will. (*Cries bitterly.*)

GEORGE: And so you may – I have no more to say to you – And so, your servant, miss – your servant.

MARIA: Ay! and by goles! my brother Bob shall fight you.

GEORGE: (*going*) What care I for your brother Bob?

MARIA: How can you be so cruel, Mr Philpot? How can you – Oh! (*Cries and struggles with him. Exit* GEORGE PHILPOT.) Ha, ha! I have carried my brother's scheme into execution charmingly, ha, ha! He will break off the match now of his own accord, ha, ha! This is charming! This is fine! This is like a girl of spirit! (*Exit.*)

ACT II

SCENE 1.   CORINNA's *apartment. Enter* CORINNA, TOM *following her.*

CORINNA: An elderly gentleman, did you say?

TOM: Yes; that says he has got a letter for you, madam.

CORINNA: Desire the gentleman to walk up stairs. (*Exit* TOM.) These old fellows will be coming after a body – but they pay well, and so – Servant, sir.
              (*Enter* OLD PHILPOT.)

OLD PHILPOT: Fair lady, your very humble servant. (*aside*) Truly, a blooming young girl! – Madam, I have a letter here for you from Bob Poacher, whom, I presume, you know.

CORINNA: Yes, sir, I know Bob Poacher. He is a very good friend of mine. (*Reads to herself.*) He speaks so handsomely of you, sir, and says you are so much of a gentleman, that, to be sure, sir, I shall endeavour to be agreeable, sir.

OLD PHILPOT: Really you are very agreeable. (*Looks at his watch.*) You see I am punctual to my hour.

CORINNA: That is a mighty pretty watch, sir.

OLD PHILPOT: Yes, madam, it is a repeater; it has been in our family for a long time. This is a mighty pretty lodging. – I have twenty guineas here, in a purse. Here they are – (*Turns them out on the table.*) – as pretty golden rogues as ever fair fingers played with.

CORINNA: I am always agreeable to anything from a gentleman.

OLD PHILPOT: (*aside*) There are some light guineas amongst them. I always put off my light guineas in this way. – You are exceedingly welcome, madam. Your fair hand looks so tempting, I must kiss it – Oh, I could eat it up! – Fair lady, your lips look so cherry, they actually invite the touch. (*Kisses.*) Really, it makes the difference of cent per cent in one's constitution. – You have really a mighty pretty foot – Oh, you little rogue! – I could smother you with kisses – Oh, you little delicate, charming . . . (*Kisses her.*)

(GEORGE PHILPOT *is heard within.*)

GEORGE: Gee-houp! Awhi! Awhi! Gallows! Awhi!

OLD PHILPOT: Hey? What is all that? Somebody is coming!

CORINNA: Some young rake, I fancy, coming in, whether my servants will or no.

OLD PHILPOT: What shall I do? I will not be seen for the world – Can't you hide me in that room?

CORINNA: Dear heart! No sir. These wild young fellows take such liberties. He may take it into his head to go in there, and then you will be detected. – Get under the table – he shan't remain long, whoever he is – here – here, sir, get under here.

OLD PHILPOT: Ay, ay; that will do – don't let him stay long. – Give me another buss. – Wounds! I could . . .

CORINNA: Hush! Make haste.

OLD PHILPOT: Ay, ay; I will, fair lady. (*Creeps under the table, and peeps out.*) Don't let him stay long.

CORINNA: Hush! Silence! You will ruin all else.

(*Enter* GEORGE PHILPOT, *dressed out.*)

GEORGE: Sharper, do your work! Awhi! Awhi! So, my girl, how dost do?

CORINNA: Very well, thank you. I did not expect to see you so soon, I thought you was to be at the club. The servants told me you came back from the City at two o'clock to dress, and so I concluded you would have stayed all night as usual.

GEORGE: No, the run was against me again, and I did not care to pursue ill fortune. But I am strong in cash, my girl.

CORINNA: Are you?

GEORGE: Yes, yes, suskins in plenty.

OLD PHILPOT: (*peeping*) Ah, the ungracious! These are your haunts, are they?

---

light guineas: coins that had been clipped or pared to steal the gold.
Gallows, Sharper: names of George's horses; see p. 132 below.
suskins: Dutch coins, hence cash.

GEORGE: Yes, yes, I am strong in cash. I have taken in old curmudgeon since I saw you.

CORINNA: As how, pray?

OLD PHILPOT: (*peeping*) Ay, as how; let us hear, pray.

GEORGE: Why, I'll tell you.

OLD PHILPOT: (*peeping*) Ay, let us hear.

GEORGE: I talked a world of wisdom to him.

OLD PHILPOT: Ay!

GEORGE: Tipped him a few rascally sentiments of a scoundrelly kind of prudence.

OLD PHILPOT: Ay!

GEORGE: The old curmudgeon chuckled at it.

OLD PHILPOT: Ay, ay; the old curmudgeon! Ay, ay.

GEORGE: He is a sad old fellow.

OLD PHILPOT: Ay! Go on.

GEORGE: And so I appeared to him as deserving of the gallows as he is himself.

OLD PHILPOT: Well said, boy, well said. Go on.

GEORGE: And then he took a liking to me. 'Ay, ay,' says he, 'ay, friendship has nothing to do with trade.' And then, as I dealt out little maxims of penury, he grinned like a Jew broker, when he has cheated his principal of an eight per cent and cried, 'Ay, ay, that is the very spirit of trade – a fool and his money are soon parted.' (*mimicking him*) And so he went on, like Harlequin in a French comedy, tickling himself into a good humour, till at last I tickled him out of fifteen hundred and odd pounds.

OLD PHILPOT: I have a mind to rise and break his bones – but then I discover myself – Lie still, Isaac, lie still.

GEORGE: Oh, I understand trap. I talked of a great house stopping payment. The thing was true enough, but I had no dealings with them.

OLD PHILPOT: Ay, ay!

GEORGE: And so, for fear of breaking off a match with an idiot he wants me to marry, he lent me the money – and cheated me, though.

OLD PHILPOT: Ay, you have found it out, have ye?

GEORGE: No old usurer in England, grown hard-hearted in his trade, could have dealt worse with me. 'I must have commission upon these bills for taking them up for the honour of the drawer – your bond – lawful interest while I am out of the money – and the difference for selling out of the stocks.' An old, miserly, good-for-nothing skin-flint.

OLD PHILPOT: My blood boils to be at him. Go on, can't you tell us a little more?

GEORGE: Pho! He is an old curmudgeon – and so I will talk no more about him. – Come give me a kiss. (*Kisses.*)

OLD PHILPOT: The young dog, how he fastens his lips to her!

GEORGE: You shall go with me to Epsom next Sunday.

CORINNA: Shall I? That's charming.

GEORGE: You shall, in my chariot – I drive . . .

CORINNA: But I don't like to see you drive.

GEORGE: But I like it! I am as good a coachman as any in England. There was my lord what d'ye call him, he kept a stage-coach for his own driving; but, Lord! he was nothing to me.

CORINNA: No!

GEORGE: Oh, no! I know my road-work, my girl, when I have my coachman's hat on – Is my hat come home?

CORINNA: It hangs up yonder; but I don't like it.

GEORGE: Let me see – ay! the very thing. Mind me when I go to work – throw my eyes about a few – handle the braces – take the off-leader by the jaw – here, you – how have you curbed this horse up? Let him out a link; do, you blood of a — Whoo, eh! Jewel! Button! Whoo, eh! Come here, you, sir; how have you coupled Gallows? You know he'll take the bar of Sharper – take him in two holes, do – there's four pretty little knots as any in England – Whoo, eh!

CORINNA: But can't you let your coachman drive?

GEORGE: No, no. See me mount the box (*climbing on to the table*) handle the reins, my wrist turned down, square my elbows, stamp with my foot – Gee-up! Off we go – Button, do you want to have us over? Do your work, do – Awhi! Awhi! There we bowl away! See how sharp they are – Gallows! Softly up the hill. (*Whistles.*) There's a public house – Give them a mouthful of water, do – And fetch me a dram – drink it off – gee-up! Awhi! Awhi! There we go, scrambling all together – Reach Epsom in an hour and forty-three minutes, all Lombard Street to an egg-shell, we do. There's your work, my girl! Eh! Damn me!

OLD PHILPOT: Mercy on me! What a profligate, debauched, young dog it is!

(*Enter* YOUNG WILDING.)

WILDING: Ha! My little Corinna. – Sir, your servant.

GEORGE: Your servant, sir.

WILDING: Sir, your servant.

GEORGE: Any commands for me, sir?

WILDING: For you, sir?

GEORGE: Yes, for me, sir.

WILDING: No, sir. I have no commands for you, sir.

GEORGE: What's your business?

WILDING: Business!

GEORGE: Ay, business.

WILDING: Why, very good business, I think; my little Corinna – my life – my little . . .

GEORGE: Is that your business? Pray, sir – not so free, sir.

WILDING: Not so free!

GEORGE: No, sir! That lady belongs to me.

WILDING: To you, sir?

GEORGE: Yes, to me.

WILDING: To you! Who are you?

GEORGE: As good a man as you.

WILDING: Upon my word! Who is this fellow, Corinna? Some journeyman tailor, I suppose, who chooses to try on the gentleman's clothes before he carries them home.

GEORGE: Tailor! What do you mean by that? You lie! I am no tailor.

WILDING: You shall give me satisfaction for that!

GEORGE: For what?

WILDING: For giving me the lie.

GEORGE: I did not.

WILDING: You did, sir.

GEORGE: You lie, I'll bet you five pounds I did not. But if you have a mind for a frolic, let me put by my sword – Now, sir, come on. (*in a boxing attitude*)

WILDING: Why, you scoundrel, do you think I want to box? Draw, sir, this moment!

GEORGE: Not I – come in.

WILDING: Draw, or I'll cut you to pieces.

GEORGE: I'll give you satisfaction this way. (*Pushes at him.*)

WILDING: Draw, sir, draw! You won't draw! There, take that, sirrah – and that – and that, you scoundrel. (*Beats him with the flat of his sword.*)

OLD PHILPOT: (*peeping*) Ay, ay; well done; lay it on.

WILDING: And there, you rascal, and there.

OLD PHILPOT: Thank you, thank you. Could not you find in your heart to lay on another for me?

CORINNA: Pray, don't be in such passion, sir.

WILDING: My dear Corinna, don't be frightened. I shall not murder him.

OLD PHILPOT: I am safe here – lie still, Isaac, lie still – I am safe.

WILDING: The fellow has put me out of breath. (*Sits down. OLD PHILPOT's watch strikes ten under the table.*) Hey! What is all this? (*Looks under the table.*) Your humble servant, sir! Turn out, pray turn out – you won't – then I'll unshell you. (*Takes away the table.*) Your very humble servant, sir.

GEORGE: (*aside*) Zounds! My father there all this time!

WILDING: I suppose you will give me the lie, too?

OLD PHILPOT: (*still on the ground*) No, sir, not I, truly; but the gentleman, there, may divert himself again, if he has a mind.

GEORGE: No, sir, not I. I pass.

OLD PHILPOT: George, you are there I see.

GEORGE: Yes, sir. And you are there I see.

WILDING: Come rise. Who is this old fellow?

CORINNA: Upon my word, I don't know – as I live and breathe, I don't. He came after my maid, I suppose. I'll go and ask her. – Let me run out of the way, and hide myself from this scene of confusion! (*Exit.*)

GEORGE: (*aside*) What an imp of hell she is!

WILDING: Come, get up, sir, you are too old to beat.

OLD PHILPOT: (*rising*) In troth so I am. But there you may exercise yourself again, if you please.

GEORGE: No more for me, sir – I thank you.

OLD PHILPOT: (*aside*) I have made but a bad voyage of it; the ship is sunk, and stock and block lost.

WILDING: Ha, ha! Upon my soul, I can't help laughing at this old Square Toes. As for you, sir, you have had what you deserved. Ha, ha! You are a kind of cull, I suppose, ha, ha! And you, reverend dad, you must come here tottering after a punk. Ha, ha!

OLD PHILPOT: Oh, George! George!

GEORGE: Oh, Father! Father!

WILDING: Ha, ha! What, father and son! And so you have found one another out, ha,

---

cull: cully or dupe.

ha! Well, you may have business, and so, gentlemen, I'll leave you to yourselves. (*Exit.*)

GEORGE: This is too much to bear! What an infamous jade she is! All her contrivance! – Don't be angry with me, sir; I'll go my ways this moment, tie myself up in the matrimonial noose, and never have anything to do with these courses again. (*going*)

OLD PHILPOT: And, harkye, George, tie me up in a real noose, and turn me off as soon as you will. (*Exeunt.*)

SCENE 2.   *A room in* SIR JASPER WILDING's *house. Enter* BEAUFORT, *dressed as a lawyer, and* SIR JASPER WILDING *with a bottle and glass in his hand.*

BEAUFORT: No more, Sir Jasper. I can't drink any more.

SIR JASPER: Why, you be but a weezen-faced drinker, Master Quagmire. Come, man, finish this bottle.

BEAUFORT: I beg to be excused. You had better let me read over the deeds to you.

SIR JASPER: Zounds! It's all about out-houses, and messuages, and barns, and stables, and orchards, and meadows, and lands, and tenements, and woods, and under-woods, and commons, and backsides. I am o' the commission for Wilts, and I know the ley; and so truce with your jargon, Mr Quagmire.

BEAUFORT: But, sir, you don't consider, marriage is an affair of importance. It is contracted between persons, first, consenting; secondly, free from canonical impediments; thirdly, free from civil impediments, and can only be dissolved for canonical causes, or levitical causes. – See Leviticus xviii and xxviii, Henry VIII, chapter vii.

SIR JASPER: You shall drink t'other bumper, an you talk of ley.
          (*Enter a servant.*)

SERVANT: Old Mr Philpot, sir, and his son.

SIR JASPER: Wounds! That's right. They'll take me out of the hands of this lawyer here. (*Exits, with the servant.*)

BEAUFORT: Well done, Beaufort! Thus far you have played your part, as if you had been of the pimplenose family of Furnival's Inn.
          (*Re-enter* SIR JASPER *with* OLD PHILPOT *and* GEORGE.)

SIR JASPER: Master Philpot, I be glad you are come: this man here has so plagued me with his ley! But now we'll have no more about it, but sign the papers at once. (*Signs.*)

OLD PHILPOT: Sir Jasper, twenty thousand pounds, you know, is a great deal of money. I should not give you so much, if it were not for the sake of your daughter's marrying my son; so that, if you will allow me discount for prompt payment, I will pay the money down.

GEORGE: Sir, I must beg to see the young lady once more before I embark, for, to be plain, sir, she appears to be a mere natural.

SIR JASPER: I'll tell you what, youngster, I find my girl is a notable wench – and here, here's zon Bob.
          (*Enter* YOUNG WILDING.)

SIR JASPER: Bob, gee us your hand. I have finished the business, and so now – here, here, here's your vather-in-law.

OLD PHILPOT: (*aside*) Of all the birds in the air, is that he?

GEORGE: (*aside*) He has behaved like a relation to me already.

SIR JASPER: Go to un, man – that's your vather . . .

WILDING: This is the strangest accident – sir – sir – (*stifling a laugh*) I – I – sir – upon my soul I can't stand this. (*Bursts out laughing.*)

OLD PHILPOT: (*aside*) I deserve it! I deserve to be laughed at.

GEORGE: (*aside*) He has shown his regard to his sister's family already.

SIR JASPER: What's the matter, Bob? I tell you this is your vather-in-law. (*Pulls* OLD PHILPOT *to him.*) Master Philpot, that's Bob – Speak to un, Bob – speak to un . . .

WILDING: Sir – I – I am . . . (*Stifles a laugh.*) I say, sir – I am, sir – extremely proud – of – of . . .

GEORGE: (*aside*) Of having beat me, I suppose.

WILDING: Of the honour, sir – of – of . . . (*Laughs.*)

GEORGE: (*aside*) Ay, that's what he means.

WILDING: And, sir, I – I – this opportunity – I cannot look him in the face. (*Bursts out into a laugh.*) Ha, ha! I cannot stay in the room . . . (*going*)

SIR JASPER: Why, the volks are all mad, I believe! You shall stay, Bob; you shall stay! (*Holds him.*)

WILDING: Sir, I – I cannot possibly – (*Whispers to his father.*)

OLD PHILPOT: George! George! What a woeful figure do we make?

GEORGE: Bad enough, of all conscience, sir.

SIR JASPER: (*Laughs heartily.*) An odd adventure, Bob!

GEORGE: Ay! There now he is hearing the whole affair, and is laughing at me.

SIR JASPER: Ha, ha! Poh, never mind it – a did not hurt un.

OLD PHILPOT: It's all discovered.

SIR JASPER: Ha, ha! I told ye zon Bob could find a hare squat upon her form with any he in Christendom – ha, ha! Never mind it, man; Bob meant no harm – Here, here, Bob – here's your vather, and there's your brother. – I should like to have zeen under the table!

WILDING: Gentlemen, your most obedient. (*stifling a laugh*)

OLD PHILPOT: Sir, your servant – He has licked George well – and I forgive him.

SIR JASPER: Well, young gentleman, which way is your mind now?

GEORGE: Why, sir, to be plain, I find your daughter an idiot.

SIR JASPER: Zee her again, then – zee her again. Here, you, sirrah, send our Moll hither.

SERVANT: Yes, sir.

SIR JASPER: Very well, then; we'll go into t'other room, crack a bottle, and settle matters there, and leave un together – Hoic! Hoic! – Our Moll – Tally over!
          (*Enter* MARIA.)

MARIA: Did you call me, papa?

SIR JASPER: I did, my girl. There, the gentleman wants to speak with you. Behave like a clever wench, as you are. – Come along, my boys – Master Quagmire, come and finish the business. (*Exit singing, with* OLD PHILPOT, WILDING *and* BEAUFORT. *Manent* GEORGE *and* MARIA.)

GEORGE: (*aside*) I know she is a fool, and so I will speak to her without ceremony. – Well, miss, you told me you could read and write!

MARIA: Read, sir? Heavens! (*looking at him*) Ha, ha, ha!

GEORGE: (*aside*) What does she laugh at?

MARIA: Ha, ha, ha, ha!

GEORGE: What diverts you so, pray?

MARIA: Ha, ha, ha! What a fine tawdry figure you have made of yourself! Ha, ha!

GEORGE: Figure, madam?

MARIA: I shall die, I shall die! Ha, ha, ha!

GEORGE: Do you make a laughing-stock of me?

MARIA: No, sir; by no means – Ha, ha, ha!

GEORGE: Let me tell you, miss, I don't understand being treated thus.

MARIA: Sir, I can't possibly help it – I – I – Ha, ha!

GEORGE: I shall quit the room, and tell your papa, if you go on thus.

MARIA: Sir, I beg your pardon a thousand time – I am but a giddy girl – I can't help it – I – I – Ha, ha!

GEORGE: Madam, this is downright insult!

MARIA: Sir, you look somehow or other – I don't know how – so comically – Ha, ha, ha!

GEORGE: Did you never see a gentleman dressed before?

MARIA: Never like you – I beg your pardon, sir – Ha, ha, ha!

GEORGE: Now, here is an idiot in spirits – I tell you, this is ignorance – I am dressed in high taste.

MARIA: Yes, so you are – Ha, ha, ha!

GEORGE: Will you have done laughing?

MARIA: Yes, sir, I will – I will – there – there – there – I have done.

GEORGE: Do so then, and behave yourself a little sedately.

MARIA: I will, sir. (*aside*) I won't look at him, and then I shan't laugh.

GEORGE: Let me tell you, miss, that nobody understands dress better than I do.

MARIA: Ha, ha, ha!

GEORGE: She's mad sure!

MARIA: No, sir, I am not mad – I have done, sir – I have done. I assure you, sir, that nobody is more averse from ill manners, and would take greater pains not to affront a gentleman – ha, ha, ha!

GEORGE: Again? Zounds! What do you mean? You'll put me in a passion, I can tell you, presently.

MARIA: I can't help it – Indeed I can't – Beat me if you will, but let me laugh – I can't help it. Ha, ha, ha!

GEORGE: I never met with such usage in my life.

MARIA: I shall die! Do, sir, let me laugh – It will do me good – Ha, ha, ha! (*Sits down in a fit of laughing.*)

GEORGE: If this is your way, I won't stay a moment longer in the room. I'll go this moment and tell your father.

MARIA: Sir, sir, Mr Philpot, don't be so hasty, sir – I have done, sir. It's over now – I have had my laugh out. I am a giddy girl, but I'll be grave. (*aside*) I'll compose myself, and act a different scene with him from what I did in the morning. I have all the materials of an impertinent wit, and I will now twirl him about the room, like a boy setting up his top with his finger and thumb.

GEORGE: Miss, I think you told me you could read and write?

MARIA: Everything.

GEORGE: You have?

MARIA: Yes, sir, I have.

GEORGE: Oh, brave! – And do you remember what you read, miss?

MARIA: Not so well as I could wish – Wits have short memories.

GEORGE: Oh! You are a wit too?

MARIA: I am – and do you know that I feel myself provoked to a simile now?

GEORGE: Provoked to a simile! Let us hear it.

MARIA: What do you think we are both like?

GEORGE: Well . . .

MARIA: Like Cymon and Iphigenia, in Dryden's fable.

GEORGE: Jenny in Dryden's fable!

MARIA: The fanning breeze upon her bosom blows;
      To meet the fanning breeze, her bosom rose.
  That's me – now you.
      He trudged along, unknowing what he sought,
      And whistled as he went (*Mimics.*) for want of thought.

GEORGE: (*disconcerted*) This is not the same girl!

MARIA: Mark again, mark again:
      The fool of nature stood with stupid eyes,
      And gaping mouth, that testified surprise.
      (*He looks foolish, she laughs at him.*)

GEORGE: (*aside*) I must take care how I speak to her, she is not the fool I took her for.

MARIA: You seem surprised, sir, but this is my way – I read, sir, and then I apply – I have read everything: Suckling, Waller, Milton, Dryden, Lansdowne, Gay, Prior, Swift, Addison, Pope, Young, Thomson . . .

GEORGE: Hey! The devil – what a clack is here! (*He walks across the stage.*)

MARIA: (*following him eagerly*) Shakespeare, Fletcher, Otway, Southerne, Rowe, Congreve, Wycherley, Farquhar, Cibber, Vanbrugh, Steele, in short everybody; and I find them all wit, fire, vivacity, spirit, genius, taste, imagination, raillery, humour, character, and sentiment. (*aside*) Well done, Miss Notable! You have played your part like a young actress in high favour with the town.

GEORGE: (*aside*) Her tongue goes like a water-mill!

MARIA: What do you say to me now, sir?

GEORGE: (*aside*) Say! I don't know what the devil to say.

MARIA: What's the matter, sir? Why, you look as if the stocks were fallen – or like London bridge at low water – or like a waterman when the Thames is frozen – or like a politician without news – or like a prude without scandal – or like a great lawyer without a brief – or like some lawyers with one – or . . .

GEORGE: Or like a poor devil of a husband henpecked by a wit, and so say no more of that. (*aside*) What a capricious piece here is!

MARIA: Oh, fie! You have spoilt all, I had not half done.

GEORGE: There is enough of all conscience. You may content yourself.

MARIA: But I can't be so easily contented – I like a simile half a mile long.

GEORGE: I see you do.

Cymon and Iphigenia: a pastoral poem written by Dryden in 1700.

MARIA: Oh, and I make verses too – verses like an angel – off hand – extempore. Can you give me an extempore?

GEORGE: What does she mean? No, miss – I have never a one about me.

MARIA: You can't give me an extempore – Oh, for shame, Mr Philpot! I love an extempore of all things; and I love the poets dearly; their sense so fine, their invention rich as Pactolus.

GEORGE: A poet rich as Pactolus! I have heard of that Pactolus in the City.

MARIA: Very like.

GEORGE: But you never heard of a poet as rich as he.

MARIA: As who?

GEORGE: Pactolus – he was a great Jew merchant – lived in the ward of Farringdon-without.

MARIA: Pactolus a Jew merchant! Pactolus is a river.

GEORGE: A river!

MARIA: Yes – don't you understand geography?

GEORGE: (*aside*) The girl's crazy!

MARIA: Oh, sir, if you don't understand geography, you are nobody. I understand geography, and I understand orthography. You know I told you I can write – and I can dance too – will you dance a minuet? (*Sings and dances.*)

GEORGE: You shan't lead me a dance, I promise you.

MARIA: Oh, very well, sir – you refuse me – remember you'll hear immediately of my being married to another, and then you'll be ready to hang yourself.

GEORGE: Not I, I promise you.

MARIA: Oh! Very well, very well – remember – mark my words. I'll do it, you shall see – Ha, ha! (*Runs off in a fit of laughing.*)

GEORGE: Marry you! I would as soon carry my wife to live in Bow Street, and write over the door 'Philpot's punch-house'.

(*Enter* OLD PHILPOT *and* SIR JASPER.)

SIR JASPER: (*singing*) 'So rarely, so bravely we'll hunt him over the downs, and we'll hoop and we'll halloo!' Gee us your hand, young gentleman. Well, what zay ye to un now? Ben't she a clever girl?

GEORGE: A very extraordinary girl indeed!

SIR JASPER: Did not I tell un zo. Then you have nothing to do but to consummate as soon as you will.

GEORGE: No; you may keep her, sir – I thank you. I'll have nothing to do with her.

OLD PHILPOT: What's the matter now, George?

GEORGE: Pho! She's a wit!

SIR JASPER: Ay, I told un zo.

GEORGE: Ay that's worse than t'other. I am off, sir.

SIR JASPER: Odds heart! I am afraid you are no great wit.

(*Enter* MARIA *with* BEAUFORT *and* WILDING.)

MARIA: Well, papa, the gentleman won't have me.

OLD PHILPOT: The numskull won't do as his father bids him; and so, Sir Jasper, with your consent, I'll make a proposal to the young lady myself.

MARIA: Ha! What does he say?

OLD PHILPOT: I am in the prime of my days, and I can be a brisk lover still! Fair lady, a glance of your eye is like the returning sun in spring – it melts away the frost of age, and gives a new warmth and vigour to all nature. (*Falls a coughing.*)

MARIA: Dear heart! I should like to have a scene with him.

SIR JASPER: Hey! What's in the wind now! This won't take. My girl shall have fair play. No old fellow shall totter to her bed! What say you, my girl, will you rock his cradle?

MARIA: Sir, I have one small doubt – Pray, can I have two husbands at a time?

GEORGE: There's a question now! She is grown foolish again.

OLD PHILPOT: Fair lady, the law of the land . . .

SIR JASPER: Hold ye, hold ye! Let me talk of law. I know the law better nor any on ye. Two husbands at once – No, no! Men are scarce, and that's downright poaching.

MARIA: I am sorry for it, sir, for then I can't marry him, I see.

SIR JASPER: Why not?

MARIA: I am contracted to another.

SIR JASPER: Contracted! To whom?

MARIA: To Mr Beaufort – that gentleman, sir.

OLD PHILPOT: That gentleman?

BEAUFORT: Yes, sir. (*Throws open his gown.*) My name is Beaufort. And I hope, Sir Jasper, when you consider my fortune, and my real affection for your daughter, you will generously forgive the stratagem I have made use of.

SIR JASPER: Master Quagmire! What, are you young Beaufort all this time?

OLD PHILPOT: That won't do, sir; that won't take.

BEAUFORT: But it must take, sir! You have signed the deeds for your daughter's marriage, and Sir Jasper by this instrument has made me his son-in-law.

OLD PHILPOT: How is this, how is this! Then, Sir Jasper, you will agree to cancel the deeds, I suppose? For you know . . .

SIR JASPER: Catch me at that, an ye can! I fulfilled my promise, and your son refused, and so the wench has looked out slyly for herself elsewhere. Did I not tell you she was a clever girl? I ben't ashamed of my girl. – Our Moll, you have done no harm, and Mr Beaufort is welcome to you with all my heart. I'll stand to what I have signed, though you have taken me by surprise.

WILDING: Bravo! My scheme has succeeded rarely!

OLD PHILPOT: And so here I am bubbled and choused out of my money. George, George, what a day's work have we made of it! Well, if it must be so, be it so. I desire, young gentleman, you will come and take my daughter away tomorrow morning. And I'll tell you what – here, here – take my family watch into the bargain; and I wish it may play you just such another trick as it has me, that's all. I'll never go intriguing with a family watch again.

MARIA: (*to* GEORGE) Well, sir, what do you think of me now? An't I a connoisseur, sir? And a virtuoso? Ha, ha!

GEORGE: Yes! And much good may't do your husband! I have been connoisseured among ye to some purpose – Bubbled at play; duped by my wench; cudgelled by

---

choused: tricked, swindled.

a rake; laughed at by a girl; detected by my father – and there is the sum total of all I have got at this end of the town.

OLD PHILPOT: This end of the town! I desire never to see it again while I live. I'll pop into a hackney-coach this moment, drive to Mincing Lane, and never venture back to this side of Temple Bar. (*going*)

GEORGE: And, sir, sir! Shall I drive you?

OLD PHILPOT: Ay, you or anybody. (*Exit.*)

GEORGE: I'll overturn the old hocus at the first corner. (*following*)

SIR JASPER: They shan't go zo, neither – they shall stay and crack a bottle. (*Exit after them.*)

MARIA: Well, brother, how have I played my part?

WILDING: ⎱
BEAUFORT: ⎰ To a miracle!

MARIA: Have I? I don't know how it is –

Love urged me on to try all wily arts

To win your (*to* BEAUFORT) – No! Not yours - to win your hearts: (*to the audience*)

Your hearts to win is now my aim alone;

There if I grow, the harvest is your own.

EPILOGUE

Spoken by OLD PHILPOT *and* GEORGE PHILPOT.

OLD PHILPOT: Oh! George, George, George! 'tis such young rakes as you,

That brings vile jokes, and foul dishonour too

Upon our city youth.

GEORGE: 'Tis very true.

OLD PHILPOT: St James's end o'th'town –

GEORGE: No place for me.

OLD PHILPOT: No truly – no – their manners disagree

With ours entirely – yet you there must run,

To ape their follies –

GEORGE: And I am undone.

OLD PHILPOT: There you all learn a vanity in vice,

You turn mere fops, your game –

GEORGE: Oh! Damn the dice.

OLD PHILPOT: Bubbled at play –

GEORGE: Yes, sir –

OLD PHILPOT: By every common cheat.

GEORGE: Ay! Here's two witnesses. (*Pulls out his pockets.*)

OLD PHILPOT: You get well beat.

GEORGE: A witness too of that (*Shows his head.*), and there's another. (*to* YOUNG WILDING)

OLD PHILPOT: You dare to give affronts.

GEORGE: Zounds, such a pother!

OLD PHILPOT: Affronts to gentlemen!

GEORGE: 'Twas a rash action.

OLD PHILPOT: (*mimicking*) 'Damn me, you lie, I'll give you satisfaction.'
      Drawn in by strumpets – and detected too!
GEORGE: That's a sad thing, sir! I'll be judged by you!
OLD PHILPOT: The dog has me there.
GEORGE: Think you it right;
      Under a table –
OLD PHILPOT: Miserable plight!
GEORGE: For grave three-score to skulk with trembling knees,
      And envy each young lover that he sees!
      Think you it fitting thus abroad to roam?
OLD PHILPOT: Would I had stayed to cast accounts at home.
GEORGE: Ay! There's another vice –
OLD PHILPOT: Sirrah, give o'er.
GEORGE: You brood for ever o'er your much loved store
      And scraping cent per cent still pine for more.
      At Jonathon's where millions are undone,
      Now cheat a nation, and now cheat your son.
OLD PHILPOT: Rascal, enough!
GEORGE: I could add, but I am loath –
OLD PHILPOT: Enough! This jury (*to the audience*) will convict us both.
GEORGE: Then to the court we'd better make submission.
      Ladies and Gentlemen, with true contrition,
      I here repent my faults – ye courtly train,
      Farewell! Farewell, ye giddy and ye vain!
      I now take up – forsake the gay and witty,
      To live henceforth a credit to the city.
OLD PHILPOT: You see me here quite cover'd o'er in shame,
      I hate long speeches – But I'll do the same;
      Come, George – to mend is all the best can boast.
GEORGE: Then let us in –
OLD PHILPOT: And this shall be our toast,
      May Britain's thunder on her foes be hurled.
GEORGE: And London prove the market of the World.
    FINIS

THREE WEEKS AFTER MARRIAGE

A comedy in two acts

by ARTHUR MURPHY

> – *otium et oppidi*
> *Laudat rura sui –*   HOR.
> *– Nugae seria ducunt*
> *In mala –*   HOR.

First performed at the Theatre Royal, Covent Garden, on 30 March 1776, with the following cast:

SIR CHARLES RACKET	Mr Lewis
DRUGGET	Mr Quick
LOVELACE	Mr Booth
WOODLEY	Mr Young
LADY RACKET	Mrs Mattocks
MRS DRUGGET	Mrs Pitt
NANCY	Miss Dayes
DIMITY	Mrs Green

Otium et oppidi: Horace, *Odes*, I, i, 16–17: 'He praises the calm and rural surroundings of his own village.'
Nugae seria: Horace, *Ars Poetica*, 451–2: 'Trifles lead to serious wrongs.'

ADVERTISEMENT

The following farce was offered to the public in January 1764; but the quarrel about a trifle, and the renewal of that quarrel after the dispute had subsided, being thought unnatural, the piece was *damned*. Mr LEWIS of Covent Garden Theatre, had the courage to revive it for his benefit in March last, with an alteration of the title, and it has been since repeated with success. A similar incident happened to VOLTAIRE at PARIS. That writer, in the year 1734, produced a tragedy, entitled ADELAIDE DU GUESCLIN, which was hissed through every act. In 1765, LE KAIN, an actor of eminence, revived the play which had lain for years under condemnation. Every scene was applauded. What can I think, says VOLTAIRE, of these opposite judgements? He tells the following anecdote. A banker in Paris had orders to get a new march composed for one of the regiments of Charles XII. He employed a man of talents for the purpose. The march was prepared and a practice of it had at the banker's house before a numerous assembly. The music was found detestable. MOURET (that was the composer's name) retired with his performance, and soon inserted it in one of his operas. The banker and his friends went to the opera; the march was applauded. Ah, says the banker, *that's what we wanted; why did you not give us something in this taste?* Sir, replied MOURET, the march which you now applaud, is the very same that you condemned before.

---

the piece was damned: when Murphy republished the Advertisement in *The Works*, he was no longer dependent on the critics, or his political enemies, for the play's reception, and so he wrote a rather more pointed explanation for its original failure. 'The following scenes were offered to the public in January 1764; but a party of that species of CRITICS, whom the love of mischief sometimes assembles at the theatre, being unwilling to hear, the piece was *damned*.'

ACT I

Enter WOODLEY *and* DIMITY.

DIMITY: Pho, pho! No such thing! I tell you, Mr Woodley, you are a mere novice in
these affairs!

WOODLEY: Nay, but listen to reason, Mrs Dimity; has not your master, Mr Drugget,
invited me down to his house here at Fulham? Has not he promised to give me his
daughter Nancy in marriage? And with what pretence can he now break off?

DIMITY: What pretence! – You put a body out of all patience! But go on your own
way, sir; my advice is lost upon you.

WOODLEY: You do me injustice, Mrs Dimity. – Your advice has governed my whole
conduct. Have not I fixed an interest in the young lady's heart?

DIMITY: An interest in a fiddlestick! You ought to have made love to the father and
mother. What! Do you think the way to get a wife, at this time of day, is by
speaking fine things to the lady you have a fancy for? That was the practice,
indeed, but things are altered now. You must address the old people, sir, and
never trouble your head about your mistress. None of your letters, and verses,
and soft looks, and fine speeches – 'Have compassion, thou angelic creature, on
a poor dying . . .' Pshaw! Stuff! Nonsense! All out of fashion. Go your ways to the
old curmudgeon, humour his whims – 'I shall esteem it an honour, sir, to be allied
to a gentleman of your rank and taste.' 'Upon my word, he's a pretty young
gentleman.' Then, wheel about to the mother: 'Your daughter, madam, is the
very model of you, and I shall adore her for your sake.' 'Here, come hither,
Nancy, take this gentleman for better or worse.' 'La, mamma, I can never consent.' – 'I should not have thought of your consent – the consent of your relations
is enough: why, how now, hussy!' So away you go to church; the knot is tied; an
agreeable honeymoon follows; the charm is then dissolved; you go to all the clubs
in St James's street; your lady goes to the Coterie; and, in a little time you both
go to Doctor's Commons; the *Morning Post* displays you in black and white;
Poet's Corner treats you with a ballad or an epigram; your friends pity you; the
town laughs at you; the lawyers abuse you; and if faults on both sides prevent a
divorce, you'll quarrel like contrary elements all the rest of your lives. That's the
way of the world now.

WOODLEY: But you know, my dear Dimity, the old couple have received every mark
of attention from me.

DIMITY: Attention! To be sure you didn't fall asleep in their company, but what then?
You should have entered into their characters, played with their humours, and
sacrificed to their absurdities.

WOODLEY: But if my temper is too frank . . .

DIMITY: Frank, indeed! I hate the word, except when I receive a letter. Yes, you have
been frank enough to ruin yourself. Have you not to do with a rich old shop-
keeper, retired from business with an hundred thousand pounds in his pocket, to

---

Doctor's Commons: the College of Doctors in Civil Law who were the specialists in matrimonial
law and divorces.
Poet's Corner: the jocular name for the poetical column of a newspaper.
I hate the word . . . letter: this weak pun was cut from the 1776 edition.

enjoy the dust of the Fulham road, which he calls living in the country? And yet you must find fault with his situation! What if he has made a ridiculous gimcrack of his house and gardens? You know his heart is set upon it; and could not you commend his taste? But you must be too frank! 'Those walks and alleys are too regular – those evergreens should not be cut into such fantastic shapes!' And thus you advise a poor old mechanic, who delights in everything that's monstrous, to follow nature. – Oh, you are likely to be a successful lover!

WOODLEY: But why should I not save a father-in-law from being a laughing stock?

DIMITY: Make him your father-in-law first.

WOODLEY: Why, he can't open his windows for the dust. He stands all day looking through a pane of glass at the carts and stage-coaches as they pass by, and he calls that living in the fresh air, and enjoying his own thoughts!

DIMITY: And could not you let him go on in his own way? You have ruined yourself by talking sense to him, and all your nonsense to the daughter won't make amends for it. And then the mother; how have you played your cards in that quarter? She wants a tinsel man of fashion for her second daughter. 'Don't you see,' says she, 'How happy my eldest girl is made by marrying Sir Charles Racket? She has been married three entire weeks, and not so much as one angry word has passed between them! Nancy shall have a man of quality, too!'

WOODLEY: And yet I know Sir Charles Racket perfectly well.

DIMITY: Yes, so do I, and I know he'll make his lady wretched at last. But what then? You should have humoured the old folks; you should have been a talking, empty fop, to the good old lady, and to the old gentleman, an admirer of his taste in gardening. But you have lost him. He is grown fond of this beau Lovelace, who is here in the house with him. The coxcomb ingratiates himself by flattery, and you are undone by frankness!

WOODLEY: And yet, Dimity, I won't despair.

DIMITY: And yet you have reason to despair, a million of reasons. Tomorrow is fixed for the wedding-day; Sir Charles and his lady are to be here this very night. They are engaged indeed at a great rout in town, but they take a bed here, notwithstanding. The family is sitting up for them. Mr Drugget will keep you all up in the next room there, till they arrive; and tomorrow the business is over; and yet you don't despair! Hush! Hold your tongue; here comes Lovelace. Step in, and I'll devise something, I warrant you. (*Exit* WOODLEY.) The old folks shall not have their own way! It's enough to vex a body, to see an old father and mother marrying their daughter as they please, in spite of all I can do. (*Exit.*)

(*Enter* DRUGGET *and* LOVELACE.)

DRUGGET: And so you like my house and gardens, Mr Lovelace?

LOVELACE: Oh! perfectly, sir. They gratify my taste in all things. One sees villas, where nature reigns in a wild kind of simplicity, but then, they have no appearance of art – no art at all.

DRUGGET: Very true, rightly distinguished. – Now, mine is all art; no wild nature here; I did it all myself.

LOVELACE: What! Had you none of the great proficients in gardening to assist you?

DRUGGET: Lack-a-day! No – ha, ha! I understand these things – I love my garden. In front of my house, Mr Lovelace, is not that very pretty?

LOVELACE: Elegant to a degree!

DRUGGET: Don't you like the sun-dial, placed just by my dining-room windows?

LOVELACE: A perfect beauty!

DRUGGET: I knew you'd like it – and the motto is so well adapted – *Tempus edax et index rerum*. And I know the meaning of it: 'Time eateth and discovereth all things.' Ha, ha! Pretty, Mr Lovelace? I have seen people so stare at it as they pass by – ha, ha!

LOVELACE: Why now, I don't believe there's a nobleman in the kingdom has such a thing.

DRUGGET: Oh no – they have got into a false taste. I bought that bit of ground, the other side of the road – and now it is a perfect beauty – I made a duck-pond there, for the sake of the prospect.

LOVELACE: Charmingly imagined!

DRUGGET: My leaden images are well!

LOVELACE: They exceed ancient statuary.

DRUGGET: I love to be surprised at the turning of a walk with an inanimate figure, that looks you full in the face, and can say nothing to you, while one is enjoying one's own thoughts – ha, ha! Mr Lovelace, I'll point out a beauty to you. Just by the haw-haw, at the end of my ground, there is a fine Dutch figure, with a scythe in his hand, and a pipe in his mouth. That's a jewel, Mr Lovelace.

LOVELACE: That escaped me. A thousand thanks for pointing it out. I observe you have two very fine yew trees before the house.

DRUGGET: Lack-a-day, sir, they look uncouth. I have a design about them. I intend – ha, ha! it will be very pretty, Mr Lovelace – I intend to have them cut into the shape of the two giants at Guildhall – ha, ha!

LOVELACE: Exquisite! Why then they won't look like trees.

DRUGGET: No, no; not in the least; I won't have anything in my garden that looks like what it is – ha, ha!

LOVELACE: Nobody understands these things like you, Mr Drugget.

DRUGGET: Lack-a-day! It's all my delight now. This is what I have been working for. I have a great improvement to make still – I propose to have my evergreens cut into fortifications; and then I shall have the Moro Castle, and the Havana; and then near it shall be ships of myrtle, sailing upon seas of box to attack the town. Won't that make my place look very rural, Mr Lovelace?

LOVELACE: Why, you have the most fertile invention, Mr Drugget.

DRUGGET: Ha, ha! This is what I have been working for. I love my garden. – But I must beg your pardon for a few moments. I must step and speak with a famous nursery-man, who is come to offer me some choice things. Do go, and join the company, Mr Lovelace. My daughter Racket and Sir Charles will be here

---

Tempus . . . rerum: the original, from Ovid's *Metamorphoses*, xv, reads *Tempus edax rerum*; the addition of & *index* is Drugget's ignorant whim.

pipe in his mouth: Hogarth painted Father Time with a pipe. He was using the smoke to darken and age a counterfeit Old Master.

giants at Guildhall: the two statues of Gog and Magog carved for the Guildhall by Richard Saunders in 1708.

Moro Castle: the chief fortification of Havana, captured by the English in 1762.

presently. I shan't go to bed till I see them. Ha, ha! My place is prettily variegated – this is all I delight in now. I fined for sheriff, to enjoy these things ha, ha! (*Exit.*)

LOVELACE: Poor Mr Drugget! Mynheer Van Thundertentrunck, in his little box at the side of a dyke, has as much taste and elegance. However, if I can but carry off his daughter, if I can but rob his garden of that flower – why, I then shall say, 'This is what I have been working for.'

(*Enter* DIMITY.)

DIMITY: Do lend us your assistance, Mr Lovelace. You're a sweet gentleman, and love a good-natured action.

LOVELACE: Why, how now! What's the matter?

DIMITY: My master is going to cut the two yew trees into the shape of two devils, I believe, and my poor mistress is breaking her heart for it. Do run and advise him against it. She is your friend, you know she is, sir.

LOVELACE: Oh, if that's all – I'll make that matter easy directly.

DIMITY: My mistress will be for ever obliged to you, and you'll marry her daughter in the morning.

LOVELACE: Oh, my rhetoric shall dissuade him.

DIMITY: And, sir, put him against dealing with that nursery-man; Mrs Drugget hates him.

LOVELACE: Does she?

DIMITY: Mortally.

LOVELACE: Say no more, the business is done. (*Exit.*)

DIMITY: If he says one word against the giants of Guildhall, old Drugget will never forgive him. My brain was at its last shift, but if this plot takes . . . So, here comes our Nancy.

(*Enter* NANCY.)

NANCY: Well, Dimity, what's to become of me?

DIMITY: My stars! What makes you up, miss? I thought you were gone to bed.

NANCY: What would I go to bed for? Only to tumble and toss, and fret, and be uneasy. They are going to marry me, and I am frightened out of my wits.

DIMITY: Why then, you're the only young lady, within fifty miles round, that would be frightened at such a thing.

NANCY: Ah! If they would let me choose for myself.

DIMITY: Don't you like Mr Lovelace?

NANCY: My mamma does, but I don't. I don't mind his being a man of fashion, not I.

DIMITY: And, pray, can you do better than follow fashion?

NANCY: Ah, I know there's a fashion for new bonnets, and a fashion for dressing the hair – but I never heard of a fashion for the heart.

DIMITY: Why then, my dear, the heart mostly follows the fashion now.

NANCY: Does it! Pray, who sets the fashion of the heart?

DIMITY: All the fine ladies in London, o'my conscience.

NANCY: And what's the last new fashion, pray?

---

fined for sheriff: paid a fine rather than undertake the duties of sheriff.
Mynheer Van Thundertentruck: a Prussian junker in Voltaire's *Candide* (1759), although Lovelace seems to take him for a Dutchman. Dutch gardens, irrigated from the dykes, were world famous, and tulip breeding was highly fashionable.

DIMITY: Why, to marry any fop, that has a few deceitful, agreeable appearances about him, something of a pert phrase, a good operator for the teeth, and a tolerable tailor.

NANCY: And do they marry without loving?

DIMITY: Oh, marrying for love has been a great while out of fashion.

NANCY: Why, then, I'll wait till that fashion comes up again.

DIMITY: And then, Mr Lovelace, I reckon . . .

NANCY: Pshaw! I don't like him. He talks to me as if he was the most miserable man in the world, and the confident thing looks so pleased with himself all the while! I want to marry for love, and not for card-playing. I should not be able to bear the life my sister leads with Sir Charles Racket. Shall I tell you a secret? I'll forfeit my new cap, if they don't quarrel soon.

DIMITY: Oh fie! No! They won't quarrel yet a-while. A quarrel in three weeks after marriage would be somewhat of the quickest. By and by we shall hear of their whims and their humours. Well, but if you don't like Mr Lovelace, what say you to Mr Woodley?

NANCY: Ah! I don't know what to say – but I can sing something that will explain my mind.

> SONG
>
> When first the dear youth, passing by,
>   Disclosed his fair form to my sight,
> I gazed, but could not tell why;
>   My heart it went throb with delight.
>
> As nearer he drew, those sweet eyes
>   Were with their dear meaning so bright,
> I trembled, and lost in surprise,
>   My heart it went throb with delight.
>
> When his lips their dear accents did try
>   The return of my love to excite,
> I feigned, yet began to guess why
>   My heart it went throb with delight.
>
> We changed the stolen glance, the fond smile,
>   Which lovers alone read aright;
> We looked, and we sighed, yet the while
>   Our hearts they went throb with delight.
>
> Consent I soon blushed, with a sigh,
>   My promise I ventured to plight;
> Come, Hymen, we then shall know why
>   Our hearts they go throb with delight.
>   (*Enter* WOODLEY.)

WOODLEY: My sweetest angel! I have heard it all, and my heart overflows with love and gratitude.

NANCY: Ah! But I did not know you was listening! You should not have betrayed me so, Dimity. I shall be angry with you.

DIMITY: Well, I'll take my chance for that. Run both into my room, and say all your pretty things to one another there, for here comes the old gentleman – make haste away! (*Exeunt* WOODLEY *and* NANCY.)

(*Enter* DRUGGET.)

DRUGGET: A forward, presuming coxcomb! Dimity, do you step to Mrs Drugget, and send her hither.

DIMITY: Yes, sir. – It works upon him, I see. (*Exit.*)

DRUGGET: My yew trees ought not to be cut, because they'll help to keep off the dust, and I am too near the road already. A sorry, ignorant fop! When I am in so fine a situation, and can see every cart, waggon and stage-coach that goes by. And then to abuse the nursery-man's rarities! A finer sucking pig in lavender, with sage growing in his belly, was never seen! And yet he wants me not to have it – But have it I will – There's a fine tree of knowledge, with Adam and Eve in juniper; Eve's nose not quite grown, but it is thought in the spring it will be very forward. I'll have that, too, with the serpent in ground ivy. Two poets in wormwood! I'll have them both. Ay, and there's a lord mayor's feast in honey suckle with the whole court of aldermen in hornbeam; and three modern beaux in jassamine, somewhat stunted. They shall all be in my garden, with the Dragon of Wantley in box – all – all – I'll have them all, let my wife and Mr Lovelace say what they will . . .

(*Enter* MRS DRUGGET.)

MRS DRUGGET: Did you send for me, lovey?

DRUGGET: The yew trees shall be cut into the giants of Guildhall, whether you will or not.

MRS DRUGGET: Sure my own dear will do as he pleases.

DRUGGET: And the pond, though you praise the green banks, shall be walled round, and I'll have a little fat boy in marble, spouting up water in the middle.

MRS DRUGGET: My sweet, who hinders you?

DRUGGET: Yes, and I'll buy the nursery-man's whole catalogue. Do you think, after retiring to live all the way here, almost four miles from London, that I won't do as I please in my own garden?

MRS DRUGGET: My dear, but why are you in such a passion?

DRUGGET: I'll have the lavender pig, and the Adam and Eve, and the Dragon of Wantley, and all of them; and there shan't be a more romantic spot on the London road than mine.

MRS DRUGGET: I am sure it's as pretty as hands can make it.

DRUGGET: I did it all myself, and I'll do more – And Mr Lovelace shan't have my daughter.

MRS DRUGGET: No! What's the matter now, Mr Drugget?

DRUGGET: He shall learn better manners than to abuse my house and gardens. You put him in the head of it, but I'll disappoint ye both. And so you may go and tell Mr Lovelace that the match is quite off.

MRS DRUGGET: I can't comprehend all this, not I, but I'll tell him so, if you please, my dear. I am willing to give myself pain, if it will give you pleasure. Must I give myself pain? Don't ask me, pray don't. I can't support all this uneasiness.

Dragon of Wantley: from Henry Carey's burlesque opera of that name, 1737.

DRUGGET: I am resolved, and it shall be so.

MRS DRUGGET: Let it be so, then. (*Cries.*) Oh, oh, cruel man! I shall break my heart if the match is broke off. If it is not concluded tomorrow, send for an undertaker, and bury me the next day.

DRUGGET: How! I don't want that neither.

MRS DRUGGET: Oh, oh!

DRUGGET: I am your lord and master, my dear, but not your executioner. Before George, it must never be said, that my wife died of too much compliance. Cheer up, my love; and this affair shall be settled as soon as Sir Charles and Lady Racket arrive.

MRS DRUGGET: You bring me to life again. You know, my sweet, what an happy couple Sir Charles and his lady are. Why should not we make our Nancy as happy?
(*Enter* DIMITY.)

DIMITY: Sir Charles and his lady, madam.

MRS DRUGGET: Oh, charming! I'm transported with joy! Where are they? I long to see them! (*Exit.*)

DIMITY: Well, sir, the happy couple are arrived.

DRUGGET: Yes, they do live happy indeed!

DIMITY: But how long will it last?

DRUGGET: How long! Don't forebode any ill, you jade! Don't, I say! It will last during their lives, I hope.

DIMITY: Well, mark the end of it. Sir Charles, I know, is gay and good humoured – but he can't bear the least contradiction, no, not in the merest trifle.

DRUGGET: Hold your tongue – hold your tongue!

DIMITY: Yes, sir, I have done; and yet there is in the composition of Sir Charles, a certain humour, which, like the flying gout, gives no disturbance to the family, till it settles in the head. When once it fixes there, mercy on everybody about him! But here he comes. (*Exit.*)
(*Enter* SIR CHARLES RACKET.)

SIR CHARLES: My dear sir, I kiss your hand. But why stand upon ceremony? To find you up at this late hour mortifies me beyond expression.

DRUGGET: 'Tis but once in a way, Sir Charles.

SIR CHARLES: My obligations to you are inexpressible; you have given me the most amiable of girls; our tempers accord like unisons in music.

DRUGGET: Ah, that's what makes me happy in my old days. My children and my garden are all my care.

SIR CHARLES: And my friend Lovelace – he is to have our sister Nancy, I find.

DRUGGET: Why, my wife is so minded.

SIR CHARLES: Oh, by all means, let her be made happy! A very pretty fellow, Lovelace. And as to that Mr – Woodley, I think you call him – he is but a plain, underbred, ill-fashioned sort of a – Nobody knows him. He is not one of us. Oh, by all means marry her to one of us.

DRUGGET: I believe it must be so. Would you take any refreshment?

SIR CHARLES: Nothing in nature – it is time to retire to rest.

---

flying gout: in which the pains move throughout the body. It was believed if it reached the head it caused madness. This diagnosis was suggested for George III's madness in 1788.

DRUGGET: Well, well! Good night, Sir Charles. Ha! Here comes my daughter –
Goodnight Sir Charles.

SIR CHARLES: *Bon repos.*

(*Enter* LADY RACKET.)

LADY RACKET: Dear Sir! I did not expect to see you up so late.

DRUGGET: (*meeting her at the door*) My Lady Racket, I'm glad to hear how happy
you are. I won't detain you now. There's your good man waiting for you. Good
night my girl! (*Exit.*)

SIR CHARLES: (*aside*) I must humour this old put, in order to be remembered in his
will.

LADY RACKET: (*coming on*) Oh la! I am quite fatigued. I can hardly move. Why
don't you help me, you barbarous man?

SIR CHARLES: There! Take my arm – 'Was ever thing so pretty made to walk.'

LADY RACKET: But I won't be laughed at. (*looking tenderly at him*) I don't love you.

SIR CHARLES: Don't you?

LADY RACKET: No. Dear me, this glove! Why don't you help me off with my glove?
Pshaw! You awkward thing, let it alone! You an't fit to be about my person. I
might as well not be married, for any use you are of. Reach me a chair. You have
no compassion for me. I am so glad to sit down! Why do you drag me to routs?
You know I hate them.

SIR CHARLES: Oh, there's no existing, no breathing, unless one does as other people
of fashion do.

LADY RACKET: But I'm out of humour. I lost all my money.

SIR CHARLES: How much?

LADY RACKET: Three hundred.

SIR CHARLES: Never fret for that. I don't value three hundred pounds to contribute
to your happiness.

LADY RACKET: Don't you? – Not value three hundred pounds to pleasure me?

SIR CHARLES: You know I don't.

LADY RACKET: Ah, you fond fool! – But I hate gaming. It almost metamorphoses a
woman into a fury. Do you know that I was frighted at myself several times
tonight? I had a huge oath at the very tip of my tongue.

SIR CHARLES: Had ye?

LADY RACKET: I caught myself at it, but I bit my lips and so I did not disgrace myself.
And then I was crammed up in a corner of the room with such a strange party at
a whist-table, looking at black and red spots. Did you mind them?

SIR CHARLES: You know I was busy elsewhere.

LADY RACKET: There was that strange unaccountable woman, Mrs Nightshade. She
behaved so strangely to her husband, a poor, inoffensive, good-natured, good
sort of a good-for-nothing kind of man; but she so teased him – 'How could you
play that card? Ah, you have a head and so has a pin! You are a numskull, you
know you are – Madam, he has the poorest head in the world, he does not know
what he is about – you know you don't – Ah, fie! I am ashamed of you!'

SIR CHARLES: She has served to divert you, I see.

'*Was ever thing so pretty . . .* ': cf. E. Young, *Love of Fame* (1728), ii, 170, 'Was ever thing so pretty
born to stand'.

LADY RACKET: And then, to crown all, there was my Lady Clackit, who runs on with an eternal larum of nothing, out of all season, time and place. In the very midst of the game, she begins – 'Lard, me'm, I was apprehensive I should not be able to wait on your ladyship – my poor little dog, Pompey – the sweetest thing in the world – a spade led! – there's the knave – I was fetching a walk, me'm, the other morning in the Park; a fine frosty morning it was; I love frosty weather of all things. Let me look at the last trick – and so, me'm, little Pompey – Oh! if your la'yship was to see the dear little creature pinched with the frost, and mincing his steps along the Mall, with his pretty little innocent face – I vow I don't know what to play – and so, me'm, while I was talking to Captain Flimsey – Your la'yship knows Captain Flimsey? – Nothing but rubbish in my hand – I can't help it – and so, me'm, five odious frights of dogs beset my poor little Pompey – the dear creature has the heart of a lion, but who can resist five at once? And so Pompey barked for assistance. The hurt he received was upon his chest. The doctor would not advise him to venture out till the wound was healed for fear of an inflammation – Pray what's trumps?'

SIR CHARLES: My dear, you would make a most excellent actress!

LADY RACKET: Why don't you hand me upstairs? Oh! I am so tired. Let us go to rest.

SIR CHARLES: (*assisting her*) You complain, and yet raking is the delight of your little heart.

LADY RACKET: (*leaning on him as she walks away*) It is you that make a rake of me. Oh, Sir Charles, how shockingly you played that last rubber, when I stood looking over you.

SIR CHARLES: My love, I played the truth of the game.

LADY RACKET: No, indeed, my dear, you played it wrong. Ah! Sir Charles, you have a head.

SIR CHARLES: Pho! Nonsense! You don't understand it.

LADY RACKET: I beg your pardon, I am allowed to play better than you.

SIR CHARLES: All conceit, my dear. I was perfectly right.

LADY RACKET: No such thing, Sir Charles, how can you dispute it? The diamond was the play.

SIR CHARLES: Pho! Riciculous! The club was the card against the world.

LADY RACKET: Oh, no, no, no! I say it was the diamond.

SIR CHARLES: Zounds, madam! I say it was the club!

LADY RACKET: What do you fly into such a passion for?

SIR CHARLES: Death and fury, do you think I don't know what I am about? I tell you once more, the club was the judgement of it.

LADY RACKET: May be so. Have it your own way. (*Walks about and sings.*)

SIR CHARLES: Damnation! You are the strangest woman that ever lived! There's no

---

that last rubber: although it is probably intentional that the rights and wrongs of the argument are very unclear, even to a whist player, it seems that Sir Charles had played a club and lost the trick. He claims that this was intentional, so as to draw out his opponents' clubs to make sure of the 'odd' (i.e. winning) trick later in the game. Lady Racket seems to think that his opponent was out of trumps (i.e. hearts) and diamonds, as he had ruffed (i.e. trumped) a diamond earlier in the game, and that he had previously finessed in clubs (i.e. won the trick with a lower card than he need have done) which left him with a master card in clubs, 'the best in the house'.

conversing with you. Look'e here, my Lady Racket, it's the clearest case in the world. I'll make it plain in a moment.

LADY RACKET: Very well, sir. To be sure you must be right. (*with a sneering smile*)

SIR CHARLES: Listen to me, Lady Racket: I had four cards left. Trumps were out. The lead was mine. They were six – no, no, no; they were seven, and we were nine; then you know the beauty of the play was to . . .

LADY RACKET: Well, now, it's amazing to me that you can't perceive; give me leave, Sir Charles. Your left-hand adversary had led his last trump, and he had before finessed the club, and roughed the diamond; now, if you had led your diamond . . .

SIR CHARLES: Zounds, madam! But we played for the odd trick!

LADY RACKET: And sure, the play for the odd trick . . .

SIR CHARLES: Death and fury! Can't you hear me?

LADY RACKET: And must not I be heard, sir?

SIR CHARLES: Zounds! Hear me, I say – will you hear me?

LADY RACKET: I never heard the like in my life. (*Hums a tune, and walks about fretfully.*)

SIR CHARLES: Why then, you are enough to provoke the patience of a Stoic. (*Looks at her; she walks about, and laughs uneasily.*) Very well, madam; you know no more of the game than your father's leaden Hercules on the top of the house. You know no more of whist than he does of gardening.

LADY RACKET: Go on your own way, sir. (*Takes out a glass, and settles her hair.*)

SIR CHARLES: Why then, by all that's odious, you are the most perverse, obstinate, ignorant . . .

LADY RACKET: Polite language, sir!

SIR CHARLES: You are, madam, the most perverse, the most obstinate – you are a vile woman!

LADY RACKET: I am obliged to you, sir.

SIR CHARLES: You are a vile woman, I tell you so, and I'll not sleep another night under one roof with you.

LADY RACKET: As you please.

SIR CHARLES: Madam, it shall be as I please– I'll order my chariot this moment. (*going*) I know how the cards should be played as well as any man in England, that let me tell you. (*going*) And when your family were standing behind counters, measuring out tapes, and bartering for Whitechapel needles, my ancestors, madam, my ancestors were squandering away whole estates at cards – whole estates, my Lady Racket! (*She hums a tune, and he looks at her.*) Why then, by all that's dear to me, I'll never exchange another word with you, good, bad or indifferent! (*Goes and turns back.*) Will you command your temper, and listen to me?

LADY RACKET: Go on, sir.

SIR CHARLES: Can't you be as cool as I am? Lookye, my Lady Racket, thus it stood: the trumps being led, it was then my business . . .

---

we were nine: as there are only thirteen tricks in a hand of whist, and he has four cards left, either Sir Charles is getting very confused, or he means that nine tricks had been played and that the score, therefore, was seven to two against him, though in that case his opponents would have already won the odd trick!

LADY RACKET: To play the diamond, to be sure.

SIR CHARLES: Damnation! I have done with you for ever, and so you may tell your father. (*going*)

LADY RACKET: What a passion the gentleman is in!

SIR CHARLES: Will you let me speak?

LADY RACKET: Who hinders you, sir?

SIR CHARLES: Once more out of pure good nature . . .

LADY RACKET: Oh, sir, I am convinced of your good nature.

SIR CHARLES: That and only that prevails with me to tell you, the club was the play.

LADY RACKET: I am prodigiously obliged to you for the information. I am perfectly satisfied, sir.

SIR CHARLES: It's the clearest point in the world. Only mind now. We were nine and . . .

LADY RACKET: And for that very reason the diamond was the play. Your adversary's club was the best in the house!

SIR CHARLES: Why then, such another fiend never existed. There is no reasoning with you. It is vain to say a word. Good sense is thrown away upon you. I now see the malice of your heart. You're a base woman and I'll part from you for ever. You may live here with your father, and admire his fantastical evergreens, till you grow fantastical yourself. I'll set out for London this moment. Your servant, madam. (*Going, turns and looks at her.*) The club was not the best in the house.

LADY RACKET: How calm you are! – Well, I'll to bed. Will you come? You had better. Not come to bed when I ask you? – Oh, Sir Charles! (*going*)

SIR CHARLES: That ease is so provoking! I desire you will stay and hear me. Don't think to carry it in this manner. Madam, I must and will be heard.

LADY RACKET: Oh, Lud! With that terrible countenance? You frighten me away. (*Runs in and shuts the door.*)

SIR CHARLES: (*following her*) You shall not fly me thus. Confusion! Open the door – will you open it? This contempt is beyond enduring. (*Walks away.*) I intended to have made it clear to her, but now let her continue in her absurdity. She is not worth my notice. My resolution is taken. She has touched my pride, and I now renounce her for ever; yes for ever; not to return, though she were to request, beseech and implore on her very knees. (*Exit.*)

LADY RACKET: (*peeping in*) Is he gone? (*Comes forward.*) Bless me! what have I done? – I have carried this too far, I believe. I had better call him back. For the sake of peace I'll give up the point. What does it signify which was the best of the play? It is not worth quarrelling about – How! – here he comes again – I'll give up nothing to him. He shall never get the better of me. I am ruined for life, if he does. I will conquer him, and I am resolved he shall see it. (*Runs in and shuts the door.*)

SIR CHARLES: (*looking in*) No, she won't open it. Headstrong and positive! – If she could but command her temper, the thing would be as clear as daylight. She has

---

That ease: from this point to the end of the act was added by Murphy to the *Complete Works*. Other editions follow the Larpent MS in which Lady Racket exits and Sir Charles says: 'That ease is so provoking. (*Crosses to opposite door where she went out.*) I tell you the diamond was the play, and here I take my final leave of you. (*Walks back as fast as he can.*) I am resolved upon it. And I know the club was not the best in the house. (*Exit.*)'

sense enough, if she would but make use of it. It were a pity she should be lost. (*Advances towards the door.*) All owing to that perverse spirit of contradiction. I must reclaim her still. (*Peeps through the key-hole.*) Not so much as a glimpse of her. (*Taps on the door.*) Lady Racket – Lady Racket –

LADY RACKET: (*within*) What do you want?

SIR CHARLES: (*laughing affectedly*) Come, you have been very pleasant. Open the door. I can't help laughing at all this. – Come, no more foolery; have done now, and open the door.

LADY RACKET: (*within*) Don't be such a torment.

SIR CHARLES: Will you open it?

LADY RACKET: (*laughing*) No – no – ho, ho!

SIR CHARLES: Hell and confusion! What a puppy I make of myself! I'll bear this usage no longer. To be trifled with in this sort by a false, treacherous – (*Runs to the door and speaks through the key-hole.*) The diamond was *not* the play. (*Walks about as fast as he can.*) I know what I am about. (*Looks back in a violent rage.*) And the club was *not* the best in the house. (*Exit.*)

ACT II

SCENE 1.   *Enter* DIMITY, *laughing violently.*

DIMITY: Oh, I shall die; I shall expire in a fit of laughing! This is the modish couple who were so happy! Such a quarrel as they have had; the whole house in an uproar! Ha, ha! A rare proof of the happiness they enjoy in high life! I shall never hear people of fashion mentioned again, but I shall be ready to crack my sides. They were both – ho, ho, ho! This is Three Weeks after Marriage, I think!
              (*Enter* DRUGGET.)

DRUGGET: Hey, how! What's the matter, Dimity? What am I called downstairs for?

DIMITY: Why, there's two people of fashion – (*Stifles a laugh.*)

DRUGGET: Why, you saucy minx! Explain this moment.

DIMITY: The fond couple have been together by the ears this half hour. Are you satisfied now?

DRUGGET: Ay! What, have they quarrelled? – What was it about?

DIMITY: Something too nice and fine for my comprehension, and yours too, I believe. People in high life understand their own forms best. And here comes one that can unriddle the whole affair. (*Exit.*)
              (*Enter* SIR CHARLES.)

SIR CHARLES: (*to the people within*) I say, let the horses be put-to this moment. So, Mr Drugget!

DRUGGET: Sir Charles, here's a terrible bustle. I did not expect this. What can be the matter?

SIR CHARLES: I have been used by your daughter in so base, so contemptible, so vile a manner, that I am determined not to stay in this house tonight.

DRUGGET: This is a thunderbolt to me! After seeing how elegantly and fashionably you lived together, to find now all sunshine vanished! Do, Sir Charles, let me heal this breach if possible.

SIR CHARLES: Sir, 'tis impossible. I'll not live with her an hour longer.

DRUGGET: Nay, nay. Don't be overhasty. Let me entreat you to go to bed and sleep
    upon it. In the morning when you are cool . . .

SIR CHARLES: Oh sir! I am very cool, I assure you– ha, ha! It is not in her power, sir,
    to – to – a – to disturb the serenity of my temper. Don't imagine that I'm in a
    passion. I am not so easily ruffled as you may imagine. But quietly and deliber-
    ately I can resent ill usage. I can repay the injury done me by an ungrateful, false,
    deceitful wife, with the serenity, and at the same time the composure, of an old
    judge hardened in his office. That man am I, sir . . .

DRUGGET: The injuries done you by a faithless wife! My daughter I hope, sir . . .

SIR CHARLES: Her character is now fully known to me, the baseness of her heart is
    known. She's a vile woman, that's all I have to say, sir.

DRUGGET: Hey, how! A vile woman! What has she done? I hope she is not
    capable . . .

SIR CHARLES: I shall enter into no detail, Mr Drugget. The time and circumstances
    won't allow it at present, but depend upon it, I have done with her. A low,
    unpolished, uneducated, false, imposing – see if the horses are put-to . . .

DRUGGET: Mercy on me! In my old days to hear this!

             (*Enter* MRS DRUGGET.)

MRS DRUGGET: Deliver me! I am all over in such a tremble. Sir Charles, I shall
    break my heart if there's anything amiss!

SIR CHARLES: Madam, I am very sorry for your sake, but to live with her is
    impossible.

MRS DRUGGET: My poor, dear girl! What can she have done?

SIR CHARLES: What all her sex can do! It needs no explanation: the very spirit of
    them all.

DRUGGET: Ay, I see how it is – She's bringing foul disgrace upon us. This comes of
    her marrying a man of fashion!

SIR CHARLES: Fashion, sir! That should have instructed her better. She might have
    been sensible of her happiness. Whatever you may think of the fortune you gave
    her, my rank in life commands respect; claims obedience, attention, truth, and
    love, from one raised in the world as she has been by an alliance with me.

DRUGGET: And, let me tell you, however you may estimate your quality, my
    daughter is dear to me.

SIR CHARLES: And, sir, my character is dear to me! It shall never be in her power to
    expose me.

DRUGGET: Yet, you must give me leave to tell you . . .

SIR CHARLES: I won't hear a word!

DRUGGET: Not in behalf of my own daughter?

SIR CHARLES: Nothing can excuse her. 'Tis to no purpose. She has married above
    her; and if that circumstance makes the lady forget herself, she shall at least see
    that I can and will support my own dignity.

DRUGGET: But, sir, I have a right to ask . . .

MRS DRUGGET: Patience, my dear; be a little calm.

DRUGGET: Mrs Drugget, do you have patience. I must and will enquire.

MRS DRUGGET: Don't be so hasty, my love. Have some respect for Sir Charles's
    rank. Don't be so violent with a man of fashion.

DRUGGET: Hold your tongue, woman, I say! You're not a person of fashion, at least. My daughter was ever a good girl.

SIR CHARLES: I have found her out.

DRUGGET: Oh! Then it is all over, and it does not signify arguing about it.

MRS DRUGGET: That ever I should live to see this hour! How the unfortunate girl could take such wickedness in her head, I can't imagine. I'll go and speak to the unhappy creature this moment. (*Exit.*)

SIR CHARLES: She stands detected now; detected in her truest colours!

DRUGGET: Well, grievous as it may be, let me hear the circumstances of this unhappy business.

SIR CHARLES: Mr Drugget, I have not leisure now. Her behaviour has been so exasperating that I shall make the best of my way to town. My mind is fixed. She sees me no more. And so your servant, sir. (*Exit.*)

DRUGGET: What a calamity has here befallen us! A good girl, and so well disposed, but the evil communication of high life, and fashionable vices, turned her to folly!
 (*Enter* LOVELACE.)

LOVELACE: Joy, joy! Mr Drugget, I give you joy!

DRUGGET: Don't insult me, sir! I desire you won't.

LOVELACE: Insult you, sir! Is there anything insulting, my dear sir, if I take the liberty to congratulate you on the approaching . . .

DRUGGET: There! There! The manners of high life for you! He wishes me joy on the approaching ruin of my daughter. She is to be in the fashion! Mr Lovelace, you shall have no daughter of mine.

LOVELACE: My dear sir, never bear malice. I have reconsidered the thing, and, curse catch me, if I don't think your notion of the Guildhall giants, and the court of aldermen in hornbeam . . .

DRUGGET: Well, well, well! There may be people at the court end of the town in hornbeam, too.

LOVELACE: Yes, faith, so there may; and I believe I could help you to a tolerable collection. However, with your daughter I am ready to venture . . .

DRUGGET: But I am not ready. I'll not venture my girl with you. No more daughters of mine shall have their minds depraved by polite vices.

LOVELACE: Strike me stupid, if I understand one word of this.
 (*Enter* WOODLEY.)

DRUGGET: Mr Woodley, – you shall have Nancy to your wife, as I promised you: – take her tomorrow morning.

WOODLEY: Sir, I have not words to express . . .

LOVELACE: What the devil is the matter with the old haberdasher now?

DRUGGET: And harkye, Mr Woodley, I'll make you a present for your garden of a coronation dinner in greens, with the champion riding on horseback, and the sword will be full grown before April next.

WOODLEY: I shall receive it, sir, as your favour.

DRUGGET: Ay, ay! I see my error in wanting an alliance with great folks. I had rather have you, Mr Woodley, for my son-in-law, than any courtly fop of them all. Is this man gone? Is Sir Charles Racket gone?

WOODLEY: Not yet, he makes a bawling yonder for his horses. I'll step and call him to you. (*Exit.*)

DRUGGET: Do so, do so, Mr Woodley. I am out of all patience. I am out of my senses. I must see him once more. Mr Lovelace, neither you nor any person of fashion shall ruin another child of mine. (*Exit.*)

LOVELACE: Droll this! Damned droll! And every syllable of it Greek to me. The queer old put is as whimsical in his notions of life as of gardening. If this be the case, I'll brush, and leave him to his exotics. (*Exit.*)

(*Enter* LADY RACKET, MRS DRUGGET *and* DIMITY.)

LADY RACKET: A cruel, barbarous man! To quarrel in this unaccountable manner, to alarm the whole house, and to expose me and himself, too.

MRS DRUGGET: Oh, child, I never thought it would have come to this. Your shame won't end here, it will be all over St James's parish before tomorrow morning.

LADY RACKET: Well, if it must be so, there's one comfort still: the story will tell more to his disgrace than mine.

DIMITY: As I'm a sinner, and so it will, madam. He deserves what he has met with.

MRS DRUGGET: Dimity, don't you encourage her. You shock me to hear you speak so. I did not think you had been so hardened.

LADY RACKET: Hardened, do you call it? I have lived in the world to very little purpose, if such trifles are to disturb my rest.

MRS DRUGGET: You wicked girl! Do you call it a trifle, to be guilty of falsehood to your husband's bed?

LADY RACKET: How! (*Turns short and stares at her.*)

DIMITY: That! That's a mere trifle indeed! I have been in as good places as anybody, and not a creature minds it now.

MRS DRUGGET: My Lady Racket, my Lady Racket, I never could think to see you come to this deplorable shame!

LADY RACKET: (*aside*) Surely the base man has not been capable of laying anything of that sort to my charge. – All this is unaccountable to me – ha, ha! – it's ridiculous beyond measure!

DIMITY: That's right, madam: laugh at it. You served him right.

MRS DRUGGET: Charlotte! Charlotte! I'm astonished at your wickedness!

LADY RACKET: Well, I protest and vow I don't comprehend all this. Has Sir Charles accused me of any impropriety in my conduct?

MRS DRUGGET: Oh, too true, he has. He has found you out, and you have behaved basely, he says.

LADY RACKET: Madam!

MRS DRUGGET: You have fallen into frailty, like many others of your sex, he says; and he is resolved to come to a separation directly.

LADY RACKET: Why, then, if he is so base a wretch as to dishonour me in that manner, his heart shall ache before I live with him again.

DIMITY: Hold to that, madam, and let his head ache into the bargain.

MRS DRUGGET: Your poor father heard it as well as me.

LADY RACKET: Then let your doors be opened for him this very moment. Let him return to London. If he does not, I'll lock myself up, and the false one shan't approach me, though he were to whine on his knees at my very door. A base, injurious man! (*Exit.*)

MRS DRUGGET: Dimity, do let us follow, and hear what she has to say for herself. (*Exit.*)

DIMITY: She has excuse enough, I warrant her. What a noise is here, indeed! I have lived in polite families, where there was no such bustle made about nothing. (*Exit.*)

(*Enter* SIR CHARLES *and* DRUGGET.)

SIR CHARLES: It's in vain, sir, my resolution is taken.

DRUGGET: Well, but consider I am her father. Indulge me only till we hear what the girl has to say in her defence.

SIR CHARLES: She can have nothing to say. No excuse can palliate such behaviour.

DRUGGET: Don't be too positive; there may be some mistake.

SIR CHARLES: No, sir, no. There can be no mistake. Did I not see her, hear her myself?

DRUGGET: Lack-a-day! Then I am an unfortunate man!

SIR CHARLES: She will be unfortunate too, with all my heart. She may thank herself. She might have been happy, had she been so disposed.

DRUGGET: Why, truly, I think she might.

(*Enter* MRS DRUGGET.)

MRS DRUGGET: I wish you'd moderate your anger a little, and let us talk over this affair with temper. My daughter denies every tittle of your charge.

SIR CHARLES: Denies it! Denies it!

MRS DRUGGET: She does indeed.

SIR CHARLES: And that aggravates her fault.

MRS DRUGGET: She vows you never found her out in anything that was wrong.

SIR CHARLES: She does not allow it to be wrong, then? Madam, I tell you again, I know her thoroughly, I have found her out, and I am now acquainted with her character. I am deceived no more!

MRS DRUGGET: Then you are in opposite stories. She swears, my dear Mr Drugget, the poor girl swears she was never guilty of the smallest infidelity to her husband in her born days.

SIR CHARLES: And what to that? What if she does say so?

MRS DRUGGET: And if she says truly, it is hard her character should be blown upon without just cause.

SIR CHARLES: And is she, therefore, to behave ill in other respects? I never charged her with infidelity to me, madam – there I allow her innocent.

DRUGGET: And did you not charge her then?

SIR CHARLES: No, sir, I never dreamt of such a thing.

DRUGGET: Why then, if she's innocent, let me tell you, you're a scandalous person . . .

MRS DRUGGET: Prithee, my dear . . .

DRUGGET: Be quiet. Though he is a man of quality, I will tell him of it. Did I not fine for sheriff? – Yes, you are a scandalous person to defame an honest man's daughter.

SIR CHARLES: What have you taken into your head now?

DRUGGET: You charged her with falsehood to your bed.

SIR CHARLES: No – never – never.

DRUGGET: I say you did.

SIR CHARLES: And I say no, no.

DRUGGET: But I say you did; you called yourself a cuckold. Did not he, wife?

MRS DRUGGET: Yes, lovey, I am witness.

SIR CHARLES: Absurd! I said no such thing.

DRUGGET: But I aver you did.

MRS DRUGGET: You did, indeed, sir.

SIR CHARLES: But I tell you no – positively no.

DRUGGET: ⎱ And I say yes – positively yes.
MRS DRUGGET: ⎰

SIR CHARLES: 'Sdeath, this is all madness!

DRUGGET: You said, she followed the ways of most of her sex.

SIR CHARLES: I said so, and what then?

DRUGGET: There, he owns it; owns that he called himself a cuckold, and without rhyme or reason into the bargain.

SIR CHARLES: I have never owned any such thing.

DRUGGET: You owned it even now – now – now – now –

MRS DRUGGET: This very moment.

SIR CHARLES: No, no; I tell you no.

DRUGGET: This instant – prove it; make your words good; show me your horns, and if you can't, it is worse than suicide to call yourself a cuckold, without proof.
(*Enter* DIMITY *in a fit of laughing.*)

DIMITY: What do you think it was all about? The whole secret is come out, ha, ha! It was all about a game of cards – Ho! Ho! Ho!

DRUGGET: A game of cards!

DIMITY: (*laughing*) It was all about a club and a diamond. (*Runs out laughing.*)

DRUGGET: And was that all, Sir Charles?

SIR CHARLES: And enough too, sir.

DRUGGET: And was that what you found her out in?

SIR CHARLES: I can't bear to be contradicted, when I'm clear that I'm in the right.

DRUGGET: I never heard such a heap of nonsense in all my life. Woodley shall marry Nancy.

MRS DRUGGET: Don't be in a hurry, my love; this will all be made up.

DRUGGET: Why does he not go and beg her pardon, then?

SIR CHARLES: I beg her pardon! I won't debase myself to any of you – I shan't forgive her, you may rest assured. (*Exit.*)

DRUGGET: Now, there, there's a pretty fellow for you.

MRS DRUGGET: I'll step and prevail on my Lady Racket to speak to him; all this will be set right. (*Exit.*)

DRUGGET: A ridiculous fop! I'm glad it's no worse, however. He must go and talk scandal of himself, as if the town did not abound with people ready enough to take that trouble off his hands. (*Enter* NANCY.) So, Nancy – you seem in confusion, my girl.

NANCY: How can one help it, with all this noise in the house? And you're going to marry me as ill as my sister. I hate Mr Lovelace.

DRUGGET: Why so, my child?

NANCY: I know these people of quality despise us all out of pride, and would be glad to marry us out of avarice.

DRUGGET: The girl's right.

NANCY: They marry one woman, live with another, and love only themselves.

DRUGGET: And then quarrel about a card.

NANCY: I don't want to be a gay lady. I want to be happy.

DRUGGET: And so you shall; don't fright yourself, child. Step to your sister; bid her make herself easy; go and comfort her, go.

NANCY: Yes, sir. (*Exit.*)

DRUGGET: I'll step and settle the matter with Mr Woodley this moment. (*Exit.*)

SCENE 2. *Another apartment.* SIR CHARLES, *with a pack of cards at a table.*

SIR CHARLES: Never was anything like her behaviour. I can pick out the very cards I had in my hand, and then it's as plain as the sun – there – there – now – there – no – damn it – no – there it was – now, let's see – They had four by honours and we played for the odd trick – damnation! honours were divided – ay! – honours were divided, and then a trump was led, and the other side had the – Confusion! – this preposterous woman has put it all out of my head. (*Puts the cards into his pocket.*) Mighty well, madam; I have done with you.

(*Enter* MRS DRUGGET.)

MRS DRUGGET: Sir Charles, let me prevail. Come with me, and speak to her.

SIR CHARLES: I don't desire to see her face.

MRS DRUGGET: If you were to see her all bathed in tears, I am sure it would melt your very heart.

SIR CHARLES: Madam, it shall be my fault if ever I am treated so again. I'll have nothing to say to her. (*Going, stops.*) Does she give up the point?

MRS DRUGGET: She does, she agrees to anything.

SIR CHARLES: Does she allow that the club was the play?

MRS DRUGGET: Just as you please. She is all submission.

SIR CHARLES: Does she own that the club was not the best in the house?

MRS DRUGGET: She does – she is willing to own it.

SIR CHARLES: Then I'll step and speak to her. I never was clearer in anything in my life. (*Exit.*)

MRS DRUGGET: Lord love them, they'll make it up now, and then they'll be as happy as ever. (*Exit.*)

(*Enter* NANCY.)

NANCY: Well! They may talk what they will of taste and genteel life, I don't think its natural. Give me Mr Woodley. – La! That odious thing coming this way!

(*Enter* LOVELACE.)

LOVELACE: My charming little innocent, I have not seen you these three hours.

NANCY: I have been very happy these three hours.

LOVELACE: My sweet angel! You seem disconcerted. And you neglect your pretty figure. No matter for the present. In a little time I shall make you appear as graceful and genteel as your sister.

NANCY: That is not what employs my thoughts, sir.

LOVELACE: Ay, but my pretty little dear, that should engage your attention. To set off and adorn the charms that nature has given you should be the business of your life.

SCENE 2: this scene change was introduced for the final version, in *The Works*. It makes good sense but may have been inconvenient in production.

NANCY: Ah, but I have learnt a new song that contradicts what you say, and, though I am not in a very good humour for singing, yet you shall hear it.

LOVELACE: By all means; don't check your fancy; I am all attention.

NANCY: It expresses my sentiments, and, when you have heard them you won't tease me any more.

> SONG.
> To dance, and to dress, and to flaunt it about,
> To run to park, play, to assembly and rout,
> To wander for ever in whim's giddy maze,
> And one poor hair torture a million of ways!
> To put, at the glass, every feature to school,
> And practise their art on each fop and each fool,
> Of one thing to think, and another to tell –
> These, these are the manners of each giddy *belle*!
>
> To smile, and to simper, white teeth to display;
> The time, in gay follies, to trifle away;
> Against every virtue the bosom to steel,
> And only of dress the anxieties to feel;
> To be at Eve's ear the insidious decoy,
> The pleasure ne'er taste, yet the mischief enjoy;
> To boast of soft raptures they never can know –
> These, these are the manners of each giddy *beau*! (*Exit.*)

LOVELACE: I must have her, notwithstanding this, for though I'm not in love, I am most confoundedly in debt.
>   (*Enter* DRUGGET.)

DRUGGET: So Mr Lovelace! Any news from above stairs? Is this absurd quarrel at an end? Have they made it up?

LOVELACE: Oh! A mere bagatelle, sir. These little fracas among the better sort of people never last long; elegant trifles cause elegant disputes, and we come together elegantly again, as you see, for here they come in perfect good humour.
>   (*Enter* SIR CHARLES *and* LADY RACKET.)

SIR CHARLES: Mr Drugget, I embrace you. You see me in most perfect harmony of spirits.

DRUGGET: What, all reconciled again?

LADY RACKET: All made up, sir. I knew how to bring the gentleman to a sense of his duty. This is the first difference, I think, we ever had, Sir Charles?

SIR CHARLES: And I'll be sworn it shall be the last.

DRUGGET: I am happy now, as happy as a fond father can wish. Sir Charles, I can spare you an image to put on the top of your house in London.

SIR CHARLES: Infinitely obliged to you!

DRUGGET: Well, well! It's time to retire now. I am glad to see you reconciled; and now I'll wish you a good night, Sir Charles. – Mr Lovelace, this is your way. Fare ye well both. I am glad your quarrels are at an end. This way, Mr Lovelace.
>   (*Exeunt* DRUGGET *and* LOVELACE.)

LADY RACKET: Ah, you're a sad man, Sir Charles, to behave to me as you have done!

SIR CHARLES My dear, I grant it; and such an absurd quarrel too – ha, ha!

LADY RACKET: Yes – ha, ha! About such a trifle!

SIR CHARLES: It's pleasant how we could both fall into such an error – ha, ha!

LADY RACKET: Ridiculous beyond expression – ha, ha!

SIR CHARLES: And then the mistake your father and mother fell into.

LADY RACKET: That, too, is a diverting part of the story – ha, ha! – But, Sir Charles, must I stay and live with my father till I grow as fantastical as his own evergreens?

SIR CHARLES: Nay, prithee don't remind me of my folly.

LADY RACKET: Ah, my relations were all standing behind counters selling Whitechapel needles, while your family were spending great estates!

SIR CHARLES: Spare my blushes. You see I am covered with confusion.

LADY RACKET: How could you say so indelicate a thing? I don't love you!

SIR CHARLES: It was indelicate, I grant it.

LADY RACKET: Am I a vile woman?

SIR CHARLES: How can you my angel?

LADY RACKET: I shan't forgive you. I'll have you on your knees for this! (*Sings and plays with him.*) 'Go naughty man.' Ah, Sir Charles!

SIR CHARLES: The rest of my life shall aim at convincing you how sincerely I love you.

LADY RACKET: (*Sings.*) 'Go naughty man, I can't abide you.' Well, come let's go to rest. (*going*) Ah, Sir Charles, now it is all over, the diamond was the play.

SIR CHARLES: Oh, no, no, no; now that one may speak, it was the club indeed.

LADY RACKET: Indeed, my love, you're mistaken.

SIR CHARLES: You make me laugh; but I was not mistaken; rely on my judgement.

LADY RACKET: You may rely on mine; you was wrong.

SIR CHARLES: (*laughing*) No! No, no, no such thing.

LADY RACKET: (*laughing*) But I say, yes, yes, yes!

SIR CHARLES: Oh, no, no; it is too ridiculous; don't say any more about it, my love.

LADY RACKET: (*toying with him*) Don't you say any more about it. You had better give it up, you had indeed.

             (*Enter* FOOTMAN.)

FOOTMAN: Your honour's cap and slippers.

SIR CHARLES: Ay, give me my night-cap, and here, take these shoes off. (*He takes them off and leaves them at a distance.*) Indeed my Lady Racket, you really make me ready to expire with laughing – ha, ha!

LADY RACKET: You may laugh, but I'm right notwithstanding.

SIR CHARLES: How can you say so?

LADY RACKET: How can you say otherwise?

SIR CHARLES: Well, now mind me, my Lady Racket, we can now talk of this matter in good humour. We can discuss it coolly.

LADY RACKET: So we can – and it is for that reason I venture to speak to you. Are these the ruffles I bought for you?

SIR CHARLES: They are, my dear.

LADY RACKET: They are very pretty. But indeed you played the card wrong.

SIR CHARLES: Pho, there is nothing so clear, if you will but hear me; only hear me.

'*Go naughty man*': from Bickerstaffe's *Love in a Village* (1762).

LADY RACKET: Ah! but do you hear me. The thing was thus. The adversary's club being the best in the house . . .

    (*Both speaking very fast and together.*)

SIR CHARLES: No, no, listen to me; the affair was thus: Mr Jenkins having never a club left . . .

LADY RACKET: Mr Jenkins finessed the club.

SIR CHARLES: (*peevishly*) How can you?

LADY RACKET: And the trumps being all out . . .

SIR CHARLES: And we playing for the odd trick . . .

LADY RACKET: If you had minded your game . . .

SIR CHARLES: And the club being the best . . .

LADY RACKET: If you had led your diamond . . .

SIR CHARLES: Mr Jenkins would of course put on a spade . . .

LADY RACKET: And so the odd trick was sure!

SIR CHARLES: Damnation! – Will you let me speak?

LADY RACKET: Well, to be sure, you're a strange man.

SIR CHARLES: Plague and torture! There is no such thing as conversing with you.

LADY RACKET: Very well, sir, fly out again!

SIR CHARLES: Look here now; here's a pack of cards. Now you shall be convinced.

LADY RACKET: You may talk till tomorrow, I know I'm right. (*Walks about.*)

SIR CHARLES: Why then, by all that's perverse, you are the most headstrong – can't you look here? Here are the very cards.

LADY RACKET: Go on; you'll find it out at last.

SIR CHARLES: Will you hold your tongue, or not? Will you let me show you? Pho, it's all nonsense! (*Puts up the cards.*) Come we'll go to bed. (*going*) Only stay one moment. (*Takes out the cards.*) Now, command yourself and you shall have demonstration.

LADY RACKET: It does not signify, sir. Your head will be clearer in the morning. I choose to go to bed.

SIR CHARLES: Stay and hear me, can't you.

LADY RACKET: (*affectedly*) No, my head aches. I am tired of the subject.

SIR CHARLES: Why then, damn the cards! (*throwing the cards about*) There, and there, and there! You may go to bed by yourself. Confusion seize me if I stay to be tormented a moment longer. (*putting on his shoes again*)

    (*Enter* DIMITY.)

DIMITY: Do you call, sir?

SIR CHARLES: No. Never, never, madam!

DIMITY: (*in a fit of laughing*) At it again!

LADY RACKET: Take your own way, sir.

SIR CHARLES: Now then, I tell you once more, you are a vile woman!

DIMITY: La, sir! – This is charming. I'll run and tell the old couple. (*Exit.*)

SIR CHARLES: (*still putting on his shoes*) You are the most perverse, obstinate, nonsensical . . .

LADY RACKET: Don't make me laugh again, Sir Charles. (*Walks and sings.*)

SIR CHARLES: Hell and the devil! Will you sit down quietly and let me convince you?

LADY RACKET: I don't choose to hear any more about it.

SIR CHARLES: Why then I believe you are possessed. It is in vain to talk sense and reason to you.

LADY RACKET: Thank you for your compliment, sir – such a man! (*with a sneering laugh*) I never knew the like. (*Sits down.*)

SIR CHARLES: I promise you, you shall repent of this usage, before you have a moment of my company again. It shan't be in a hurry, you may depend, madam – Now, see here – I can prove it to a demonstration. (*Sits down by her, she gets up.*) Lookye there again now; you have the most perverse and peevish temper. I wish I had never seen your face. I wish I was a thousand miles off. Sit down but one moment.

LADY RACKET: I'm disposed to walk about, sir.

SIR CHARLES: Why then, may I perish if ever – a blockhead, an idiot I was to marry. (*Walks about.*) Such a provoking, impertinent – (*She sits down.*) Damnation! I am so clear in the thing. She is not worth my notice – (*Sits down, turns his back and looks uneasy.*) Is it not very strange, that you won't hear me?

LADY RACKET: Sir, I am very ready to hear you.

SIR CHARLES: Very well then, very well. You remember how the game stood? (*Draws his chair near her.*) I'll write it down and send it to Arthur's, and if the best judges there . . .

LADY RACKET: I wish you'd untie my necklace, it hurts me.

SIR CHARLES: Why can't you listen?

LADY RACKET: I tell you it hurts me terribly.

SIR CHARLES: Death and confusion! (*Moves his chair away.*) There is no bearing this. (*Looks at her angrily.*) It won't take a moment, if you will but listen. (*Moves towards her.*) Can't you see that by forcing the adversary's hand, Mr Jenkins would be obliged to . . .

LADY RACKET: (*moving her chair away from him*) Mr Jenkins had the best club, and never a diamond left.

SIR CHARLES: (*rising*) Distraction! Bedlam is not so mad. Be as wrong as you please, and may I never hold four by honours, may I lose everything I play for, may fortune eternally forsake me, if I ever endeavour to set you right again. (*Exit.*)

    (*Enter* MR *and* MRS DRUGGET, WOODLEY, LOVELACE *and* NANCY.)

MRS DRUGGET: Gracious! What's the matter now?

LADY RACKET: Such another man does not exist. I did not say a word to the gentleman, and yet he has been raving about the room and storming like a whirlwind.

DRUGGET: And about a club again! I heard it all. Come hither, Nancy. Mr Woodley, she is yours for life.

MRS DRUGGET: My dear, how can you be so passionate?

DRUGGET: It shall be so. Take her for life, Mr Woodley.

WOODLEY: My whole life shall be devoted to her happiness.

LOVELACE: The devil! And so I am to be left in the lurch in this manner, am I?

LADY RACKET: Oh, this is only one of those polite disputes which people of quality, who have nothing else to differ about, must always be liable to. This will be made up tomorrow.

DRUGGET: Never tell me; it's too late now. Mr Woodley, I recommend my girl to

---

Arthur's: a fashionable gaming house.

your care. I shall have nothing to think of, but my greens, and my images and my shrubbery. Though, mercy on all married folks, say I, for these wranglings are, I am afraid, what they must all come to.

LADY RACKET: (*coming forward*)

What we must all come to? What? – Come to what?
Must broils and quarrels be the marriage lot?
If that's the wise, deep meaning of our poet,
The man's a fool! a blockhead! and I'll show it.

    What could induce him in age so nice,
So famed for virtue, so refined from vice,
To form a plan so trivial, false and low?
As if a belle could quarrel with a beau;
As if there were, in these thrice happy days,
One who from nature, or from reason strays!
There's no cross husband now, no wrangling wife,
The man is downright ignorant of life.

    'Tis the millennium this: devoid of guile,
Fair gentle Truth, and white robed Candour smile.
From every breast the sordid love of gold
Is banished quite – no boroughs now are sold!
Pray tell me, sirs, – (for I don't know, I vow,)
Pray, is there such a thing as gaming now?
Do peers make laws against the giant vice?
And then at Arthur's break them in a trice?

    No, no; our lives are virtuous all, austere and hard;
Pray, ladies – do you ever see a card?
Those empty boxes show you don't love plays;
The managers, poor souls! get nothing nowadays.
If here you come – by chance – but once a week,
The pit can witness that you never speak:
Pensive Attention sits with decent mien;
No paint, no naked shoulders, to be seen!

    And yet this grave, this moral, pious age,
May learn one useful lesson from the stage.
Shun strife, ye fair, and once a contest o'er,
Wake to blaze the dying flame no more.
From fierce debate fly all the tender loves;
And Venus, cries, 'Coachman, put-to my doves.'
The genial bed no blooming Grace prepares,
'And every day becomes a day of cares.'

4 Mrs Mattocks delivering the epilogue to *Know Your Own Mind*
at Covent Garden, 1777

KNOW YOUR OWN MIND

A comedy

by ARTHUR MURPHY

> *– Pugnat sententia secum;*
> *Quod petiit, spernit; repetit quod nuper omisit;*
> *Aestuat, et vitae disconvenit ordine toto.*   HOR.
>
> *Ut callidum ejus ingenium, ita anxium judicium.* TAC.

First performed at the Theatre Royal, Covent Garden, on 2 February 1777, with the following cast:

MILLAMOUR	Mr Lewis
DASHWOULD	Mr Lee-Lewis
MALVIL	Mr Wroughton
BYGROVE	Mr Aickin
CAPTAIN BYGROVE, *his son*	Mr Booth
SIR JOHN MILLAMOUR	Mr Fearon
SIR HARRY LIZARD	Mr Whitfield
CHARLES, servant to Millamour	Mr Wewitzer
LADY BELL	Mrs Mattocks
LADY JANE	Miss Dayes
MRS BROMLEY	Mrs Jackson
MISS NEVILLE	Mrs Hartley
MADAM LA ROUGE	Miss Ambrose
TRINKET	
FOOTMEN etc. [WILLIAM, ROBERT, RICHARD]	

Pugnat sententia: Horace, *Letters*, I, i: 'Sense strives against itself; scorns what it desired; returns to what it threw away before; it changes like the tide, and the whole order of life is in disarray.'
Ut callidum: Tacitus, *Annals*, I, lxxx: 'By nature shrewd, but in judgement anxious'.

PROLOGUE

Spoken by Mr Lewis

> Through the wide tracts of life, in every trade,
> What numbers toil with faculties decay'd?
> Worn out, yet eager, – in the race they run,
> And never learn – when proper to have done.
>
> What need of proofs? Ev'n Authors do the same,
> And rather than desist, decline in fame.
> Like Gamesters thrive at first, then bolder grow,
> And hazard all upon one desperate throw.
>
> This truth to feel, perhaps too much inclin'd
> Our Bard, long hackney'd, trembles there behind,
> Lest he should prove – another VANISHED MIND.
> Long has this play lain hid, suppress'd by fears,
> Beyond the critic's rule ABOVE NINE YEARS!
> And now he comes, 'tis the plain simple truth,
> This night to answer for his sins of youth.
>
> The piece, you'll say, should now perfection bear;
> But who can reach it after all his care?
> He paints no monsters for ill judg'd applause:
> Life he has view'd, and from that source he draws.
> Here are no fools, the Drama's standing jest!
> And WELSHMEN now, NORTH-BRITONS too, may rest.
> HIBERNIA's sons shall here excite no wonder,
> Nor shall St PATRICK blush to hear them blunder.
> By other arts he strives your taste to hit,
> Some plot, some character, he hopes, some wit.
> And if the piece should please you like the past,
> Ye Brother Bards! forgive him – 'tis his last.
>
> Lost are the friends who lent their aid before,
> Roscius retires, and BARRY is no more.
> Harmonious BARRY! with what varied art
> His grief, rage, tenderness assail'd the heart?
> Of plaintive OTWAY now no more the boast!
> And SHAKESPEARE grieves for his OTHELLO lost.
> Oft on this spot the tuneful swain expir'd,
> Warbling his grief; – you listen'd and admir'd.
> 'Twas then but fancied woe; now every Muse,
> Her lyre unstrung, with tears his urn bedews.

Roscius: the name applied to Garrick, who had retired in June 1776.
BARRY: Spranger Barry, who had died in 1777, had appeared with his wife Ann Dancer in several of Murphy's plays, in particular *The Grecian Daughter*, and had supported Murphy in frequent arguments with Garrick.

For this night's scenes e'en WOODWARD too is fled,
Stretch'd by pale sickness in his languid bed,
Nor can THALIA raise her favourite's head.

For them our Author lov'd the tale to weave;
He feels their loss; and now he takes his leave;
Sees new performers in succession spring,
And hopes new poets will expand their wing.
Beneath your smile his leaf of laurel grew;
Gladly he'd keep it; – for 'twas giv'n by you.
But if too weak his art, if wild his aim,
On favours past he builds no idle claim;
To you once more he boldly dares to trust;
HEAR, and pronounce; – he KNOWS you will be just.

ACT I

SCENE 1.   *The house of* SIR JOHN MILLAMOUR. *Enter* CHARLES *in violent haste.*
CHARLES: Here William, William! Where are you running?
          (*Enter* WILLIAM.)
WILLIAM: Why, there's the gentleman that comes from the corporation to sell master a seat in parliament. I am going to tell him he must wait.
CHARLES: You must do just the contrary; tell him he may go.
WILLIAM: And t'other that comes about a company in a marching regiment?
          (*Enter* ROBERT.)
ROBERT: Mr Charles, Mr Charles!
CHARLES: What's the matter, Robert?
ROBERT: You must order the chariot. (*Exit.*)
CHARLES: Very well. What did you say, William?
WILLIAM: The commission broker, must he go too?
CHARLES: Yes, he may go.
WILLIAM: Well, I'll give 'em both their answer. (*Exit.*)
CHARLES: Hurry, hurry! Nothing but hurry! Get me this, get me that, get me t'other. 'Bring me the blue and silver. Scoundrel, what do you fetch me this for? Let me have the brown and gold!' A poor servant does not know which way to turn himself in this house.
          (*Enter* RICHARD.)
CHARLES: Well, Richard, what are you about?
RICHARD: Why, a man in a whirlwind may as well tell what he is about. Going to get him his boots. I think he intends to ride. (*Exit.*)

WOODWARD: the comic actor who had starred in Murphy's early farces, *The Apprentice* and *The Citizen*. Murphy's footnote: 'Mr WOODWARD was to have played the part of DASHWOULD: in his last illness he lamented to the Author, that he could not close his theatrical life with that character: he died a few weeks after the play appeared; for years the life of the comic scene, and in his end regretted as a worthy and an honest man.'

CHARLES: And a good ride to him, say I. No rest till his back is turned. What a life to lead! I had rather be a country curate, than go on upon these terms.
>   (*Enter* ROBERT.)
ROBERT: Richard, Richard! Where is he gone?
CHARLES: What's in the wind now?
ROBERT: Why the wind's in another quarter; he intends to dress.
CHARLES: There again now! Not a crane-neck carriage in town can give a short turn with him. I wish he'd marry, and sit down to some regular plan of life.
ROBERT: His father, Sir John, would be glad to see it; but I doubt young Mr Millamour will be always going on from one thing to another, and end in nothing at last.
CHARLES: I don't know what to say to that, Robert. Some day or other, before he has time to change his resolution, he may be caught. Last night, as he was going to bed, I touched upon the subject, dropped a hint or two, that it is now time to think of raising heirs to himself, enlarged upon the comforts of matrimony, and I think with no small degree of eloquence.
ROBERT: I dare say, but no effect, Mr Charles.
CHARLES: Oh yes! A very visible effect. He composed himself in bed, listened with great attention, and fell asleep.
ROBERT: I thought as much.
>   (*Enter* RICHARD, *with boots.*)
CHARLES: You may take 'em back; he does not want 'em now.
RICHARD: Wounds! To be tossed to and fro, from pillar to post in this manner!
CHARLES: Never stand talking, but to business.
RICHARD: If a body could but know one's business. (*Exit.*)
CHARLES: A worrying kind of life, Robert, and an odd sort of character this same Mr Millamour.
ROBERT: I'd as soon live upon board wages with a weather cock.
CHARLES: I don't know what to make of him. This morning early he rings his bell. 'Charles,' says he, 'I have been considering what passed last night. I shall visit the young ladies, and I believe I shall marry one of them.' I fly immediately to get him his things ready to dress, and . . .
>   (*Enter* WILLIAM.)
WILLIAM: Mr Charles, you must come to my master.
CHARLES: I am coming.
WILLIAM: He wants you directly. (*Exit.*)
CHARLES: Very well, tell him I am coming. I got him his things to dress and returned in an instant. 'Charles', says he, then tossed himself back in his chair, beat the ground with his heel and fell areading. 'Won't your Honour get ready to visit the ladies?' 'The ladies, what ladies, you blockhead?' 'My Lady Bell and Lady Jane, your honour, Mrs Bromley's handsome nieces.' 'Po! You are a numskull', says he, with an oblique kind of a smile, stretched his arms, yawned, talked to himself, and bade me go about my business.

---

crane-neck carriage: a carriage slung from curved iron springs, which was particularly manoeuvrable.

ROBERT: I guess it would end so. (*A bell rings.*)

CHARLES: There, not a moment's patience. Do you step and tell the coachman to be in the way. (ROBERT *goes.*) And harkye, Robert – (*Bell rings.*) 'Sdeath I must be gone. So, so, there come more misfortunes, his father and that carping, cavilling, morose, old . . . I'll take care of a single rogue and get me out of their way. (*Exit.*)

(*Enter* SIR JOHN MILLAMOUR *and* BYGROVE.)

BYGROVE: Why then I'd marry again, and disinherit him.

SIR JOHN: Brother Bygrove, I beg your pardon for a moment. Charles, Charles, this way. (*Enter* CHARLES.) Well Charles, what is he about?

CHARLES: Very busy, sir, a thousand things in hand.

BYGROVE: And all at the same time, I'll warrant.

SIR JOHN: Have you spoke to him as I bade you?

CHARLES: I have, sir, and he has now ordered the chariot. He says he will marry, sir, and is now going to pay a visit at Mrs Bromley's.

SIR JOHN: Well, that's well. Anybody with him?

CHARLES: A power of people have been here this morning, and there are several with him now. There's Sir Harry Lizard, and . . .

BYGROVE: Ay, Sir Harry Lizard! I am glad he is of age, and that I am no longer his guardian. He has not had a new idea in his head since he was five years old; and yet the blockhead affects to be lively. He runs after wits, who do nothing but laugh at him. He repeats scraps and sentences, a mere retailer of what falls from other people, and with this stock he sets up for a wit.

CHARLES: He is with my master, sir, and there's Mr Malvil and Mr Dashwould. (*Bell rings.*) He rings, sir, you will pardon me, I must be gone, sir. (*Exit.*)

BYGROVE: And that fellow Dashwould, he is the ruin of your son, and of poor Sir Harry into the bargain. He is the Merry Andrew of the Town. Honour has no restraint upon him, truth he sets at nought, and friendship he is ever ready to sacrifice to a joke.

SIR JOHN: Po! Mere innocent pleasantry. Dashwould has no harm in him.

BYGROVE: No harm in him! I grant you, the fellow has a quick sense of the ridiculous, and draws a character with a lucky hit; but everything is distorted by him. He has wit to ridicule you, invention to frame a story of you, humour to help it about, and when he has set the town a laughing, he puts on a familiar air and shakes you by the hand. And yet your son has no other adviser. Sooner than I would permit it, as I told you already, I'd marry again and disinherit him!

SIR JOHN: Brother Bygrove, you think too severely in these matters.

BYGROVE: Severely, Sir John? If I had a mind that my son should marry, why should not he do as I would have him?

SIR JOHN: Allowance must be made for inclination. The success of our children depends upon the manner in which we set them out upon the world. They are like bowls, which, if delivered out of hand, with a due regard to their bias, our aim is answered, if otherwise, they are short or wide of the mark in view, or perhaps rush wildly out of the green.

BYGROVE: Well argued, truly! He, that should obey, is to judge for himself, and you, that are his governor, are to be directed by him.

SIR JOHN: Why, he is chiefly interested in the end, and the choice of the means may be fairly left to himself. I can't but be tender of George, a plant of my own rearing, and the tree will hereafter be known by its fruit.

BYGROVE: It is a tree that will bear nothing without grafting, and if I could not inoculate what will make it thrive and flourish, it should not encumber a foot of my land.

SIR JOHN: Your system and mine differ widely, brother Bygrove. My son is of an enlarged and liberal understanding, and I a father of mild authority.

BYGROVE: Authority! Your son's word is a law to you. Now, there is my young graceless; he is in the army, and why? Because I chose it. I had a mind he should serve, and so he went to be shot at. No arguing with me – if I see anything wrong I accost him directly: 'Lookye, sir, do you think to go on in this fashion? Not during my life, I promise you. I will acknowledge you no longer than you prove worthy, and if you can't discern what is benefitting you, I, at least, will judge what is proper on my part.'

SIR JOHN: Well, George and I have lived together as friends. From a boy, I endeavoured to subject him rather to his reason than his fears. If any little irregularity happened, he was no sooner sensible of it, than his cheek coloured, and the blush of youth not only looked decent, but expressed an ingenuous and well-disposed mind.

BYGROVE: But the consequence of all this? Has he a settled opinion? A fixed principle for a moment? He is grown up in caprice; his judgement has not vigour to be decisive upon the merest trifle; he is distracted by little things, and, of course, is perishing little by little.

SIR JOHN: Oh no, all from a good cause: his knowledge of life occasions quick reflection, quick reflection shows things in a variety of lights. I am not angry – he will settle in the world – you will see him married before long.

BYGROVE: In what a variety of lights his wife will appear to him!

(*Enter* SIR HARRY LIZARD, *laughing violently.*)

SIR HARRY: Ha, ha, ha! I shall certainly expire one day in a fit of laughing.

SIR JOHN: What's the matter, Sir Harry?

BYGROVE: What fool's errand brings him hither?

SIR HARRY: That fellow Dashwould will be the death of me. The very spirit of whim, wit, humour and raillery possess him.

BYGROVE: Ay, wit and humour for the meridian of your understanding.

SIR HARRY: By the shade of Rabelais! He is the most entertaining creature! He has played off such a firework of wit! I'll tell you what he said this moment . . .

BYGROVE: No, sir, no. If you are a pedlar in smart sayings and brisk repartees, we don't desire you to unpack for us.

SIR HARRY: A plague on him, for an agreeable devil! And then the rogue has so much ease!

BYGROVE: Yes, the ease of an executioner. He puts all to death without remorse. He laughs at everything, as if heaven intended to make its own work ridiculous. He has no relish for beauty, natural or moral. He is in love with deformity, and never better pleased than when he has most reason to find fault.

SIR HARRY: There is a picture of as harsh feature as any in Dashwould's whole collection.

BYGROVE: But the picture is true – no exaggeration in it.

SIR HARRY: He gave us a miniature of you, this morning, my dear guardian, and you shall have it. Dashwould has made a discovery, Sir John – What reason do you think he gives for Mr Bygrove's railing forever at your son's inconstancy of temper?

BYGROVE: Ay, now! now!

SIR HARRY: You shall hear it. Mr Bygrove's desires being all rusted to a point, looking directly toward the land of matrimony . . .

BYGROVE: Matrimony! Now gild the pill with humour and down it goes.

SIR HARRY: Dashwould has found you out. Mr Bygrove's desires being all collected and fixed on matrimony, he rails at the variety of my friend Millamour's whimsies, like Sir George Bumper, with chalkstones on his knuckles as big as nutmegs, hobbling along, and thanking Doctor le Fevre that he has no small humours flying about him.

SIR JOHN: That's a discovery indeed!

BYGROVE: Sir John, can you mind what such a fellow says? Everything that passes through the medium of his fancy, appears deformed, as the straightest stick looks crooked in troubled water.

SIR HARRY: Well dashed out, upon my soul, with tolerable spleen and some vivacity!

BYGROVE: Po! If you had taken my advice, Sir Harry, and renounced his acquaintance long ago, you had been now a young man coming into life with some promise of a character. Continue in dissipation, sir. For my part, it is a rule with me, neither to give, nor to take a joke.

SIR HARRY: Ha, ha, ha! a pleasant rule positively – ha! ha! ha! Dashwould shall have it this moment; do you take the consequence, and in the mean time I'll leave you to the practice of your social humour. (*Exit.*)

BYGROVE: It is such coxcombs as that butterfly that encourage him to fix his pasquinades upon every man's character. Matrimony! A licentious – No, Sir John, I still cherish the memory of your sister. She was the best of wives – 'Sdeath! Interrupted again by that – No, it's my friend Malvil; he is a man of true value.

SIR JOHN: Dashwould would say he is a compound of false charity and real malice.

BYGROVE: And it is enough for you that Dashwould says it. Malvil is a man of honour, sir, and an enemy to all scandal, though wit prove a palatable ingredient in the poison.

(*Enter* MALVIL.)

MALVIL: Intolerable! There is no being safe where he is. A licentious railer! All truth, all morality sacrificed to a jest! Nothing sacred from his buffoonery!

BYGROVE: I told you, Sir John, how it is.

MALVIL: Oh, such indiscriminate satire!

BYGROVE: Yes, the fellow runs amuck and nothing escapes him.

MALVIL: There is no enduring it. Ridicule is a very unfair weapon, Mr Bygrove. It is by no means the test of truth, Sir John.

SIR JOHN: Nay, but you are too grave about this matter.

MALVIL: Too grave! Shall he wantonly stab the reputation of his neighbour, and then tell you he was in jest? For my part, I had rather throw a veil over the infirmities of my friend than seek a malicious pleasure in the detection – That's my way of thinking.

SIR JOHN: I fancy you are right. This son of mine does so perplex me! (*Walks aside.*)

MALVIL: Pray, Mr Bygrove, give me leave – I am sorry to hear certain whispers about a friend of ours.

BYGROVE: About whom? The widow, Mrs Bromley?

MALVIL: Oh, no, no! I have a great respect for her, though I – Pray, don't you think she throws out the lure for a young husband?

BYGROVE: For a husband, yes, but not too young a one. You can serve my interest in that quarter.

MALVIL: I know it, rely upon my friendship. But have you heard nothing of an eminent Turkey merchant?

BYGROVE: Mr Freeport?

MALVIL: I say nothing – I don't like the affair. – Have you really heard nothing?

BYGROVE: Not a syllable.

MALVIL: So much the better, though it is fit you should be put on your guard. Any money of yours in his hands?

BYGROVE: Pho! As safe as the bank.

MALVIL: I may be mistaken – I hope I am – I was in company the other night – several members of parliament present – they did not speak plainly – hints and innuendoes only – you won't let it go any further? – His seat in the house, they all agreed, is perfectly convenient at this juncture – I hope the cloud will blow over. I shall remember you with the widow.

BYGROVE: One good turn deserves another; I shan't be unmindful of your interest.

MALVIL: There, now you hurt me – you know my delicacy. Must friendship never act a disinterested part? I esteem you, Mr Bygrove, and that's sufficient. Sir John, give me leave to say, the man who busies himself about other people's affairs is a pragmatical character and very dangerous in society.

BYGROVE: So I have been telling Sir John. But to laugh at everything is the fashion of the age. A pleasant, good-for-nothing fellow is by most people preferred to modest merit. A man like Dashwould, who runs on with an eternal confusion! So! Here comes Scandal in folio.

    (*Enter* DASHWOULD.)

DASHWOULD: Sir John, I rejoice to see you – Mr Bygrove, I kiss your hand. Malvil, have you been uneasy for any friend since?

MALVIL: Pho! Absurd! (*Walks away.*)

DASHWOULD: I have been laughing with your son, Sir John. – Pray, have I told you about Sir Richard Doriland?

BYGROVE: You may spare him, sir, he is a very worthy man.

DASHWOULD: He is so – great good nature about him – I love Sir Richard. You know he was divorced from his wife, a good fine woman, but an invincible idiot.

MALVIL: Lookye there now, Mr Bygrove!

BYGROVE: My Lady Doriland, sir, was always accounted a very sensible woman.

DASHWOULD: She was so; with too much spirit to be ever at east, and a rage for pleasure that broke the bubble as she grasped it. She fainted away upon hearing that Mrs Allnight had two card tables more than herself.

BYGROVE: Inveterate malice!

His seat in the house . . . : parliamentary privilege protected members from arrest in civil cases.

DASHWOULD: They waged war a whole winter, for the honour of having the greatest number of fools gazing at black and red spots. – First, Mrs Allnight kept Sundays; her ladyship did the same – Mrs Allnight had forty tables; her ladyship rose to fifty – Then one added, then t'other, till every room in the house was crammed like the black hole at Calcutta, and at last, upon casting up the account, Sir Richard sold off fifteen hundred acres, to clear incumbrances.

SIR JOHN: Ridiculous! And so they parted upon this?

DASHWOULD: Don't you know the history of that business?

MALVIL: Now mark him – now.

DASHWOULD: Tender of reputation, Malvil! – The story is well known. She was detected with – the little foreign count – I call him the Salamander – I saw him five times in one winter upon the back of the fire, at Bath, for cheating at cards.

MALVIL: Go on, sir, abuse everybody. My lady was perfectly innocent. I know the whole affair – a mere contrivance to lay the foundation of a divorce.

DASHWOULD: So they gave out. Sir Richard did not care a nine-pin for her while she was his. You know his way; he despises what is in his possession, and languishes for what is not. Her ladyship was no sooner married to – what's his name? – His father was a footman, and Madam Fortune, who, every now and then loves a joke, sent him to the East Indies, and in a few years brought him back at the head of half a million, for the jest's sake.

MALVIL: Mr Dashwould, upon my word, sir – Families to be run down in this manner!

DASHWOULD: Mushroom was his name. My Lady Doriland was no sooner married to him, but, up to his eyes, Sir Richard was in love with her. He dressed at her – sighed at her – danced at her; she is now libelled in the Commons, and Sir Richard has a crim. con. against him in the King's Bench.

MALVIL: Pshaw! I shall stay no longer to hear this strain of defamation. (*Exit.*)

DASHWOULD: Malvil, must you leave us? A pleasant character, this same Mr Malvil.

BYGROVE: He has a proper regard for his friends, sir.

DASHWOULD: Yes, but he is often present where their characters are canvassed, and is anxious about whispers which nobody has heard but himself. He knows the use of hypocrisy better than a court chaplain.

BYGROVE: There, call honesty by a burlesque name, and so pervert everything.

DASHWOULD: Things are more perverted, Mr Bygrove, when such men as Malvil make their vices do their work under a mask of goodness, and with that stroke we'll dismiss his character.

SIR JOHN: Ay, very right; my brother Bygrove has a regard for him, and so change the subject. My son, Mr Dashwould, what does he intend?

DASHWOULD: Up to the eyes in love with Lady Bell, and determined to marry her.

SIR JOHN: I told you so, Mr Bygrove – I told you, you would soon see him settled in the world. Mr Dashwould, I thank you. I'll step and confirm George in his resolution. (*Exit.*)

DASHWOULD: A good-natured man, Sir John, and does not want credulity!

BYGROVE: Ay, there! the moment his back is turned!

DASHWOULD: Gulliver's Travels is a true history to him! His son has strange flights.

---

foreign count: Baron Newman (*Biographia Dramatica*, vol. II, p. 359).

– First, he was to be a lawyer, bought chambers in the Temple, ate his commons, and was called to the bar. Then the law is a damned, dry, municipal study; the army is fitter for a gentleman, and as he was going to the war-office to take out his commission, he saw my Lord Chancellor's coach go by; in an instant back to the Temple, and no sooner there, 'Pho! Pox! Hang the law! Better marry and live like a gentleman.' Now marriage is a galling yoke, and he does not know what he'll do. He calls his man, Charles – sends him away – walks about the room, sits down, asks a question – thinks of something else – talks to himself, sings, whistles, lively, pensive, pleasant, and melancholy, in an instant. He approves, finds fault; he will, he will not; and, in short, the man does not know his own mind for half a second. – Here comes Sir John. (*Enter* SIR JOHN MILLAMOUR.) You find him disposed to marry, Sir John?

SIR JOHN: I hope so, he wavers a little, but still I . . .

BYGROVE: Pho! I have no patience – my advice has been all lost upon you – I wish it may end well. A good morning, Sir John. (*going*)

DASHWOULD: Mr Bygrove, yours. Sir John will defend you in your absence.

BYGROVE: If you will forget your friends in their absence, it is the greatest favour you can bestow upon them. (*Exit.*)

DASHWOULD: Did I ever tell you what happened to him last summer, at Tunbridge?

SIR JOHN: Excuse me for the present. This light young man! – I must step and talk with my lawyer.

DASHWOULD: I'll walk part of the way with you. A strange medley, this same Mr Bygrove: with something like wit, he is always abusing wit. You must know, last summer at Tunbridge . . .

SIR JOHN: Another time, if you please. (*Exit.*)

DASHWOULD: (*following* SIR JOHN) The story is worth your hearing: a party of us dined at the Sussex . . .

     (*Enter* CHARLES.)

CHARLES: Mr Dashwould! Mr Dashwould!

DASHWOULD: What's the matter, Charles?

CHARLES: My master desires you won't go.

     (*Enter* SIR HARRY LIZARD.)

SIR HARRY: Hey! What, going to leave us?

DASHWOULD: Only a step with Sir John. Strange vagaries in your master's head, Charles! – Sir Harry! Going to wait upon Miss Neville, I suppose. She has beauty, and you have a heart.

SIR HARRY: Pshaw! There you wrong me now! Why will you?

DASHWOULD: Very well, be it so. I can't see, to be sure! But take my word for it, you will marry that girl, and that's my prophecy. Come, I follow you.

SIR HARRY: I must not part with you. I had rather lose the whole college of physicians. (*Exit.*)

DASHWOULD: March on, Sir Harry. (*Turns to* CHARLES.) Did you ever see such a baronet! This fellow, Charles, is as ridiculous himself as any of them. (*Exit.*)

---

ate his commons: residence at an Inn of Court was proved by a student's presence at the common dinners.

CHARLES: Now have I but one man in the house, and he will be fifty different men in a moment! (*Enter* RICHARD.) Well, Richard what are you about?

RICHARD: Going to order the coachman to put up. He intends to change his dress and walk to the Temple. (*Exit.*)

CHARLES: What does he mean by talking of the Temple again? I hope we are not going to take up our studies once more. I hate the law. There is not a footman in the Temple has a grain of taste. All mere lawyers! They have not an idea out of the profession.

(*Enter* ROBERT.)

ROBERT: Richard! Richard! It is another shift. He has been writing verses, as he calls them, ever since the company left him. He has torn a quire of paper, I believe, and now wants the carriage directly. (*Exit.*)

CHARLES: Run and order it. (*Bell rings.*) What is he at now?

MILLAMOUR: (*within*) Charles! Who answers there?

CHARLES: Ay, now for the old work.

(*Enter* MILLAMOUR.)

MILLAMOUR: Is the chariot ready?

CHARLES: At the door, sir.

MILLAMOUR: Do you step to Mrs Bromley's and – perhaps it would be better to – No, do you step, Charles, and – you need not mind it – another time will do as well. (*Exit.*)

CHARLES: There again now! This is the way from morning to night.

(*Enter* MILLAMOUR.)

MILLAMOUR: The sooner, the better. I promised Sir John, and I will pay this visit. (*Reads from paper.*)

   'I look'd and I sigh'd and I wish'd I could speak,
     And fain would have paid adoration.'

Lady Bell reigns sovereign of my heart. That vivacity of mind!

   'Quick as her eyes, and as unfixed as those.'

CHARLES: She is by far preferable to her sister, your honour.

MILLAMOUR: Po! You are illiterate in these matters. The sober graces of Lady Jane! – Lady Bell advances like a conqueror and demands your heart; Lady Jane seems unconscious of her charms, and yet enslaves you deeper.

CHARLES: Which of them does your honour think . . .

MILLAMOUR: Which of them, Charles? – Is the chariot at the door? (*Reads.*)

   'But when I endeavoured the matter to break,
     Still then I said least of my passion.'

Do you step, Charles, and – 'Sdeath, where are the other copies? Confusion! I left them – (*Reads.*) 'Than live with forbearing to love her.' (*Exit.*)

CHARLES: There, now he begins. What will he do next?

(*Re-enter* MILLAMOUR, *three papers in his hand.*)

MILLAMOUR: I have the papers here. Which is the best copy? No matter. – I shall certainly marry, Charles.

(*Enter* WILLIAM.)

'*I look'd* . . . ': William Congreve, 'Song'.
'*Quick as her eyes* . . . ': Pope, *The Rape of the Lock*, II, 10.

WILLIAM: Captain Bygrove, sir.

MILLAMOUR: That's unlucky. I am not at home; tell him I went out an hour ago. (*Enter* CAPTAIN BYGROVE.) My dear Bygrove, I longed to see you. But why that pensive air? Still in love, I suppose. (*Exeunt* CHARLES *and* ROBERT.)

CAPT. BYGROVE: My dear Millamour, you have guessed it. I am in love, and glory in my chains.

MILLAMOUR: Shall I tell you a secret? I suspect myself plaguily. Everything is not as quiet here as it used to be.

CAPT. BYGROVE: Indulge the happy passion. Let wits and libertines say what they will, there is no true happiness, but in the married state.

MILLAMOUR: Why, I have thought much upon the subject of late, and, with a certain refinement, I don't know but a man may fashion a complying girl to his taste of happiness. Virtuous himself, he confirms her in her virtue; constant, he secures her fidelity; and, by continuing the lover, instead of commencing the tyrant husband, he wins from her the sweetest exertion of tenderness and love. I shall most positively marry. Who is your idol? My dear boy, impart.

CAPT. BYGROVE: There I beg to be excused. You know my father. I must not presume to think for myself. I must contrive some stratagem, to make him propose the match. Were it to move first from me, I should be obliged to decamp from before the town at once.

MILLAMOUR: I wish you success. My resolution is taken, and with the most amiable of her sex. She romps about the room like one of the Graces, and deals about her wit with such a happy negligence . . .

CAPT. BYGROVE: An agreeable portrait, but mine is the very reverse. That equal serenity in all her ways! Wit she has, but without ostentation; and elegance itself seems the pure effect of nature.

MILLAMOUR: (*aside*) I don't know whether that is not the true character for a wife. And pray, what progress have you made in her affections?

CAPT. BYGROVE: Enough to convince me that I am not quite unacceptable. My dear Millamour, I had rather fold that girl in my arms than kiss his majesty's hand for the first regiment of guards.

MILLAMOUR: I am a lost man. I shall most positively marry. We will wonder at each other's felicity, and be the envy of all our acquaintance.

(*Enter* DASHWOULD.)

DASHWOULD: I am as good as my word, you see. Most noble Captain, your father was here this morning. A good agreeable old gentleman, and about as pleasant as a nightmare. Millamour, whom do you think I met since I saw you?

MILLAMOUR: Who?

DASHWOULD: Our friend Beverley, just imported from Paris, perfectly frenchified and abusing everything in this country – 'Oh! There is no breathing their English atmosphere. – Roast beef and liberty will be the death of me!'

MILLAMOUR: Ha, ha! Poor Beverley! I saw him, last summer, at Paris, dressed in the style of an English fox-hunter, he swore there was not a morsel to eat in their country, kept an opera-singer upon beef-steaks and oyster sauce, drove to his villa every Saturday in a phaeton, and returned on the Monday like a young buck just come upon town.

DASHWOULD: He has done his country great honour abroad.

CAPT. BYGROVE: He will settle at home now: he is going to be married.

DASHWOULD: Yes, I hear he is in love, and much good may it do him. I wish I may die, if I know so ridiculous a thing as love! – 'My life! – My soul! – Hybla dwells upon her lips; ecstasy and bliss! blank verse and pastoral nonsense!' In a little time, the man wonders what bewitched him: an armchair after dinner, and a box and dice till five in the morning, make all the comforts of his life.

MILLAMOUR: Very true! Love is a ridiculous passion indeed.

CAPT. BYGROVE: Do you take up arms against me? But a moment since, just as you came in, he was acknowledging to me . . .

MILLAMOUR: No, not I, truly, I acknowledge nothing. Marriage is not to my taste, I promise you. The handsome wife! – She is all affectation; routs, drums, hurricanes and intrigue!

DASHWOULD: And the ugly! She makes it up with good sense, pronounces upon wit, and talks you dead with maxims, characters and reflections.

MILLAMOUR: And for the woman of high birth! She produces her pedigree as her patent for vice and folly. 'Seven's the main', and away goes your whole fortune!

CAPT. BYGONE: Mere commonplace.

DASHWOULD: And the tender mawkin! She dotes upon you. 'Don't drink any more, my dear', 'You'll take cold near that window, my love', 'Pray don't talk so much, you'll flurry your spirits.' – And then kisses you before company.

MILLAMOUR: And the sick madam! She has the vapours, and she finds she has nerves. – 'I wish I had none. – But it is too true that I have nerves as slight as so many hairs.'

DASHWOULD: Ha, ha! The whole sex is divided into so many classes of folly.

MILLAMOUR: Right! So it is. Ha, ha, ha! (*Both laugh.*)

CAPT. BYGROVE: You play finely into one another's hands.

MILLAMOUR: (*laughing*) Now mark the champion of the sex!

DASHWOULD: (*laughing*) Yes; he'll throw down the gauntlet for them.

CAPT. BYGROVE: Nay, decide it your own way. Since you won't hear, gentlemen, there is a clear stage for you. (*Exit.*)

DASHWOULD: Fare ye well, most noble Captain! A facetious companion! Did you ever hear him say anything?

MILLAMOUR: He is in for it; and my father would fain reduce me to the same condition, with one of Mrs Bromley's nieces. A good fine woman, Mrs Bromley!

DASHWOULD: Has been! Were she now to rub her cheek with a white handkerchief, her roses and lilies would go to the clear starcher.

MILLAMOUR: Ha, ha! And yet she sets up for the rival of her nieces.

DASHWOULD: The young ladies are pretty well in their way too. Lady Bell has a brisk volubility of nothing, that she plays the pretty idiot with; and Lady Jane, a sly piece of formality, ready to go post to Scotland, with the first red coat that asks her the question. We all dine at the widow's today; are you to be with us?

MILLAMOUR: Yes, to meet you. The party will be diverting.

DASHWOULD: Observe old Bygrove. He pronounces with rigour upon the conduct of others, and hopes his own follies lie concealed. His whole struggle is to escape

---

routs, drums, hurricanes: all names for afternoon or evening parties.
'*Seven's the main*': a call in the dice game of hazard.

detection. He hoodwinks himself and thinks he blinds you. Positive and dog-matical in his opinions, yet a dupe to the designs of others, and, flattering himself that a peevish and censorious spirit hides every defect, he gives you the full ridicule of his character.

MILLAMOUR: I have marked him before now.

DASHWOULD: Mark him with the widow. You will see him sighing for his deceased wife and Mrs Bromley's charms at the same time. One eye will weep for the dead and the other ogle the living.

MILLAMOUR: Ha, ha! And then Malvil laying siege to Miss Neville!

DASHWOULD: Miss Neville is the best of them. Mrs Bromley has taken her into her house, as a poor relation, whom she pities, and her pity is no more than the cruel art of tormenting an unhappy dependant upon her generosity.

MILLAMOUR: But she has generosity. She has promised Miss Neville a fortune of five thousand pounds.

DASHWOULD: And so the hook is baited for Malvil. The widow flings out a snare to counteract Sir Harry.

MILLAMOUR: Sir Harry!

DASHWOULD: Yes, he is in love with Miss Neville, and the best of the story is, he is afraid I shall think him ridiculous. If I say the word and promise not to laugh at him, he breaks his mind at once. Miss Neville sees clearly that he admires her, and, of course, will not listen to Malvil. The self-interested designs of that fellow shall be disappointed, and Mrs Bromley will have the mortification of seeing that girl, whom she delights in tormenting, raised to a level with herself.

MILLAMOUR: Admirable! Thou art a whimsical fellow. Come, I attend you. A pleasant group they are altogether. It is as you say,

> Our passions sicken, and our pleasures cloy;
> A fool to laugh at is the height of joy. (*Exeunt.*)

ACT II

SCENE. *A room in* MRS BROMLEY's *house. Enter* MRS BROMLEY *and* MISS NEVILLE.

MRS BROMLEY: Why, to be sure, Neville, there is something in what you say: one is so odd, and I don't know how, in a morning.

MISS NEVILLE: Certainly, madam. And then people of your turn, whose wit over-flows in conversation, are likely to a waste of spirits, and the alteration appears sooner in them.

MRS BROMLEY: So it does. You observe very prettily upon things. Heighho! I am as faded as an old lute-string today.

MISS NEVILLE: No indeed, madam, you look very tolerable, considering.

MRS BROMLEY: (*aside*) Considering! She grows pert, I think. – I am glad you think me not altogether intolerable.

MISS NEVILLE: Ma'am!

MRS BROMLEY: (*aside*) Tolerably! She is Lady Bell's prime agent. – Has Sir Harry given you hopes lately?

MISS NEVILLE: Sir Harry! I really don't understand you, Ma'am.

MRS BROMLEY: Do you think it will be a match? You must be a baronet's lady, indeed. And have you made up your quarrel with Lady Bell?

MISS NEVILLE: The sweetness of her disposition reconciles everything.

MRS BROMLEY: And is Millamour reconciled to Lady Bell?

MISS NEVILLE: There was only a slight mistake, which I explained.

MRS BROMLEY: Oh! You explained? That was prudently done; I am glad to hear this: and do you think he loves her? Tell me. (*Sits down.*) Tell me all. Why? Why do you think he loves her?

MISS NEVILLE: He cannot be insensible to her merit, and the other day he asked me if you were likely to approve of his proposing for Lady Bell.

MRS BROMLEY: And you told him – Well! – What did you tell him?

MISS NEVILLE: That you, no doubt, would be ready to promote the happiness of so amiable a young lady.

MRS BROMLEY: You told him so? (*Rises and walks about.*) And so you are turned match-maker: you busy yourself in my family? – Hey! – Mrs Start-up! You are dizened out, I think. My wardrobe has supplied you.

MISS NEVILLE: Your pardon, ma'am; I had these things in the country, when you first showed so much goodness to me.

MRS BROMLEY: What airs! You know I hate to see creatures give themselves airs! Was not I obliged to provide you with everything?

MISS NEVILLE: You have been very kind. I always acknowledge it.

MRS BROMLEY: Acknowledge it! Does not everybody know it?

MISS NEVILLE: Yes, ma'am, I dare say everybody does know it.

MRS BROMLEY: That's maliciously said. I can spy a sneer upon your false face. You suppose I have made my brags. That's what lurks in your ambiguous meaning. I deserve it. Deliver me from poor relations!

MISS NEVILLE: (*aside*) Now the storm begins! I am sure I have said nothing to offend you. I am helpless, it is true, but your relation, and by that tie a gentlewoman still.

MRS BROMLEY: I made you a gentlewoman. Did not I take you up in the country, where you lived in the parsonage house, you, and your sister, with no other company to converse with than the melancholy tombstones, where you read the high and mighty characters of John Hodge and Deborah his wife? While your father's miserable horse, worn to a shadow with carrying double to the next market town, limped about, with a dull alms-begging eye, in quest of the wretched sustenance, that grew thriftily between the graves? Did I not take you out of that misery?

MISS NEVILLE: (*in a softened tone*) You did, ma'am.

MRS BROMLEY: Did I not bring you home to the great house?

MISS NEVILLE: You did, ma'am. (*Weeps aside.*)

MRS BROMLEY: And I am finely thanked for it! Warm the snake, and it will turn upon you.

MISS NEVILLE: (*aside*) I cannot bear to be insulted thus!

MRS BROMLEY: So! Your spirit is humbled, is it?

MISS NEVILLE: Give me leave to tell you, madam, that when people of superior fortune, whom Providence has enabled to bestow obligations, claim a right, from the favour they confer, to tyrannise over the hopes and fears of a mind in distress, they exercise a cruelty more barbarous than any in the whole history of human malice.

MRS BROMLEY: Is this your gratitude?

MISS NEVILLE: I could be thankful for happiness, if you permitted me to enjoy it, but when I find myself, under colour of protection, made the sport of every sudden whim, I have a spirit, madam, that can distinguish between real benevolence and the pride of riches.

MRS BROMLEY: Oh brave! That is your spirit!

MISS NEVILLE: A spirit, give me leave to say, that would rather, in any obscure corner, submit to drudgery, for a slender pittance, than continue to be an unhappy subject, for cruelty to try its experiments upon. (*Weeps.*)

MRS BROMLEY: I fancy I have been too violent. After all this sour, I must sweeten her a little. Come, dry up your tears. You know I am good-natured in the main. I am only jealous that you don't seem to love me.

MISS NEVILLE: Were that left to my heart, every principle there would attach me to you. But to be dunned for gratitude!

MRS BROMLEY: You are right, the observation is very just. I am in the wrong. – Come, let us be friends. I have a great regard for you Neville. (*Walks aside.*) The creature should visit with me, only she looks so well. – How! Did not I hear Mr Malvil's voice? Yes, it is he; I am visible; I am at home; show him in. Walk in Mr Malvil.

(*Enter* MALVIL.)

MALVIL: To a person of sentiment, like you,madam, a visit is paid with pleasure.

MRS BROMLEY: You are very good to me. Neville, do you step and bring me the letter that lies upon my table. (*Exit* MISS NEVILLE.) I am obliged to go out this morning. (*Smiles at* MALVIL.) She looks mighty well. I have been speaking for you; our scheme will take. Sir Harry will not be able to rival you: she will be your reward for all your services to me.

MALVIL: Your generosity is above all praise, and so I was saying this moment to Mr Bygrove. He is coming to wait on you.

MRS BROMLEY: That's unlucky! I wanted to have some talk with you. Well, have you seen Millamour?

MALVIL: Yes, and I find him apt: I have hopes of succeeding.

MRS BROMLEY: Hush! – Not so loud! – You think me mad, I believe. May I hazard myself with that wild man?

MALVIL: Your virtue will reclaim him. I have a friendship with Millamour, and that is my reason for counteracting the designs of my friend Bygrove. – Mr Bygrove has desired me to speak favourably of him to your ladyship.

MRS BROMLEY: Oh! But he kept his last wife mewed up in the country. I should certainly expire in the country.

MALVIL: Why, I can't say much for country life: you are perfectly right. Rooks and crows about your house; fox-hounds in full cry all the morning; the country squires as noisy at dinner as their own hounds; disputes about the game; commissioners of turnpikes, justices of the peace, and pedigrees of horses! 'Oroonoko, brother to White Surry, got by Brisk Lightning, his dam by Bold Thunder.' – That's the whole of their conversation.

MRS BROMLEY: Deliver me! It would be the death of me! But I don't tell Mr Bygrove: amuse him with hopes.

MALVIL: He is a very worthy man. I am sorry to see some oddities in him; but that is very common in life. Vices always border upon virtues. Dashwould says – but there's no believing his slander – he says Mr Bygrove's sorrow for his dead wife is mere artifice, to weep himself into the good graces of another. But I don't believe it.

MRS BROMLEY: I hear him coming. Do you go and take care of your interest with Neville.

MALVIL: (*going*) I obey your commands.

MRS BROMLEY: I shall make her fortune five thousand. Be sure you speak to Millamour. Go, go; success attend you. (*Exit* MALVIL.)
　　　　　　(*Enter* MR BYGROVE.)

BYGROVE: (*bowing*) Madam!

MRS BROMLEY: This attention to one in my forlorn state is obliging . . .

BYGROVE: It is a favour on your part to receive a lost, dejected, sprightless . . .

MRS BROMLEY: I admire your sensibility, Mr Bygrove. That tender look, which you are forever casting back to a beloved, but irrecoverable object, shows so amiable a sorrow! Oh! There is something exquisite in virtuous affection.
　　　　　　(*Enter* MISS NEVILLE.)

MISS NEVILLE: Is this the letter you want, madam? (*Gives it her.*)

MRS BROMLEY: I thank you, Neville. Yes, there is a luxury in hankering after a valuable person, who has been snatched away. I have found a pleasing indulgence in contemplations of that sort. Have not I, Neville?

MISS NEVILLE: Ma'am?

MRS BROMLEY: Ma'am! Are you deaf? Are you stupid? I was telling Mr Bygrove what a taking I was in, when poor dear Mr Bromley died.

MISS NEVILLE: I was not with you then, ma'am.

MRS BROMLEY: Was not with me! What memories some folks have! – Go, and try if you can recover your memory. Leave the room.

MISS NEVILLE: Ungenerous narrow-minded woman! (*Exit.*)

MRS BROMLEY: Oh! You little know what a profusion of goodness I have lavished on that creature. She returns it all with sullenness, with ill-humour, with aversion. She perfectly remembers the affliction I was in, when I lost the best of men.

BYGROVE: I have had my trials too. Heigho!

MRS BROMLEY: I beg your pardon. I am recalling your afflictions. You should not give way; you should struggle a little. Heaven knows how I have struggled. I have appeared, indeed, with an air, but it was all struggling. (*Looks and smiles.*) I could divert you this morning. Do you know that your son is in love with Lady Jane?

BYGROVE: In love! Has he said anything?

MRS BROMLEY: I don't know as to that, but I can see what is working in his heart. He is above stairs now. But I don't like his choice. Lady Bell is the proper match for him, and her fortune is the best. An estate, you know, must come to her by the family settlement. You should direct his choice.

BYGROVE: This comes of his presuming to think for himself. Has he declared himself?

MRS BROMLEY: I fancy not; but he has hinted something to me about a match in my family.

BYGROVE: (*Looks at her, and smiles.*) Why, a match in your family has diverted me of late – Heigho! – It is the only thing that has entertained me for a long time.

MRS BROMLEY: I have had my fancies too. I should like to talk further, but I am engaged abroad this morning. Can I set you down? Will you trust yourself with me?

BYGROVE: You encourage a smile, madam.

MRS BROMLEY: We shall be the town talk; but let them talk; what need we mind? I will just step and say a word to Neville. – You should not be so solitary.

BYGROVE: So my friends tell me.

MRS BROMLEY: I shall be with you in a moment. (*Returns.*) Do you know that we are very like each other in our tempers? After all, that is the true foundation of lasting friendships. Poor, dear Mr Bromley! (*Going, returns.*) It was similitude of temper brought us together, and if ever I could be prevailed upon again, similitude of temper must do it. Well, you have diverted me this morning. Here comes your son, talk to him now. (*Exit.*)

(*Enter* CAPTAIN BYGROVE.)

BYGROVE: Well, sir, what brings you to this house?

CAPT. BYGROVE: A morning visit, sir, merely to kill half an hour.

BYGROVE: There is nothing I hate so much as hypocrisy. I know your errand; you must pretend to be in love.

CAPT. BYGROVE: I, sir!

BYGROVE: What have you been saying to Lady Jane? I thought I had cautioned you against presuming to think for yourself.

CAPT. BYGROVE: You have been very kind in that way.

BYGROVE: See what comes of your friend Millamour's being left to his own discretion. The ass in the fable, between two bundles of hay, divided in his choice, and still doubting on, till it is too late to resolve, gives but a faint image of him.

CAPT. BYGROVE: And if I, sir, to avoid his irresolution . . .

BYGROVE: You are in the opposite extreme: he thinks too much, and never decides, you never think at all, and so resolve without judgement. Take the advice of your friends before you come here to play the antic tricks of love; to kneel, cringe, fawn, flatter, and make yourself ridiculous. Do you know enough of the world to judge for yourself? Can you tell what they are all doing in the gay sphere of life? The young are all bred up under the veterans of vice and folly. They see their mothers, with autumnal faces, playing the agreeable, and forgetting they are no longer young. The men are advanced beyond all former bounds, and the women press close after them. A club for ladies! Intrepidity is now the female charm: to complete their career, there is nothing left but to build a turf coterie at Newmarket, and ride their own matches over the four-mile course.

CAPT. BYGROVE: An admirable picture, sir! Dashwould could not colour it higher.

BYGROVE: Dashwould! He is all buffoonery! What I say is true, and remember, I tell you, you know nothing of the world. After all, sir, Lady Bell is the person I wish to see you married to. – Go, and pay your addresses to her. I will settle that matter for you. You may then marry the person, to whom you have not degraded yourself, by pining, sighing, love verses, and I know not what.

CAPT BYGROVE: This is all unaccountable to me, sir. If you will but hear me . . .
>   (*Enter* MR MALVIL.)
BYGROVE: No, sir, no; I won't allow you to fetch a single sigh, till I say the word; when I give leave, you may then go and sigh till your heart is ready to break. I'll hear no more; no parleying with me. Leave the house this moment.
CAPT. BYGROVE: I obey. (*Exit.*)
MALVIL: I interrupt you.
BYGROVE: No, no; I am glad to see you. Well, have you had any opportunity with the widow?
MALVIL: I have; she surprises me a little: she has dropped the mask. I did not think she had been so eager to marry. We had some talk about you. You know my heart: I am always true to my friends. I see but one difficulty: she will never agree to live in the country.
BYGROVE: The lover need not dispute that point, whatever the husband may do hereafter.
MALVIL: Very true; and besides, though I am not inclined, with the malicious part of the world, to suspect her virtue, yet this town has temptations. It grieves me to see the ways of this great city; fine women without principle; friends without sincerity; marriages today, divorces tomorrow; whole estates set upon the cast of a die; real knowledge despised; frivolous talents admired; masquerades without wit or humour; new comedies that make you cry, and tragedies that put you to sleep. It grieves me to see all this. You are in the right to prefer good sense and tranquillity in the country.
>   (*Enter* MRS BROMLEY *and* MISS NEVILLE.)
MRS BROMLEY: I beg your pardon, gentlemen. Neville, mind what I say to you: don't let those giddy girls go out in my absence, to walk in the Green Park, or run to hideous painters, under the pretence of seeing odious pictures, that they may have an interview with more odious originals. Keep them at home. I will reward your pains. Allons, Mr Bygrove. (*Exit* BYGROVE.) Come, Mr Malvil.
MALVIL: Had not I better stay, and . . .
MRS BROMLEY: No, no; come now, you may return to her. (*Exit.*)
MALVIL: (*to* MISS NEVILLE) You see that I am torn from you, but I shall return as soon as possible. (*Exit.*)
MISS NEVILLE: Tyrannical woman! Some virtues she has, but they are overshadowed by their opposite qualities. Her love of praise is a gross appetite of flattery. She oppresses with kindness, and her very civilities are sure to be disobliging.
>   (*Enter* TRINKET.)
TRINKET: The young ladies desire your company, ma'am.
MISS NEVILLE: Very well.
TRINKET: Madam La Rouge, the French milliner, is with them.
MISS NEVILLE: (*in a peevish manner*) Well, I'll come directly.
TRINKET: (*aside*) An ill-natured, proud, good-for-nothing puss. Because she has been puffed by my mistress, she must go for to snub me, must she? I'll go my ways downstairs, and ding away at all the rest of the family, so I will. (*Exit.*)
MISS NEVILLE: I am not in spirits for the young ladies. This state of dependence is intolerable. Would Sir Harry were in earnest, but my ill stars will have it otherwise. I must not aspire so high, I have no pretensions.

(*Enter* LADY JANE.)

LADY JANE: Miss Neville, I am very angry with you. What is the matter? Has anything made you uneasy?

MISS NEVILLE: No, I am not remarkable for high spirits, you know.

LADY JANE: Why would not you give us your company? How can you be so cross?
That sister of mine is the veriest madcap!

MISS NEVILLE: Lady Bell is rather lively to be sure.

LADY JANE: But when she once begins, she hazards everything, and talks sometimes
like a very libertine.

MISS NEVILLE: The overflowing of gaiety and good humour.

LADY JANE: I wish she would restrain herself a little. She called me a thousand
prudes, and will have it that nothing runs in my head but a lover.

MISS NEVILLE: I don't know but she may be right – we are apt to deceive ourselves.
We talk of vapours and fidgets and retirements, but it is often artful, sly, insinuating man, that lurks at the bottom.

LADY JANE: Well, I vow you'll make me hate you!

MISS NEVILLE: Has Captain Bygrove made no disturbance in your heart?

LADY JANE: How can you? You are as great a plague as my sister. – As I live and
breathe, the giddy romp is coming! You must take my part.

(*Enter* LADY BELL.)

LADY BELL: Yes, I'm in love, I own it now,
      And Caelia has undone me;
    And yet, I swear, I can't tell how,
      The pleasing plague stole on me.

What would I give to have some miserable swain talk in that style to me? 'Belinda
has undone me.' – Charming!

MISS NEVILLE: A lively imagination is a blessing, and you are happy, Lady Bell.

LADY BELL: I am so, but then I am not talked of. I am losing all my time.

LADY JANE: Why, you bold creature! I hate to hear you talk with so much intrepidity.

LADY BELL: Prudery, my dear sister! Downright prudery! I am not for making
mysteries of what all the world knows.

LADY JANE: And how do I make mysteries, pray?

LADY BELL: Why, you confident thing, I'll prove it against you.

LADY JANE: But what? What? What will you prove?

LADY BELL: That you are ready to jump out of your little wits, for a husband, my
demure, sober sister. Miss Neville, a poet is not more eager for the success of a
new comedy, nor one of his brother poets more desirous to see it fail, than that
girl is to throw herself into the arms of a man.

LADY JANE: All scandal, sister.

LADY BELL: Miss Neville shall be judge.

LADY JANE: Your story is mere invention.

LADY BELL: Was there ever such a wrangler!

LADY JANE: You'll not make good your words.

LADY BELL: (*Pats her hand.*) Hold your tongue, miss, will you?

LADY JANE: Very well, go on.

Yes, I'm in love . . . : William Whitehead, 'A Song', *The Museum*, 10 May 1746.

LADY BELL: Will you have done? Now mind, Miss Neville. She does not want to be married, she says. The other night, my young madam, whose thoughts are always composed and even, went to sleep as soon as we got to bed, and then her busy imagination went to work with all the vivacity of an intriguing chambermaid.

LADY JANE: And how can you tell that, pray?

LADY BELL: Out of your own mouth you shall be judged. Miss Neville, she talked in her sleep, like a beauty in a side-box, and then fell a singing,

> No, no, he is true, and I believe;
> He look'd, he sigh'd, he can't deceive;
> No, no, I have conquer'd; he is mine;
> My heart is touch'd, and I resign.

LADY JANE: Oh, you scurrilous creature!

MISS NEVILLE: Fairly caught, Lady Jane.

LADY JANE: All odious slander! You judge of me by yourself.

LADY BELL: I do so. I mean to be married, and am frank enough to own it. But you may let 'concealment feed on your damask cheek'. My damask cheek, I hope, was made for other purposes.

LADY JANE: Gracious – there is no bearing this! What a mad girl you are!

LADY BELL: Not in the least; a natural character. One would not, to be sure, tell a hideous man that one loves him, but, when one has encouraged him by degrees, and drawn him on, like a new glove, and perhaps done him a mischief in the doing it, why then one would draw him off again, and maybe ask a pretty fellow to help a body; and then the wretch looks so piteous and kneels at your feet! – Then rises in a jealous fit – 'I take my lasting farewell! never to return – no, never! What! to her? who encouraged me? – encouraged him? who primised? – broke her promise? The treacherous, faithless, dear deluding' – Then returns in an instant, hands dangling – eyes imploring – tongue faltering – 'Lady Bell, – Lady Bell, – when you know that I adore you!' And I burst out into a fit of laughter in his face. Oh, that's my joy, my triumph, my supreme delight!

LADY JANE: And is there not a kind of cruelty in all this?

LADY BELL: Oh, your very humble servant, my sweet Lady Graveairs! Cruelty! The difference between you and me, sister, is this: you deny your love to your female friends, and own it to the man; now I deny it to him, but among ourselves, I fairly own that Miss Neville is not more impatient to be married to Sir Harry, than I to . . .

MISS NEVILLE: Who, I? Spare me, I beg you! – Why Sir Harry?

LADY JANE: Now, now, your turn is come. Never spare her, sister.
  (*Enter* TRINKET.)

TRINKET: Madam La Rouge desires to know if you have any commands.

LADY JANE: She has the sweetest point eyes ever beheld. I must go and cheapen it.

MISS NEVILLE: No, let me speak to her. I'll beat down the price. (*Exit with* TRINKET.)

LADY JANE: And pray, sister, are you really in love?

LADY BELL: Over head and ears.

LADY JANE: With whom?

---

the sweetest point: decorative point lace.

LADY BELL: Not with Captain Bygrove. How alarmed you are! With Millamour, sister.

LADY JANE: Fix that roving temper, if you can; he will be on his knees to you, and the first pair of black eyes that enters the room will be through his heart.

LADY BELL: As to that, I give myself very little trouble; but if I could once catch him paying his adoration to me, my aunt Bromley does not raise and sink poor Miss Neville's spirits with such exquisite skill in the art of tormenting, as I should his. I should use him as the men do their punch: a little more sweet, a little more sour, a little more spirit, more acid again, then perhaps say it's good for nothing, and then perhaps . . .

LADY JANE: What?

LADY BELL: Sip it up at last, as you would do at first. You wicked girl! How could you ask me such a question? Law! What am I about? I have a thousand things to do.

(*Enter* MISS NEVILLE *and* MADAM LA ROUGE.)

LA ROUGE: Ah! My lady! Always so gay! English climate no effect upon you. De maniers de Paris for all de vorl. En vérité, vous est charmante.

LADY BELL: Oh, Madam la Rouge, you say such polite things! But you rob me of all my money. My sister is rich, you had better deal with her. Sister, you'll be married before me. (*Sings.*) 'Yes, I'll have a husband, ay marry.' (*Exit.*)

LADY JANE: Was ever anything so crazy!

LA ROUGE: It is all vivacity! And, my lady, you have ver great wit en partage; vous avez les graces; you have de grace; but you no deal vid me.

LADY JANE: I shall call at your house in Pall Mall. Miss Neville, you joined against me! I am very angry with you. (*Exit.*)

LA ROUGE: (*following her*) Let me have l'honneur to say two, tree words. (*returning*) Mademoiselle, I tell you, persuade my lady to have de lace, and you come to my house, me give you ver pretty present.

MISS NEVILLE: Oh, you have a national talent for applying a little bribery.

LA ROUGE: Diantre; 'tis false delicatesse. You know de manières of de vorl. Ah! Monsieur Malvil!

(*Enter* MALVIL.)

MALVIL: Madam la Rouge, I did not expect this pleasure.

LA ROUGE: It is always pleasure to see mes amis – to see my friends, and I glad to see you here vid de lady. You have ver good choice; and I can tell you, make de despatch – you have rival.

MALVIL: Rival!

LA ROUGE: You not know? Sir Harry have taste as well as you. Mademoiselle, you are ver great favourite.

MISS NEVILLE: A favourite! Keep your vivacity for some other subject; don't make me the town talk.

LA ROUGE: It is ver true. He come to my house in Pall Mall, and say ver fine ting of Mademoiselle Neville, and Monsieur Dashwould praise you ver much.

MALVIL: (*aside*) Ay, his malice is at work.

LA ROUGE: Monsieur, you lose all your time. (*Goes to him and speaks low.*) You wait de fortune from Madam Bromley; Sir Harry vil take her vidout any money at all. Vat you slow for?

MALVIL: Are the apartments kept ready at your house?

LA ROUGE: De apartment it is ready. You take it two, tree week ago, and pay de rent for noting. – I leave you vid de lady, and I go mind mes affairs. Bon voyage. (*Exit.*)

MALVIL: I have disengaged myself, to have the honour of attending you.

MISS NEVILLE: Your attention is thrown away. Did I not hear Mr Millamour's voice?

MALVIL: Yes, he came with me. He is gone into the next room to pay his compliments to Lady Jane. I am sorry to see him forever distracted, always resolving, and yet every day beginning the world over again. You look chagrined, what has disturbed you?

MISS NEVILLE: The old story, Mrs Bromley's eternal whims.

MALVIL: She is not spoken of as I could wish. Good-natured and arrogant, generous and cruel, obliging and oppressive at the same time.

MISS NEVILLE: There cannot surely be a more distressful situation than to remain under daily obligations, and yet not be able to esteem your benefactress.

MALVIL: Your delicacy charms me – It has fixed me yours. I long for nothing so much as to see you out of her power. They have a strange report about town – people will be talking – the whisper goes that Mr Bygrove, amidst all his grief, is in a hurry for another wife. Mrs Bromley, they say, encourages him, and, at the same time, has a design upon my friend Millamour.

MISS NEVILLE: The world is not always wrong.

MALVIL: Malice will be busy and does not spare the young ladies.

MISS NEVILLE: If anything is said to their disadvantage, believe me, they do not deserve it.

MALVIL: I dare say not; I don't think they are too forward. I am sorry to see, in one of the papers today, a character of Sir Harry not at all favourable. His little follies one does not mind. He may run after Dashwould, that only makes him ridiculous, but it grieves me to hear that perfidy stains his character, and, as I am told, the worst of perfidy. To be the ruin of beauty and innocence is his ruling passion.

MISS NEVILLE: This is very odd. Somebody has been at the trouble of sending me an anonymous letter to that very effect: and why to me? I am not able to decipher.

MALVIL: I don't like anonymous letters. In general they aim at mischief – but this, perhaps, is meant as a caution to you. It must be a friend that sent it.

MISS NEVILLE: No, I can guess the quiver from whence that arrow comes.

MALVIL: Dashwould, perhaps?

MISS NEVILLE: I don't say that.

MALVIL: Nor I, I never charge anybody; but, upon recollection, the letter in the newspaper is imputed to him. Mrs Bromley, I know, has no opinion of Sir Harry: his designs with regard to you she does not think honourable. My heart interests me for you. You know I am all heart. The plan which Mrs Bromley has proposed – Hark! I think I hear Millamour coming – I'll follow you upstairs.

MISS NEVILLE: Oh, sir, you have frightened me out of my wits! (*Exit.*)

MALVIL: She loves Sir Harry, I see, and yet she shan't slip through my hands. I can set on Mrs Bromley to lead her a weary life, and if I can prevail upon Millamour to drop Lady Bell and marry the widow, my business is done. When Miss Neville is heartily tormented by Mrs Bromley, affliction softens the mind and I may then decoy her away and stand upon terms with the family. But Dashwould's wit will

fly about. No matter, he is a sad scoundrel, and does not mind how he murders
reputations. So, here comes Millamour! I must get clear of him, and talk further
with Miss Neville.
>   (*Enter* MILLAMOUR.)

MILLAMOUR: From this moment I blot all other women from my memory. Malvil
>   wish me joy – the perplexity of choice is now at an end.

MALVIL: Why, what has happened?

MILLAMOUR: Lovely Lady Jane! 'And yield her charms of mind with sweet delay.' –
>   I can't stay to tell you now.

MALVIL: Nor will I stay to interrupt your raptures. You know I wish you success.
>   (*Exit.*)

MILLAMOUR: With what a lovely attention she received me! She has touched my
>   heart, and so I'll go and tell my father directly.
>   (*Enter* LADY BELL, *reading.*)

LADY BELL: 'Who yields too soon, must her lover lose,
>   Would you restrain him long? Then long refuse.'

MILLAMOUR: (*Looks at her and smiles.*) There is something commanding in that air
>   of vivacity.

LADY BELL: (*Reads.*) 'Oft at your door let him for entrance wait,
>   There let him . . .'
>   How! Millamour here! How could you surprise me so? You horrid thing! How
>   long have you been here?

MILLAMOUR: Been, madam? I have been – I have been in the next room, paying my
>   respects to your sister.

LADY BELL: And never inquired for poor Lady Bell?

MILLAMOUR: Your ladyship wrongs me. You do injustice to your own charms: they
>   can never be forgot.

LADY BELL: I see how it is. The other day you was listed in my service, and now a
>   deserter to my sister! You are right, you would have been upon hard duty with
>   me.

MILLAMOUR: Any duty but a forlorn hope would be . . .

LADY BELL: Hope! Why sure you would not have had the intolerable assurance to
>   entertain the smallest degree of hope? My sister, I suppose, has given you some
>   hope? Ay, that's her way, she moves by settled rules and shines with equal light.
>   – Now I – I am a mere comet, I blaze of a sudden –dazzle for a while, then wheel
>   away, and am thought of no more.

MILLAMOUR: (*aside*) That gaiety of hers is charming! – The impression your ladyship
>   makes . . .

LADY BELL: Words, mere words. No, I am a strange piece of wild nature, never the
>   same for two minutes together. Now my sister, she is a Prussian blue, holds
>   her colour, and is always the same. I – I am a changeable silk, I shift about and
>   display my wit, and my folly, so curiously blended, that nobody can tell where one
>   begins or the other ends. I am not worth your notice. (*Walks and hums a tune.*)

'And yield her charms . . . ': Edward Young, *Love of Fame*, 1728.
'Oft at your door . . . ': Congreve, *Ovid's Ars Amoris*, III.

MILLAMOUR: (*looking at her*) She has described herself admirable; without variety a woman is a downright piece of insipidity.

LADY BELL: Yes, I have my whims – never the same for two minutes together. Now I love to give a scope to folly, and the men say, 'Curse catch her, she pleases more when in the wrong, than other women when they are in the right.' Then good sense is the word, and the next moment I can't bear the fatigue of thinking – why won't somebody write a comedy to divert me? Then all spirit, and I long to lead up the ball. (*Sings and moves a minuet.*)

> Ladies, like variegated tulips show,
> 'Tis to their weakness all their charms they owe.

MILLAMOUR: (*aside*) Lady Jane is mere mediocrity compared to her!

LADY BELL: Lord, how I run on! Well, au revoir. (*going*)

MILLAMOUR: A moment longer – You must not leave me. You possess my heart, possess it without a rival.

LADY BELL: Hey! What's the matter now?

MILLAMOUR: Do not trifle with a passion sincere as mine. I adore you, my Lady Bell – adore your matchless charms; thus on my knees adore . . .

LADY BELL: Stay, stay; let me see what the poet says. (*Reads quickly.*)

> 'Oft at your door, let him for entrance wait,
> There let him kneel, and threaten, and entreat.'

There, stay there, don't offer to stir. Now put up both your hands and – pray, pray have compassion, Lady Bell. (*Exit laughing.*)

MILLAMOUR: She flies, disdainful, from her lover's view,
> Yet looks and bids him, as she flies, pursue. (*Exit.*)

ACT III

SCENE. *An apartment at* MRS BROMLEY's. *Enter* LADY JANE *and* CAPTAIN BYGROVE.

LADY JANE: And laid his commands upon you to address my sister?

CAPT. BYGROVE: Most peremptorily.

LADY JANE: You have obeyed him, I hope?

CAPT. BYGROVE: You don't hope any such thing, I flatter myself you don't. You know your power too well; you know that I am devoted to you, and that my happiness depends upon the promise you have made me.

LADY JANE: There, that is always the way with you men: our smiles are sure marks of approbation, and every civil thing we say is construed into a promise.

CAPT. BYGROVE: And have not you promised?

LADY JANE: (*Looks at him and smiles.*) Need I answer that question? How easily frightened you are! But you have some reason to be alarmed, Millamour has been on his knees to me, breathing such raptures . . .

CAPT. BYGROVE: Ay! Who set him on? – What can be at the bottom of this? And have you listened to him? Here comes Dashwould; he, perhaps, can explain.

LADY JANE: He will only laugh at us, and so I'll make my escape. (*going*)

Ladies, like variegated . . . : cf. Pope, *Moral Essays*, II, 41–2.

CAPT. BYGROVE: (*Takes her hand.*) Not to hear Millamour again, I hope.

LADY JANE: Well, well, to purchase my liberty, you need not fear. I have received his vows, delivered with such ardour – how terrified you look – I have listened to him, to alarm my sister with an idea of Millamour's growing passion for me. If her jealousy is once touched, it may fix her resolution; at present, she is as volatile as Millamour himself.

(*Enter* DASHWOULD.)

DASHWOULD: As volatile as Millamour! What can that be? I never knew anything that would bear a comparison.

LADY JANE: What think you of my sister?

DASHWOULD: Lady Bell has her whims. I left her above stairs in close conference with Millamour. He has deserted your ladyship already. Mrs Bromley will be next, I hope. Your father, Captain, would grieve more for that, than for his deceased wife.

LADY JANE: And then Miss Neville's turn may come.

DASHWOULD: Oh, no. To sport with her would be inhumanity, but a brisk widow is fair game.

CAPT. BYGROVE: Yes, and it may help to cure my father of his folly.

LADY JANE: It would be sport, but I despair of it. You know, Mr Dashwould, you allow that Millamour has understanding.

DASHWOULD: But he does not act from his understanding. Fits and starts of passion govern him. If, in any one pursuit of real use, he had half the alacrity of mind, with which he runs from one folly to another, he would be a man for the ladies to pull caps for. But he lives forever in inconsistencies. One action of his life is the sure forerunner of the contrary. First, Malvil is his favourite – then arm in arm with me. Can any two things be more opposite? It is the same among the ladies; they all have him by turns, and the whim of one moment is sure to find a ridiculous antithesis in the next.

LADY JANE: He sat for that picture, I'll swear. Well, there's a gentleman wants your advice, so I'll leave you together. (*Exit.*)

CAPT. BYGROVE: My dear Dashwould, you must assist me!

DASHWOULD: What distresses you?

CAPT. BYGROVE: My evil genius is at work. You know what my father has resolved on? Lady Bell is his favourite.

DASHWOULD: I know all that business: a counterplot of the widow's fertile brain, to disappoint Lady Bell and wreak her malice on Millamour.

CAPT. BYGROVE: But the malice falls on me only. – Why will not Millamour know his own mind? Lady Bell loves him, I know she does. – I am thwarted in the tenderest point. What must be done?

DASHWOULD: Do as they would have you – you ensure success. Millamour's jealousy takes fire upon the first alarm, and while the passion holds, he will have vigour enough to act decisively.

CAPT. BYGROVE: May I hazard the experiment?

DASHWOULD: It's a sure card, take my advice.

(*Enter* MISS NEVILLE.)

MISS NEVILLE: Mrs Bromley's coach has just stopped at the door. Had not you better step upstairs, gentlemen?

(*Enter* SIR HARRY LIZARD.)

SIR HARRY: Dashwould, you are absent too long. They are all as dull as a funeral above stairs.

DASHWOULD: (*aside to* CAPTAIN BYGROVE) How the baronet follows Miss Neville from room to room! Come, Captain, I'll play a game of picquet with you before dinner. Allons! (*Exit with* CAPTAIN BYGROVE.)

SIR HARRY: If I might have the liberty, ma'am, to . . .

MISS NEVILLE: Another time, if you please, Sir Harry. Mrs Bromley is coming. I hear her voice.

SIR HARRY: And you promise me the hearing?

MISS NEVILLE: You are entitled to me, sir. I beg you'll leave me now.

SIR HARRY: I obey your commands. I am gone. You'll remember? (*Exit.*)

MISS NEVILLE: Here she comes, and, I think, in good humour.
(*Enter* MRS BROMLEY.)

MRS BROMLEY: Oh, I am heartily tired! I have been paying visits to people, who have never been let into my house, and who, I hope, will never be at home for me. I hate them all, but out of civility, we must keep up an acquaintance. Where are the girls? Has nobody been here?

MISS NEVILLE: Mr Millamour, ma'am, and the rest of the gentlemen that dine here. They are all above stairs.

MRS BROMLEY: Stupidity! Did not I give orders – How long has Millamour been here?

MISS NEVILLE: About an hour.

MRS BROMLEY: With Lady Bell, I suppose? Thou base ingratitude! And Sir Harry is here too, I reckon? Does your match go on? You shall go back to the country, I promise you. You'll be the ruin of those girls. They shall have no visitors when my back is turned. I'll give orders to all the servants this very moment. (*going*)
(*Enter* SIR JOHN MILLAMOUR.)

SIR JOHN: To see Mrs Bromley looking so well . . .

MRS BROMLEY: You are very polite, sir. Business calls me now, Sir John. I beg your pardon. (*Exit.*)

SIR JOHN: Has my son been here today?

MISS NEVILLE: He is above stairs, with Lady Bell, sir.

MRS BROMLEY: (*within*) Miss Neville! Neville, I say!

MISS NEVILLE: You'll excuse me, Sir John. What can she want? (*Exit.*)

SIR JOHN: This visit portends some good, I hope. I shall be happy if he has declared himself. I'll step and see what he is about. (*going*)
(*Enter* MILLAMOUR)

MILLAMOUR: Exquisite! Lovely angel!

SIR JOHN: Well! – How! – What!

MILLAMOUR: I beg your pardon, sir, I am not at leisure. I am in the third region, and can't descend to the language of the nether world.

SIR JOHN: Then you are in love, George?

MILLAMOUR: She is a sister of the graces, and surpasses the other three. I am fixed, unalterably fixed, and am going about the marriage articles directly.

SIR JOHN: They are at my lawyer's, ready engrossed, and only wait for the lady's name, to fill up the blanks.

MILLAMOUR: I know it, sir. I must step for them. I have it through my heart; I feel it here. I am your humble servant, sir. (*going*)

SIR JOHN: No, no; do you stay here. I'll step for Mr Copyhold. The writings shall be here in ten minutes. (*Exit.*)

MILLAMOUR: The sooner the better, sir.

Let those love now, who never loved before;

Let those who always loved, now love the more!

(*Sings.*) Lol, tol, lol.

(*Enter* MR MALVIL.)

MALVIL: Bravo! You seem in prodigious spirits!

MILLAMOUR: I am so. I am happy in myself, and happy in my friends, and happy in every circumstance, and in tip-top spirits, and my dear Malvil, yours down to the ground. Congratulate my felicity, I am ready to run wild with joy!

MALVIL: Methinks I sympathise with you. When our friends are happy, the sensation is well called a fellow feeling.

MILLAMOUR: Malvil, I thank you; your turn of mind is formed for lasting friendships. With Dashwould it is all dissipation and giddy mirth, the mere bubble of pleasure. To you I may talk seriously. The topic of the day is enough for Dashwould. I can now tell you that I shall be happy for life. But for Dashwould, I would have been settled long ago. That fellow has led me into a thousand errors.

MALVIL: He has his admirers, and not without reason. He thinks me his enemy, but he is mistaken. I never harbour resentment.

MILLAMOUR: You are growing grave, and I am a flight above common sense at present.

MALVIL: Dashwould, notwithstanding all his faults, does hit the mark sometimes. I don't usually laugh at his pleasantry; I don't like to encourage him too much, but it must be owned, he is often right. Behind his back, I cannot help being diverted by him. He has a quick insight into characters.

MILLAMOUR: No want of penetration there.

MALVIL: No, no; he says, and perhaps rightly, your lively ladies often want common prudence, and, giddy in the pursuit of pleasure, they are frequently miserable in the end.

MILLAMOUR: But Lady Bell's good sense, that refinement of understanding . . .

MALVIL: There are false refinements, the shadow for the substance. Who is it that observes, we all discover early symptoms of the disease, by which our minds and bodies go to ruin?

MILLAMOUR: Po! With Lady Bell there can be no risk.

MALVIL: I don't know whether Dashwould is good authority. – You know him best. He says . . .

MILLAMOUR: Well?

MALVIL: He is a shrewd observer.

MILLAMOUR: Nobody more so.

MALVIL: If he has a regard for anybody, it is for you. You are the only man I never heard him speak ill of. A match with Lady Bell is not to his mind. He talked seriously on the subject. Has not he told you?

Let those love . . . : T. Parnell, *The Vigil of Venus.*

MILLAMOUR: Not a syllable.

MALVIL: I wonder at that. Lady Bell, he says, showed herself early. Impatient of advice, attentive to nothing but her beauty! Whole days at her looking glass – I repeat his very words – he seemed to speak out of downright regard for you – at her toilette every feature had its instructions how to look; but no instruction for the mind. And then, says he, that terrible love of gaming!

MILLAMOUR: Gaming!

MALVIL: Don't you know it? I can't say I ever saw it myself. Time will determine her character.

MILLAMOUR: If she loves gaming, it is pretty well determined already.

MALVIL: Perhaps not. I still hope for the best.

MILLAMOUR: Why, yes. A man of sense may form her mind, and then the gentler affections may take their turn.

MALVIL: The very thing I said. But our pleasant friend had an answer ready – Gentle affections! says he, don't you see that it is with people that once love play, as with people addicted to strong cordials? They never return to cooler liquors.

MILLAMOUR: There is some truth in that. I am forever obliged to you. It is ingenuous, it is friendly of you to convey the hint.

MALVIL: Don't build too much upon it. I have told you my author, and you know his way. He may deny it all.

MILLAMOUR: Shall I talk to him?

MALVIL: I don't know what to say to that. In his vein of pleasantry he may give it another turn.

MILLAMOUR: He may so. I am glad to know all this. But my Lady Jane, there's a model for her sex to imitate.

MALVIL: Have you watched her well? People should appear what they really are. Let a precipice look like a precipice. When covered over with flowers it only serves to deceive the unwary. Mrs Bromley has been very communicative about Lady Jane.

MILLAMOUR: You alarm me. My dear friend, explain.

MALVIL: To do Lady Bell justice, she is above disguise. And though she has her faults, I have seen her please by those very faults.

MILLAMOUR: (*smiling*) And so have I. Her very blemishes are beauty spots.

MALVIL: No frankness about the youngest girl. It is friendship for you that makes me speak. Her character is all forced, studied, put on with her rouge.

MILLAMOUR: Does she paint?

MALVIL: A little; the prudent touch. I am sorry for her. When she is settled in the world, many qualities, which now lie concealed, will break out into the open day-light.

MILLAMOUR: What a masked battery there will be to play off upon a husband!

MALVIL: Their aunt told me all in confidence. You may judge how painful it is to her. I have known the family for some time. I can't but be sorry for the young ladies.

MILLAMOUR: And since this is the case, I don't care how little I know of them, or their family.

MALVIL: No occasion to quarrel with the family. Great merit about Mrs Bromley. She made an admirable wife, and that at an early period. She was but seventeen when she married.

MILLAMOUR: No more?

MALVIL: Not an hour. She is not thirty. An estate in her own right, and the command of half a borough. No opposition there: the old houses have the vote. A man may get a seat without trouble. Does not Sir John want to see you in parliament?

MILLAMOUR: It would give him pleasure.

MALVIL: Well, you will judge for yourself. Were I you, I should know what course to take. Here she comes! A good fine woman! A man may there sit down to his happiness at once.

(*Enter* MRS BROMLEY.)

MRS BROMLEY: (*Curtsies.*) Mr Millamour, Mr Malvil, what have you done with Mr Bygrove?

MALVIL: I parted with him where you set us down. (*Speaks to her aside.*) I have talked to Millamour, and I think it will do.

MRS BROMLEY: (*aside to* MALVIL) Go you upstairs.

MALVIL: How charmingly you look! Like Lady Bell's eldest sister!

MRS BROMLEY: Po! You are laughing at me.

MALVIL: Not I truly: I appeal to Millamour. I'll take the liberty to join the company above. (*aside to* MILLAMOUR) She is the best of the family. (*Exit.*)

MRS BROMLEY: A valuable man Malvil is! He has a great esteem for you, sir. His sincerity is unequalled. You seem thoughtful, Mr Millamour.

MILLAMOUR: Thoughtful, ma'am! – There are certain subjects that – (*aside*) What Malvil says is true – a man may marry her and sit down to his happiness at once.

MRS BROMLEY: Sir John has been saying a great deal to me about you.

MILLAMOUR: Has he, ma'am? There is a circumstance, which he is as yet a stranger to – a circumstance, which to communicate will perhaps – It is what I have long wished, and . . .

MRS BROMLEY: (*aside*) Faltering! Hesitating! – I interrupt you.

MILLAMOUR: There is a circumstance, ma'am – the affair is – my father for a long time – Sir John for a long time – Sir John has wished . . .

MRS BROMLEY: To see you married?

MILLAMOUR: To see me married, ma'am – and – he has – he has wished it much. – And a settlement, by way of jointure – long ready for the lady's name – that is – any lady, who shall honour me with her affection – and . . .

MRS BROMLEY: No lady can be insensible of your pretensions.

MILLAMOUR: You are very good, ma'am. And, after long observation, and a lasting passion grafted on it, which, though silent hitherto, yet working secretly – when disclosed at length – may, to the person in the world – who, already formed by experience, may in every respect – and if, without presuming too far . . .

MRS BROMLEY: (*aside*) What a delicate confusion he is in!

MILLAMOUR: And if this paper, ma'am . . .

MRS BROMLEY: (*taking the paper*) When given by you, sir . . . (*Enter* BYGROVE.) Perverse and cruel! (*She walks aside.*)

BYGROVE: You both look grave. Nothing amiss, I hope.

MRS BROMLEY: Everything is as it should be, sir.

---

command of half a borough: in the unreformed Houses of Parliament many seats were returned by 'pocket boroughs', in which voting was restricted to a few specific households. The infamous Old Sarum had an electorate of seven burgages.

MILLAMOUR: (*aside*) Not if he knew all.

BYGROVE: Sir John has been complaining . . .

MRS BROMLEY: Pass that by. Advise your own son. Had you not better step upstairs? Mr Millamour will do what is right. (*smiling at him*) You may leave all to him. Trust to his judgement.

(*Enter* SIR HARRY LIZARD.)

SIR HARRY: Millamour, I have such a story for you: Malvil and Dashwould have been quarrelling about you, and . . .

BYGROVE: Po! And here they come. I knew the substance could not be far off, when the shadow projected before it.

(*Enter* LADY BELL, DASHWOULD *and* MALVIL.)

LADY BELL: Mr Dashwould, do you think I'll bear this? What liberty will you take next? You think, because I laugh, that I am not offended. – Aunt, I receive a letter, and he has attempted to snatch it from me.

DASHWOULD: Why, it brings a little cargo of ridicule from the country, and my friend Malvil sees no joke in it.

MALVIL: When my friend's name is brought in question, sir . . .

LADY BELL: It is diverting, notwithstanding. – Aunt, what do you think? My cousin, Cynthia, you know, was married to Sir George Squanderstock. Her mother opposed it, and broke off the match, and now it's come out that she was all the time the clandestine rival of her own daughter!

MILLAMOUR: (*aside*) Not inapplicable to the present business!

MRS BROMLEY: Go, you giddy girl, no such thing!

SIR HARRY: (*Goes up to* BYGROVE.) And Dashwould has been saying . . .

BYGROVE: Po! Repeat none of his sayings to me

LADY BELL: Did you say anything, Mr Dashwould? What was it?

DASHWOULD: Oh! Nothing. Sir George Squanderstock is my very good friend.

MALVIL: And for that reason, you might spare him. No man is without his faults.

DASHWOULD: Ay, allow him his faults out of tenderness.

BYGROVE: Sir George is a valuable man, sir, and represents his county to great advantage.

DASHWOULD: He does so; takes a world of pains; nothing can escape him. Manilla ransom not paid; there must be a motion about the matter; he knots his handkerchief to remember it. – Scarcity of corn! Another knot – triennial parliaments – (*Knots.*) Juries, judges of law as well as fact. (*Knots.*) National debt. (*Knots.*) Bail in criminal cases. (*Knots.*) And so on he goes, till his handkerchief is twisted into questions of state, the liberties and fortunes of all posterity dangling like a bede roll, he puts it in his pocket, drives to the gaming table, and the next morning his handkerchief goes to the wash, and his country and the minority are both left in the suds.

Sir George Squanderstock: M.C. White in an unpublished thesis, *Arthur Murphy: his Life and Works* (University of Washington, 1936, p. 382) suggests Sir George was a satirical portrait of Charles James Fox, who was twenty-eight in 1777, and better known as a gamester than a potential statesman.

Manilla ransom: when the Philippines were captured from the Spanish in 1762, the citizens of Manilla promised a cash ransom to spare the city from being sacked. The other political issues were of perennial concern to the radical Whigs, at this time a minority in parliament.

LADY BELL: (*laughing*) What a description!

SIR HARRY: (*laughing*) Hey! Lively Lady Bell!

MILLAMOUR: Ho, ho! I thank you, Dashwould.

MRS BROMLEY: (*aside to* MILLAMOUR) How can you encourage him? Let us leave them to themselves.

MALVIL: You see, Mr Bygrove . . .

BYGROVE: Ay! Thus he gets a story to graft malice upon, and then he sets the table in a roar at the next tavern.

SIR HARRY: Never be out of humour with Dashwould, Mr Bygrove. He keeps me alive; he has been exhibiting pictures of this sort all the morning, as we rambled about the town.

DASHWOULD: Oh, no! No pictures. I have shown him real life.

SIR HARRY: Very true, Dashwould: and now mind him, he will touch them off to the life for you.

MRS BROMLEY: (*aside*) Millamour so close with Lady Bell! The forward importunity of that girl. (*She goes to* MILLAMOUR.)

DASHWOULD: There is positively no such thing as going about this town without seeing enough to split your sides with laughing. We called upon my friend Sir Volatile Vainlove. He, you know, shines in all polite assemblies, and is, if you believe himself, of the first character for intrigue. We found him drinking valerian tea for breakfast, and putting on false calves.

SIR HARRY: And the confusion he was in, when we entered the room!

DASHWOULD: In the next room we found Jack Spinbrain, a celebrated poet, with a kept mistress at his elbow, writing lampoons for the newspapers; one moment murdering the reputation of his neighbours, and the next a suicide of his own. We saw a young heir, not yet of age, granting annuity bonds, and five Jews and three Christians, duped by their avarice to lend money upon them. A lawyer . . .

SIR HARRY: Hear, hear. It is all true. I was with him.

DASHWOULD: A lawyer taking notes upon Shakespeare, a deaf nabob ravished with music, and a blind one buying pictures. Men without talents rising to preferment, and real genius going to gaol. An officer in a marching regiment with a black eye, and a French hairdresser wounded in the sword arm.

SIR HARRY: Oh, ho, ho! By this light, I can vouch for every word!

BYGROVE: Go on, Sir Harry; set up for a wit, like the monkey in the fable that must handle a razor, because he sees his master do it. You know the consequences.

SIR HARRY: Well now, that is too severe. Dashwould, defend me from his wit. You know I swallow all your good things.

DASHWOULD: You have a good digestion, Sir Harry, for they never rise again.

MALVIL: Friend or foe, it is all alike.

LADY BELL: (*coming forward*) And where is the mighty harm? I like pulling to pieces, of all things.

MILLAMOUR: (*following* LADY BELL) To be sure, it is the life of conversation. Does your ladyship know Sir George Squanderstock's sister?

---

nabob: nouveau riche, having made a fortune in India.
Sir George Squanderstock's sister: Mrs Cathrine Macaulay, a notorious republican, see James Boaden, *Memoires of Sarah Siddons* (1827), vol. I, p. 102.

LADY BELL: I have seen her.

MILLAMOUR: She is a politician in petticoats, a fierce republican; she talks of the dagger of Brutus, while she settles a pin in her tucker, and says more about ship-money than pin-money.

BYGROVE: And now you must turn buffoon?

DASHWOULD: I know the lady. She scolds the loyalists, gossips against the Act of Settlement, and has the fidgets for Magna Carta.

MILLAMOUR: She encourages a wrinkle against bribery, flirts her fan at the ministry, and bites her lips at taxes and at standing arms.

MALVIL: Mr Bygrove, will you bear all this?

(*Enter* MISS NEVILLE, *and whispers to* MRS BROMLEY.)

MRS BROMLEY: Very well, Neville, I'll come presently. (*Exit* MISS NEVILLE.)

MALVIL: (*looking at* MISS NEVILLE) I shall stay no longer. Mr Bygrove, will you walk? (*Exit.*)

BYGROVE: No, sir, I shall not leave the enemy in this room behind me. A bad translator of an ancient poet is not so sure to deface his original, as his licentious strain to disparage every character.

DASHWOULD: Sir Harry, he will neither give nor take a joke.

SIR HARRY: No, I told you so.

BYGROVE: Let me tell you, once for all, sir . . .

DASHWOULD: I wish you would.

BYGROVE: Why interrupt? Do you know what I was going to say?

DASHWOULD: No. Do you?

MILLAMOUR: I'll leave them all to themselves. (*He steals out.*)

BYGROVE: Let me tell you, sir, that your wit will one day cost you dear.

MRS BROMLEY: (*aside*) Millamour gone! (*Exit.*)

BYGROVE: And what does all this mighty wit amount to? The wit in vogue exposes one man, makes another expose himself, gets into the secrets of an intimate acquaintance and publishes the story to the world, belies a friend, puts an anecdote, a letter, an epigram into the newspaper, and that is the whole amount of modern wit.

DASHWOULD: A strain of morose invective is more diverting, to be sure.

BYGROVE: (*looking about for* MRS BROMLEY) Well, sir, we'll adjourn the debate. You may go on, misrepresent everything, if there is nothing ridiculous, invent a story, and when you have done it, it is but a cheap and frivolous talent. Has a lady a good natural bloom? Her paint must be an expensive article. Does she look grave? She will sin the deeper. Is she gay and affable? Her true character will come out at the Commons. That is the whole of your art, and I leave you to the practice of it. (*going*)

DASHWOULD: Satirical Bygrove! Now the widow has him in tow.

BYGROVE: (*turning back*) Could not you stay till my back was fairly turned? (*Exit.*)

DASHWOULD: What a look was there!

LADY BELL: At what a rate you run on! You keep the field against them all.

DASHWOULD: Sir Harry, step up, and watch him with the widow.

SIR HARRY: I will. Don't stay too long.

Commons: Doctor's Commons, that is, in a divorce case.

DASHWOULD: I'll follow you, and hark, make your party good with Miss Neville.

SIR HARRY: You see, Lady Bell, a fling at everybody! (*Exit.*)

DASHWOULD: The baronet does not want parts. That is to say, he has very good materials to play the fool with. I shall get him to marry Miss Neville.

LADY BELL: Bring that about, and you will for once do a serious action, for which everybody will honour you.

DASHWOULD: In the mean time, do you watch your aunt Bromley: she is your rival.

LADY BELL: Rival! That would be charming.

DASHWOULD: It is even so. Now Millamour's understanding is good, but his passion is quick. If you play your cards right . . .

LADY BELL: Are you going to teach me how to manage a man?

DASHWOULD: Coquetry will never succeed with him. A quicksand does not shift so often as his temper. You must take him at his word, and never give him time to change and veer about.

LADY BELL: Totally out of nature.

DASHWOULD: Oh, very well! I give up the point. (*Exit.*)

LADY BELL: You may leave the man to my management. My aunt Bromley rival me! That would be delightful! (*Enter* LADY JANE.) Well, sister!

LADY JANE: Can you be serious for a moment?

LADY BELL: Well, the solemnity of that look! Must I set my face by yours, and contract a wrinkle by a formal economy of features, which you, like the rest of the world, mistake for wisdom?

LADY JANE: Will you hear me? They are hurrying this match too fast, I think. Sir John is come and his lawyer is expected every moment. He wants to conclude the affair this day, and my aunt does not oppose it. But I don't like all this hurry.

LADY BELL: And why need you be concerned about it?

LADY JANE: Do you think Millamour capable of love?

LADYB BELL: For the moment. It will be difficult to fix him.

LADY JANE: What would you have me do?

LADY BELL: Do? – Nothing.

LADY JANE: How silly! You know it is not of my seeking.

LADY BELL: What are you about? Talking in your sleep again? Lady Jane, wake yourself. What have you taken into your head?

LADY JANE: Why, since Mr Millamour has prevailed with me . . .

LADY BELL: His affections, then, are fixed upon you? – Ho, ho! Why, the man has been dying at my feet, with a face as rueful as a love elegy.

LADY JANE: You will permit me to laugh in my turn.

LADY BELL: Oh! I can laugh with you, and at you, and at him too. This gives spirit to the business: here are difficulties, and difficulties enhance victory, and victory is triumph.

LADY JANE: Very well! Oh, brave! Laugh away! You will be undeceived presently. – If this does not take, I am at the end of my line. (*Exit.*)

LADY BELL: What does all this mean? Rivalled, outwitted by my sister! Insupportable! This begins to grow serious.

> (*Enter* MILLAMOUR.)

MILLAMOUR: 'Sdeath, she here! Sir John is quite impatient, and I am going for his attorney.

LADY BELL: And Lady Jane is impatient too. She is the object of your choice.

MILLAMOUR: Lady Jane! You are pleasant, very pleasant!

LADY BELL: She has told me with inflexible gravity!

MILLAMOUR: She is a great wit, and great wits have great quickness of invention, and so a story is easily dressed up. I could crack my sides with laughing. If trifling civilities have been received as a declaration of love . . .

LADY BELL: And is that the case? Very whimsical indeed!

MILLAMOUR: Yes, very whimsical! I am eternally yours, ma'am, and I am on the wing, and your ladyship's adorer. (*going*)
        (*Enter* LADY JANE.)

LADY JANE: (*aside*) Now to plague them both. – Sister, you may hear it from himself.

MILLAMOUR: Confusion!

LADY BELL: That lady, sir, has the strangest notion . . .

LADY JANE: You will be so good as to explain all to my sister.

MILLAMOUR: (*aside*) Both upon me at once! – I have explained, madam, and all further talk about it is unnecessary.

LADY BELL: Only to satisfy her curiosity.

LADY JANE: To show my sister her mistake.

MILLAMOUR: (*to* LADY JANE) I have made everything clear, ma'am – (*to* LADY BELL) Have not I, Lady Bell? And a – (*Turns to* LADY JANE.) everything now is upon a proper footing.

LADY JANE: Very well. Only give her to understand . . .

MILLAMOUR: Your understanding is admirable. (*Turns to* LADY BELL.) I told you she would talk in this style. (*Turns to* LADY JANE.) You are perfectly right, and nobody understands things better. (*Turns to* LADY BELL.) Nobody whatever. (*Looks and laughs at both by turns.*)

LADY BELL: But give me leave. You must speak out, sir.

MILLAMOUR: (*aside to* LADY BELL) Never argue about it, it is not worth your while.

LADY JANE: There is some mystery in all this.

MILLAMOUR: No, all very clear. (*to* LADY JANE) Drop it for the present.

LADY BELL: But I desire no doubt may remain.

LADY JANE: And I don't like to be kept in suspense. (*Both pull him by the arm.*)

MILLAMOUR: Distraction! I am like a lawyer that has taken fees on both sides. You do me honour, ladies, but, upon my soul, I can't help laughing. It will divert us some day or other, this will. Oh, ho, ho! I shall die with laughing! (*Breaks from them.*)
        (*Enter* MRS BROMLEY *and* SIR JOHN MILLAMOUR.)

MRS BROMLEY: What is all this uproar for?

MILLAMOUR: Another witness of my folly! (*Runs to the other side of the stage.*)
        (*Enter* DASHWOULD.)

DASHWOULD: Millamour, I give you joy. Mr Copyhold, your attorney, is come with the deeds. What's the matter?

MILLAMOUR: The strangest adventure! I can't stay now. The ladies have been very pleasant. You love humour, and they have an infinite deal. I'll come to you in a moment. (*Exit.*)

SIR JOHN: George, don't run away. Let us finish the business.

DASHWOULD: If he says he'll marry, you may depend upon him. A poet, determined
    to write no more, or a gamester forswearing play, is not so sure to keep his word.
    I wish I may die, if I don't think him as much to be relied upon as a prime minister!

LADY BELL: Aunt! Would you believe it? The demure Lady Jane . . . (*Bursts into a
    laugh.*) She has taken such a fancy into her head! Millamour, she thinks, is up to
    the eyes in love with her.

MRS BROMLEY: Ha, ha, ha! Poor Lady Jane!

LADY JANE: And my sister's pride is hurt. She carries it with an air, as if she had made
    a conquest of Millamour.

MRS BROMLEY: How ridiculous the girls are! Your son has opened his mind to you,
    Sir John?

SIR JOHN: He has, and I approve of his choice. I hope it is as agreeable to you, as to
    his father.

MRS BROMLEY: I don't know how to refuse my consent.
                (*Enter* BYGROVE, *listening.*)

BYGROVE: (*aside*) What does all this mean?

DASHWOULD: (*seeing* BYGROVE, *aside*) As I could wish. There he is.

MRS BROMLEY: Since it has your approbation, Sir John, I believe I must yield my
    consent. I never thought to marry again, but since you will have it so . . .

SIR JOHN: Lady Bell, I understand, is willing to do me the honour of being my
    daughter-in-law.

LADY BELL: Oh, ho, ho, ho! This makes amends for all. My dear aunt Bromley, are
    you imposed upon? Did you listen to the traitor's vows? The dear, perfidious?
    (*Laughs violently.*)

DASHWOULD: He will soon be settled, Sir John, since there are now three rival
    goddesses contending for him. Mr Bygrove, you are come in good time.

BYGROVE: (*coming forward*) What fool's part are you to play now?

MRS BROMLEY: Sir John, I desire I may not be made your sport. Have not I here,
    under his hand, a declaration of his mind. Here, in this copy of verses, given to
    me by himself as earnest of his affection?

LADY BELL: Verses, aunt!

LADY JANE: Verses to you?

MRS BROMLEY: Verses to me. Only hear, Sir John. (*Reads.*)
        'I look'd, and I sigh'd, and I wish'd I could speak,
        And fain would have paid adoration.'

LADY BELL: Stay, stay. Mine begins the same way. (*Takes out a paper.*)

LADY JANE: The very words of mine. (*Takes out a paper.*)

MRS BROMLEY: Will those girls have done? (*Reads.*)
        'But when I endeavour'd the matter to break . . .'

LADY BELL: (*Reads.*)
        'Still then I said least of my passion . . .'

MRS BROMLEY: Will you be quiet? (*Reads.*)
        'Still then I said least of my passion;
        I swore to myself . . .'

LADY BELL: (*Reads fast.*)
        'And resolv'd I would try . . .'

MRS BROMLEY *and* LADY BELL: (*reading together*)
    'Some way my poor heart to recover.'
MRS BROMLEY, LADY BELL *and* LADY JANE: (*reading eagerly together*)
    'But that was all vain, for I sooner could die,
    Than live forbearing to love her.'
LADY BELL: Oh, ho, ho, ho! Mr Dashwould, what a piece of work has he made?
DASHWOULD: And the verses copied from Congreve!
LADY BELL: Copied from Congreve! (*Laughs heartily.*)
MRS BROMLEY: There, Sir John, there is your son's behaviour!
DASHWOULD: There, Mr Bygrove, there is the widow's behaviour!
BYGROVE: And now, Mr Dashwould, now for your wit.
MRS BROMLEY: (*to* SIR JOHN) I am not disappointed in the least, sir.
SIR JOHN: I never was so covered with confusion!
LADY BELL: I never was so diverted in all my days!
DASHWOULD: He has acted with great propriety upon this occasion.
MRS BROMLEY: He has made himself very ridiculous. He has exposed nobody but
    himself. Contempt is the only passion he can excite. A crazy, mad, absurd . . .
    (*tearing her paper*)
LADY JANE: An inconstant, wild, irresolute . . . (*tearing her paper*)
LADY BELL: Ha, ha, ha! So whimsical a character! (*Kisses her paper.*)
MRS BROMLEY: (*throwing fragments about*) This behaviour will give him prodigious
    lustre! He will shine after this! I hope his visits will cease at this house.
BYGROVE: (*to* MRS BROMLEY) If ever you marry again, similitude of temper must
    do it.
MRS BROMLEY: Distraction! Must you plague me too?
BYGROVE: You have appeared with an air, but it was all struggling.
MRS BROMLEY: I cannot bear this.
BYGROVE: Heaven knows how you have struggled!
MRS BROMLEY: And you too! (*Mimics him.*) 'A match in your family has diverted
    me of late.' I renounce you all. Come, Lady Bell, Lady Jane, and let us leave
    them to themselves. (*Exit.*)
LADY JANE: You would not believe me, sister. (*Exit.*)
LADY BELL: Oh! This to me is as good as a comedy! (*Exit.*)
DASHWOULD: (*to* BYGROVE) What shall I give you for your chance?
BYGROVE: More than I'll give you for your wit. And there's your answer. (*Exit.*)
DASHWOULD: The old pike is hooked, and struggles at the end of her line.
SIR JOHN: Mr Dashwould, speak to this silly young man. You have influence over
    him. Keep him to dinner. You will forever oblige me. I must go and pacify the
    ladies. (*Exit.*)
DASHWOULD: Poor Millamour! Dryden has painted him to a hair:
    'Blest madman, who can ev'ry hour employ,
    With something new to wish, or to enjoy.' (*Exeunt.*)

Blest madman: Dryden, *Absolem and Achitophel*, I, 553–4.

ACT IV

SCENE.   *An apartment at* MRS BROMLEY'*s. Enter* DASHWOULD *and* SIR HARRY.

DASHWOULD: This way, Sir Harry. While they are all engaged in the pleasures of the table, I want a word with you in private.

SIR HARRY: With that face of importance! What is coming now?

DASHWOULD: Listen to me: know a little of the subject, before you give your opinion.

SIR HARRY: I am all attention.

DASHWOULD: Did you mark Miss Neville, at dinner?

SIR HARRY: You know I did. And when Mrs Bromley railed at her . . .

DASHWOULD: She railed at her with a littleness of spirit that disgraced wealth and affluence, and gave to poverty the superior character. You must have seen in the behaviour of that girl, though treated with pride and arrogance, a propriety that was elegant, and went even further; it interested every heart for her. She is the best of the group. Were I, at the head of such a fortune as yours, to choose a wife, she should be the object of my affection.

SIR HARRY: You have some scheme in all this.

DASHWOULD: I have; to serve you. I should mortify the pride of Mrs Bromley by placing a valuable, but helpless, young lady upon a level with her at once.

SIR HARRY: (*Bursts into a laugh.*) This is to end in some joke!

DASHWOULD: Wait for the wit before you laugh. I am in serious earnest. Her understanding is the best among them. The others are still artificial, she is a natural character, and, if I am not mistaken, has a heart. If I wanted heirs to my estate, she should be the mother of my children.

SIR HARRY: Were I to be the dupe of all this how you would laugh at me! Ha, ha, ha! I know you too well.

DASHWOULD: Again! Laughing without the provocation of a joke. Don't be the dupe of your own cunning. I know you love her, and will it not be a generosity worthy of you to extricate merit out of distress? Nay, the merit which you admire? The merit which would do honour to the choice of any man in England?

SIR HARRY: (*Laughs heartily.*) Well, I cannot contain!

DASHWOULD: What's the matter?

SIR HARRY: The scrape in which you involved Millamour with the widow!

DASHWOULD: Foolish! That was Malvil's doing. You'll hear more of it by and by. There is an underplot in all his actions. I advise you for the best. Here is a lady in question, untainted by the fashions of the age. Make her your own. She has no fortune, what then? Show yourself superior to the sordid views that govern the little mercenary spirits of the world.

SIR HARRY: (*Laughs.*) I have just recollected what you said of Jack Invoice upon his marriage.

DASHWOULD: Jack Invoice? He never was intended for anything but to be laughed at. Upon the death of a rich uncle in the city, he comes to the West End of the town, with a plumb in his pocket, and not an idea in his head, marries a fantastical

---

plumb: £100,000.

woman of rank, and with a sovereign contempt of all his former acquaintance, mixes with lords and people of quality, who win his money, and throw his wig in the fire to divert themselves. He laughs at their wit, and thinks himself in good company.

SIR HARRY: Admirable! (*laughing heartily*) You have him to a hair!

DASHWOULD: (*laughing*) Hey! The picture is like – (*Laughs.*) Pretty well, is not it?

SIR HARRY: Oh, ho, ho! The very thing! Poor Jack Invoice! You have hunted him down.

DASHWOULD: Have I? (*Laughs.*) Yes, I think I have been pleasant upon him. But come, to our point: in marrying Miss Neville there is nothing ridiculous. You like her, that's clear.

SIR HARRY: But she does not like me, and that's as clear. Somebody has done me a prejudice there. She received this letter, and gave it me to read.

DASHWOULD: 'To Miss Neville – ' (*Opens it.*) Without a name?

SIR HARRY: A poisoned arrow in the dark.

DASHWOULD: (*Reads.*) 'Anonymous letters are generally the effect of clandestine malice; this comes from a friend. If your honour, your virtue, and your peace of mind are worth your care, avoid the acquaintance of Sir Harry. He is the deceiver of innocence, and means to add your name to the list of those whom his treachery has already ruined. Make use of this hint, and act accordingly.' A pretty epistle – (*Pauses.*) Don't I know this hand? – So, so! I understand it. I can trace this. Say no more, Sir Harry. Pursue Miss Neville the closer for this. Will you let such a fellow as Malvil rob you of a treasure?

SIR HARRY: You don't suspect him?

DASHWOULD: Leave it all to me. Assure Miss Neville that this shall be cleared up. Hush! We are interrupted! Go and join the company.
(*Enter* MR MALVIL.)

SIR HARRY: Pshaw! Pox! The company without you . . .

DASHWOULD: Very well; leave me now. (*Exit* SIR HARRY.) What's the matter, Malvil?

MALVIL: It will be over presently, a sudden sensation. I can't bear to see others made unhappy. Mrs Bromley is a very valuable woman, but at times rather violent.

DASHWOULD: And that's much to be lamented, is not it?

MALVIL: You may laugh at it, sir, but I think it a serious matter. I left poor Miss Neville in a flood of tears, and – here she comes!
(*Enter* MISS NEVILLE.)

DASHWOULD: Not rising from table so soon?

MISS NEVILLE: Excuse me, sir, I had rather not stay.

DASHWOULD: Never mind Mrs Bromley's humours. Come, we will take your part.

MISS NEVILLE: I am not fit for company, sir.

DASHWOULD: I am sorry to lose you. I'll leave you with my worthy friend. He will administer consolation. (*Exit.*)

MISS NEVILLE: Was ever such inhuman tyranny? Insulted before the whole company!

MALVIL: It hurts me to the quick. I could not have believed her capable of such violence.

MISS NEVILLE: You saw that I gave her no provocation.

MALVIL: It pains me to see what I do.

MISS NEVILLE: She breaks out in such passionate insults, and never considers that an overbearing pride is the worst of cruelty to an ingenuous mind.

MALVIL: There are few who know how to confer an obligation. A disinterested action gives such moments of inward pleasure! Oh! There are moments of the heart, worth all the giddy pleasures of life. One benevolent action pays so amply and yields such exquisite interest, that I wonder people are not fond of laying out their money in that way.

MISS NEVILLE: During the whole of dinner it was one continued invective against me . . .

MALVIL: Millamour's behaviour had disconcerted her. But that is no excuse. Goodness by fits, and generosity out of mere whim, can never constitute a valuable character. I am sorry to see you so afflicted.

MISS NEVILLE: You are very good, sir.

MALVIL: No, I have no merit in it. The instincts of my nature leave me no choice. I have studied myself, and I find I am only good by instinct. I am strangely interested in you. I have thought much of your situation. Our time is short, they will be rising from the table presently. Attend to what I say: since Mrs Bromley is so incessant in her tyranny, do as I already hinted to you. Withdraw from this house at once. Madam La Rouge has an apartment ready for you. You may there remain concealed. In the mean time I shall be at work for you. I shall prevail upon Mrs Bromley to keep her word about the five thousand pounds. That, added to what is in my power, will make a handsome settlement for you.

MISS NEVILLE: You heard what she said to Sir Harry?

MALVIL: I can't discover all I know. She wants to drive you to some act of despair. Perhaps to give you up as a sacrifice to Sir Harry's loose desires.

MISS NEVILLE: Are you so clear about Sir Harry?

MALVIL: (*aside*) 'Sdeath! I see she loves him. – Hereafter, I will open a scene to astonish you. (*Pauses, and looks at her.*) Sir Harry is a bad man. You can never be happy under this roof. Mrs Bromley will make this quarrel up, I know she will. The whole of her virtue consists in repentance, but what kind of repentance? A spurious promise to reform her conduct, and a certain return to the same vices.

MISS NEVILLE: She has made me desperate. I can stay here no longer. I'll go back to the country. I shall there be at peace.

MALVIL: You will be there too much out of the way. When you are settled at Madam La Rouge's the haughty Mrs Bromley will see to what she has driven you, and, for the sake of her character, will begin to relent. Sir Harry must not know where you are. He means your ruin. I am sorry to say it, but can give you such convincing proof . . .

(*Enter* MRS BROMLEY.)

MRS BROMLEY: Do you go to your room, madam; let me see you no more today.

MALVIL: It was a mere unguarded word that fell from Miss Neville. (*Speaks to* MRS BROMLEY *aside.*) Millamour is ashamed of his conduct. He is under my influence still. I shall mould him to your wishes.

MRS BROMLEY: (*aside to him*) I am a fool to think any more about him. Go to him; watch him all day; you will not find me ungrateful. (*aloud*) I shall let you know when coffee is ready. And pray tell those girls to come upstairs. (*Exit* MALVIL.)

Mighty well, madam. You must sit next to Sir Harry. You have no pretensions, have you? And you must vouch for Lady Bell too? She does not love gaming, that story is all calumny. Bespeak yourself a place in the stage-coach, you shall quit this house, I promise you.

MISS NEVILLE: It will be the last time I shall receive those orders, madam. Your favours are so embittered, there is such a leaven of pride, even in your acts of bounty, that I cannot wish to be under any further obligations. If doing justice to Lady Bell, if avowing my sentiments in the cause of so amiable a friend, can give you umbrage, I am not fit to remain in this house. (*Exit.*)

MRS BROMLEY: Oh brave! You shall travel. Give her a fortune! No, let Lady Bell reward her. How! – Millamour, as I live!
> (*Enter* MILLAMOUR.)

MILLAMOUR: Deliver me, fate! She here! – Madam – I – I – you are not going to leave us, I hope?
> (*Enter* SIR JOHN MILLAMOUR.)

MRS BROMLEY: (*smiling at* MILLAMOUR) And how can you look me in the face?

MILLAMOUR: (*seeing* SIR JOHN) I am glad you are come, sir, I wanted to . . .

MRS BROMLEY: (*aside*) Perverse! What brings Sir John! – I shall expect you above stairs, gentlemen. (*aside*) I'll go and dress from top to toe and try once more to fix that irresolute, inconstant man. (*Exit.*)

SIR JOHN: What a day's work have you made here!

MILLAMOUR: Sir!

SIR JOHN: Can you expect any good from all this? Forever doing and undoing. These proceedings are terrible to your father.

MILLAMOUR: You know, sir, that to gratify you is the height of my ambition.

SIR JOHN: For shame! Don't imagine that you can deceive me any longer. Are you to be forever in suspense? Always resolving and yet never deciding? Never knowing your own mind for five minutes?

MILLAMOUR: I have not been hasty to determine, that is very true.

SIR JOHN: My indulgence has made me as ridiculous as you are yourself, by your eternal levity. You will force me to tell you my mind in harsher terms than I ever thought I should have occasion to do.

MILLAMOUR: What has happened today was but a mere frolic, and it has all passed off in a little raillery.

SIR JOHN: And do you think that sufficient? While you remain insensible of your folly, transferring your inclinations from one object to another, hurried away by every casualty, you will prove the jest on all your acquaintance. You will cease to live, before you have begun.

MILLAMOUR: This is rather too much, sir. If I have, in a few instances, departed from a resolution that seemed fixed, you know very well it is not uncommon, and when a person means an extraordinary leap, he retires back to take advantage of the ground and springs forward with greater vigour.

SIR JOHN: And thus you amuse yourself, compounding upon easy terms for the folly of every hour. There is no relying upon you.

MILLAMOUR: After all, sir, it is the prudent part to consider everything. The ladies were rather hasty in their conclusions. In our moments of reflection, as objects pass before us, opinion will wear different colours.

SIR JOHN: The very chameleon has that merit. But is there to be nothing inward? No
self-governing principles? A ship without a pilot, without rudder or compass, is
as likely to avoid rocks and quicksands, as you to steer clear of ruin.

MILLAMOUR: You seem exasperated, but I really don't see the cause.

SIR JOHN: No! Can't you feel how absurd it is to be always beginning the world?
Forever in a doubt? Day after day embarking on new projects; nay, twenty
different projects in one day, and often in an hour?

MILLAMOUR: Spare my confusion. I feel my folly. I feel it all, and let my future
conduct . . .

SIR JOHN: George, can I take your word? I know you have been at the gaming table.

MILLAMOUR: The gaming table!

SIR JOHN: Say no more, I know it all. After the indulgence I have shown you, I now
see that my hopes are all to be disappointed. If you have a mind to atone for what
is past, pursue one certain plan, and be somebody. The time now opens a new
scene and calls for other manners. Reform your conduct and I shall be happy. But
I am tired of this eternal levity, my patience is wore out. I shall stay no longer in
this house to be a witness of your absurdity. (*Exit.*)

MILLAMOUR: I have made myself very ridiculous here. – I can't show my face any
more in this family. I'll go back to the Temple, and not marry these ten years.
The law leads to great things: a seat in parliament, a vote or two against your
conscience, a silk gown, and a judge. That's the course of things. – I'll pursue my
ambition. – (*Calls to a* SERVANT.) Honest friend! Honest friend, will you be so
good as just to get my hat?

(*Enter* DASHWOULD.)

DASHWOULD: No, I bar hats. What, going to desert us? The sport is just beginning.
Bygrove has been lecturing his son, and quarrelling with Malvil. The integrity of
that honest gentleman is suspected at last. He was the worthiest man in the world
this morning, as good a creature as ever was born, but now he has sold himself to
the widow. Lady Bell has been lively upon the occasion, and Malvil, to support
his spirits, has plied the burgundy till he looks the very picture of hypocrisy, with
a ruddy complexion and a sparkling eye.

MILLAMOUR: You may divert yourself, sir. I have done with them all.

DASHWOULD: But I can't part with you – you shall join us. Malvil shall have no
quarter, till his charity for his neighbour begins to stagger. Then off drops the
mask. He will have courage enough to rail at mankind, and his true character will
come forth, like letters in lemon juice before the fire.

MILLAMOUR: Po! Absurd! I am on the rack. Why did you force me to stay dinner? I
have been so weak, so frivolous!

DASHWOULD: How so? Because you changed your mind? There is nothing more
natural. Don't you see men doing the same every day? Down goes the old mansion, a new one rises, exotic trees smile on the landscape and enjoy the northern
air, and when the whole is finished, in less than a twelvemonth, Mr Christie sells
it by auction to the highest bidder, who pays his money, gets possession, and runs
away the next morning with a figure dancer, to take the tour of Europe.

Mr Christie: James Christie, founder of the famous auction rooms.

MILLAMOUR: (*laughing*) Why, yes, we see these things every day.

DASHWOULD: No doubt; men are fickle and inconstant.

MILLAMOUR: Very true. It is the way through life, in the lowest rank as well as the highest. You shan't see a journeyman weaver, but he has his disgust, like a lord, and changes his lodging, his barber and his field preacher.

DASHWOULD: Certainly, and then there is a real charm in variety. Besides, what you did today was a mere frolic.

MILLAMOUR: Nothing more. And that fellow, Malvil, was the occasion of it. My heart never rightly warmed to that man. I shall never consult him again. Affairs were in a right train, if he had not interposed.

DASHWOULD: You shall have your revenge. I have a mine to spring, will blow him up. (*Laughs.*) His advice today has served to produce the widow's character.

MILLAMOUR: Yes, it has given a display of her. (*Laughs.*) How could she think me in earnest? Marry her! I would go into the army sooner!

DASHWOULD: A good, pretty trade, the army. If you are killed in battle, it is your affair; if you conquer, the general reaps the advantage.

MILLAMOUR: Very true. The law is a more certain road.

DASHWOULD: A good, agreeable life, the law is; forever entangled in the cobwebs of Westminster Hall, and you help to spin them yourself into the bargain.

MILLAMOUR: And at the end of twenty years, you are thought a good, promising young man.

DASHWOULD: In the mean time, you are constantly tiring out your lungs, and ever in a passion about other people's affairs.

MILLAMOUR: And travelling circuits in hopes of finding each county distracted, with a barbarous, bloody murder in every gaol, and so live upon the calamities of mankind.

DASHWOULD: Like physicians, when a north-east wind, a Lord Mayor's feast or a gaol distemper has made a good sickly time of it. (*Both laugh.*)

(*Enter* LADY BELL *and* LADY JANE.)

LADY BELL: Come, sister, leave the men to themselves. Mr Dashwould, has their wit frightened you away?

MILLAMOUR: (*laughing at her*) 'Look in her face, and you forget them all.'

DASHWOULD: Won't your ladyship have compassion on that gentleman?

LADY BELL: Compassion! My sister and I hope to have his protection!

(*Enter* CAPTAIN BYGROVE.)

CAPT. BYGROVE: When you go away from company, Lady Bell, you draw every-body in your train.

LADY BELL: Oh, you have so overpowered me with civil and tender things!

MILLAMOUR: (*aside*) What does he follow her for?

LADY BELL: A l'honneur, gentlemen. (*Goes up to* MILLAMOUR.) Uncle! Uncle Millamour, when you are married to my aunt, I hope you will be kind to us both. (*Curtsies.*)

MILLAMOUR: (*turning away*) Confusion! Daggers! Daggers!

LADY JANE: (*curtseying*) May I salute you, uncle?

'*Look in her face . . .* ': Pope, *The Rape of the Lock*, II, 18.

MILLAMOUR: Po! This foolery! (*Walks away.*)

LADY BELL: Let us give him all his titles! – Brother, when you marry my sister . . . (*Makes a low curtsey.*)

MILLAMOUR: How can you, Lady Bell!

LADY JANE: Uncle! Brother! (*Laughs.*)

LADY BELL: And Brother Uncle! (*Laughs.*)

MILLAMOUR: (*breaking away from them*) This is too much – no patience can endure it. (*Turns to* LADY BELL.) Madam, this usage . . .

(LADY BELL *and* LADY JANE *both laugh aloud.*)

LADY JANE: Come, sister, let us leave him. (*Exit.*)

LADY BELL: Oh! Oh! Oh! I shall expire! (*going*)

MILLAMOUR: (*taking her by the hand*) Why will you torment me thus? Am I to be forever made your sport?

LADY BELL: Oh! You would not have me laugh. To be sure, when one considers, it is a serious matter! And, though Captain Bygrove (*pointing to him*) has orders to be in love with me – and though he has declared himself in the warmest terms . . .

CAPT. BYGROVE: I have, I have vowed eternal constancy and love.

LADY BELL: You have so, and, yet, after all, Mr Millamour, after all your promises, when my heart was perhaps a little touched.

MILLAMOUR: (*aside*) Jealous of me, by this light!

LADY BELL: After all your faithless vows, to break them as you have done, like a Turk, or a Jew, or a Mahomeddan! (*crying*) And leave me, like Dido and Aeneas, it is enough to break a young girl's heart! (*crying bitterly*) So it is, it is – There, will that please you? (*Bursts into a laugh.*) Well, Captain Bygrove, adieu; I shall see you at tea.

CAPT. BYGROVE: To attend you, Lady Bell, is the pride and pleasure of my life. (*aside to* DASHWOULD) This will do, I believe. (*Exit* LADY BELL.)

(*Enter* SIR HARRY LIZARD.)

SIR HARRY: Did not I hear somebody crying?

MILLAMOUR: Yes, and laughing too. Captain Bygrove, you said something to Lady Bell, what was it, sir?

CAPT. BYGROVE: What I desire the world to know: I love her, I adore her! My father has ordered it, Mrs Bromley approved, Lady Bell encourages me, and I shall be the happiest of mankind.

MILLAMOUR: You and I must talk apart, sir. You know my prior claim. Attempt my life rather than my love. You must think no more of her, sir. She is mine by every tie, and so I shall tell her this moment. (*Exit.*)

DASHWOULD: Now hold that resolution, if you can.

CAPT. BYGROVE: I have managed it well?

DASHWOULD: Admirably!

SIR HARRY: Come, Dashwould, you are wanted in the next room. Malvil is in for it, he sits toasting Miss Neville, while every idea fades away from his countenance, all going out one by one, and his eyes sink into the dim vacuity of a brisk no meaning at all.

DASHWOULD: I'll look in upon them. (*aside*) Bygrove, I see Miss Neville; let us give Sir Harry his opportunity.

(*Enter* MISS NEVILLE.)

MISS NEVILLE: I thought Lady Bell was here: I beg your pardon, gentlemen.

DASHWOULD: Your company is always agreeable, is not it, Sir Harry? The gentleman will speak for himself. Come, Bygrove, I have occasion for you. (*Exit with* CAPTAIN BYGROVE.)

SIR HARRY: May I now presume, madam . . .

MISS NEVILLE: You choose your time but ill, Sir Harry. I have so many things to distract me, I cannot listen to you now.

SIR HARRY: (*Takes her hand.*) But you promised to hear me. I have long beheld your sufferings.

MISS NEVILLE: They do not warrant improper liberties. I can be humble, as becomes my station. I hope you will not oblige me to show that spirit, which virtue is as much entitled to as the proudest fortune in the kingdom.

SIR HARRY: I mean you no disrespect. That letter is a black artifice to traduce my character. The fraud shall be brought to light, you may rely upon it, nor will you be so ungenerous as to believe the dark assassin of my honour.

MISS NEVILLE: I know not what foundation there is for it, nor is it for me to charge you with anything. I have no right to take that liberty.

SIR HARRY: Why harbour suspicions unworthy of you? In me you behold a warm admirer, who aspires at the possession of what he loves, and trembles for the event.

MISS NEVILLE: I must take the liberty to doubt your sincerity. I know my own deficiencies, and I beg leave to withdraw.

SIR HARRY: By all that's amiable in your mind and person, my views are honourable as ever yet inspired a lover's heart.

MISS NEVILLE: I would fain express my gratitude. (*Weeps.*)

SIR HARRY: Why these tears?

MISS NEVILLE: Your character, I dare say, sir, will come out clean and unsullied. You will permit me to take care of mine. It is all I have to value. I shall not continue any longer in this house. Mrs Bromley has made it impossible. I wish you all happiness, sir.

SIR HARRY: That resolution I approve of. Let me provide you a retreat, and in a few days . . .

MISS NEVILLE: I must beg to be excused: that I can never think of.

SIR HARRY: By heaven, I mean to raise you to that independence, which your merit deserves. I would place you in that splendour, which Mrs Bromley may envy.

MISS NEVILLE: I can only return my thanks. Lady Bell will know where I am. I feel no ambition. I do not want to give pain to Mrs Bromley. I seek humble content, and ask no more.

SIR HARRY: You do injustice to yourself and me. – Hey! All breaking up from table!

MISS NEVILLE: You must not detain me now, Sir Harry. I humbly take my leave. (*Exit.*)

SIR HARRY: I wonder what Dashwould will say to all this. I shall like to hear him; he will turn it to a joke, I warrant him. No end to his pleasantry!

        (*Enter* MALVIL, *in liquor*, BYGROVE *and* DASHWOULD.)

MALVIL: Very well, make the most of it. Since you force me to speak, I say her character is a vile one.

BYGROVE: Here is a fellow whom wine only inspires with malice!

DASHWOULD: Po! Malice! Malvil has no harm in him.

MALVIL: You may talk of Mrs Bromley, but she is as vile a character as pride and insolence and avarice and vanity and fashionable airs and decayed beauty can jumble together.

BYGROVE: Here's a return for her hospitality!

MALVIL: Marry her, I say, marry her and try.

BYGROVE: You shall not have a shilling with Miss Neville.

MALVIL: There, the secret's out: you want to marry her, and make her break her word. Mankind's a villain! A medley of false friends, eloping wives, stock-jobbers, and usurers. Wits that won't write, and fools that will. (*Sings.*)

> Yes, give me wine, there's naught below
> > Naught else that can content us.
> Wine chases care, the balm of woe,
> > Best gift the Gods have sent us.

BYGROVE: Dashwould, you are a panegyrist compared to this man.

SIR HARRY: Yes, he takes your trade out of your hands.

MALVIL: She is Mrs Bromley, the widow, and you are Mr Bygrove, the widower, and so bite the biter, that's all.

BYGROVE: His wit soars above you, Mr Dashwould.

MALVIL: Wit is a bad trade. Letters have no friends left in these degenerate times. Show a man of letters to the first of your nobility and they will leave him to starve in a garret. Introduce a fellow, who can sing a catch, write a dull political pamphlet, or play off fireworks, and he shall pass six months in the country by invitation. Maecenas died two thousand years ago, and, most noble Captain, you are not historian enough to know it.

SIR HARRY: Dashwould, he makes a bankrupt of you!

BYGROVE: I have found him out. I know him now. A pretended friend, that he may more surely betray you. Go and get some coffee, to settle your head. (*Exit.*)

MALVIL: Mrs Bromley will settle your head.

DASHWOULD: Let us take him upstairs. He'll tumble over the tea-table, to show his politeness.

SIR HARRY: (*taking him by the arm*) Come, the ladies wait for us.

MALVIL: Mankind, I say, is a villain! (*Sings.*)

> From stuccoed roofs, fell Care inpends,
> > It mounts the Attic story;
> Not the first Regiment defends,
> > Great George from Whig and Tory.
> > > (*Enter* LADY BELL.)

LADY BELL: Bless me, Mr Malvil!

MALVIL: All Dashwould's doing, to expose a body. Do you look to Millamour, that's what I say to you.

DASHWOULD: He shan't stay to plague your ladyship. – Come, Malvil, let us go, and be tender of reputation above stairs.

MALVIL: I am always tender, and you are scurrilous. (*Sings, and exit, led by* DASHWOULD *and* SIR HARRY.)

LADY BELL: How Millamour follows me up and down! Charming! Here he comes!
> (*Enter* MILLAMOUR.)

MILLAMOUR: Lady Bell, allow me but one serious moment.

LADY BELL: This bracelet is always coming off. (*Fiddles with it.*)

MILLAMOUR: Whatever appearances may have been, I burn with as true a passion as ever penetrated a faithful heart.

LADY BELL: (*aside and smiling*) I know he is mine. – This silly, obstinate bauble! What were you saying? – Oh, making love again!

MILLAMOUR: By this dear hand, I swear . . .

LADY BELL: Hold, hold, no violence! Give me my liberty – and thus I make use of it. (*Runs away from him.*)
　　　　　(*Enter* CAPTAIN BYGROVE.)

LADY BELL: (*meeting him*) Oh, I have been wishing for you! How could you stay so long?

CAPT. BYGROVE: They detained me against my will; but you see I am true to my appointment.

MILLAMOUR: (*aside to* BYGROVE) Are you so? You shall keep an appointment with me.

LADY BELL: I was surrounded with darts and flames. That gentleman was for renewing the old story, but it was so ridiculous! (*Walks up the stage with* CAPTAIN BYGROVE.)

MILLAMOUR: Distraction! To be insulted!

LADY BELL: (*as she walks up*) You have prevailed upon me to be in earnest at last. Since your father has proposed it, and since you have declared yourself, why, if I must speak, get my aunt's consent and mine follows of course.

MILLAMOUR: (*listening*) If ever I forgive this . . .

CAPT. BYGROVE: Mrs Bromley has consented. (*then aside to* LADY BELL) He has it; this will gall his pride.

MILLAMOUR: No end of her folly. I was bent on marriage, but now it's all her own fault. And yet she knows my heart is fixed upon her.

LADY BELL: (*walking down with* CAPTAIN BYGROVE) You are so obliging and I have so many things to say to you! But if people will not perceive when they interrupt private conversation . . .

MILLAMOUR: If ever I enter these doors again, may the scorn of the whole sex pursue me. (*Exit.*)

CAPT. BYGROVE: We have carried this too far.

LADY BELL: The barbarous man! When he should have taken no denial, but have lain on the ground imploring, beseeching – Delightful! Here he comes again. (*Goes to* CAPTAIN BYGROVE.)
　　　　　(*Enter* MILLAMOUR.)

MILLAMOUR: (*walking up to* LADY BELL) Is it not strange that you can't know your own mind for two minutes together?

LADY BELL: Ho! Ho! The assurance of that reproach! (*Walks away.*)

MILLAMOUR: (*to* BYGROVE) Appoint your time and place – I must have satisfaction for this.

CAPT. BYGROVE: Tomorrow morning, when the marriage ceremony is over.

MILLAMOUR: I shall expect you, sir. (*going*)
　　　　　(*Enter* LADY JANE.)

MILLAMOUR: This is lucky – I was in quest of your ladyship.

LADY JANE: In quest of me, sir?

MILLAMOUR: In quest of you, ma'am. I have been waiting for an opportunity, and, if the sincerest sorrow can expiate past offences – Here's a chair, ma'am. (*Hands a chair.*)

CAPT. BYGROVE: (*to* LADY BELL) We may drive him to extremities with Lady Jane. I'll leave you to recover your wanderer. (*Exit.*)

MILLAMOUR: (*sitting down*) If you will permit me to assure you . . .

LADY JANE: But while my sister is my rival . . .

MILLAMOUR: Your sister's charms carry their own antidote with them. If there is faith in man, I mean to atone for what is past.

LADY JANE: (*aside*) Now to prove her pride. – It were vain to disguise, sir, that your accomplishments have an irresistible power over all, and when the heart has once felt your influence . . .

LADY BELL: (*coming forward*) Oh mighty well! Did you speak to me, Mr Millamour?

MILLAMOUR: There was a time, ma'am! (*Turns to* LADY JANE.) Now she wants to interrupt us – don't let us mind her, and she'll withdraw.

LADY BELL: Wear the willow, Lady Bell? Not a word, sir, you are in the right, my spirits are too violent for you, and though what I say is not absolutely wit – Do you like wit? I am sure you ought, for it is undefinable, like yourself.

MILLAMOUR: (*smiling*) That is not ill said.

LADY BELL: (*Sits at a distance.*) Horrid! I shall be vapoured up to my eyes. I'll try my song to banish melancholy. Where is that foolish guitar? (*Goes for it.*)

MILLAMOUR: (*aside*) Now her jealousy is at work. I knew she would be mortified. (*aloud to* LADY JANE) Your ladyship has fixed me your eternal admirer.

LADY BELL: Though I can't sing, it diverts a body to try. (*Sits down and sings.*)
    Sabrina, with that sober mien,
    The converse sweet, the look serene;
    Those eyes that beam the gentlest ray,
    And though she loves, that sweet delay;
    Unconscious, seems each heart to take,
    And conquers for her subject's sake.

MILLAMOUR: Vastly well! (*Listens, smiles, looks at her, draws his chair near her, and beats time on her knee.*)

LADY BELL: (*Sings.*)
    The tyrant Cynthia wings the dart,
    Coquetting with a bleeding heart;
    Has cruelty, which all adore,
    Flights that torment, yet please the more;
    Her lover strives to break his chain,
    But can't, such pleasure's in the pain.

MILLAMOUR: Oh, charming! Charming! (*Kisses her hand.*)

LADY BELL: What are you about, you wretch? Only look, sister. – I suppose, sir, when you have done, you will give me my hand again?

LADY JANE: And I suppose, sister, when you have done, you will lend the gentleman to me again. (*aside*) Now, if this succeeds, my sister will thank me for it. (*Exit.*)

Wear the willow: a willow garland was traditionally the sign of mourning for the loss of a beloved.

LADY BELL: How she flung out of the room! (*Rises and walks about.*)

MILLAMOUR: You know, Lady Bell, that I am yours, by conquest. I adore you still
and burn with a lover's faithful fires.

LADY BELL: Come and have a dish of tea to cool you.

MILLAMOUR: Hear me but a moment. It is now time you should be tired of this
eternal display of your power. Your power is sufficiently acknowledged and felt
by all. You may triumph over adoring crowds, but one lover, treated with
generosity, will be more to your honour and your happiness.

LADY BELL: Pretty, very pretty! I have read all that in one of the poets:
'By our distress, you nothing gain;
Unless you love, you please in vain'.
Come upstairs and I'll show you the whole poem.
'And one adorer kindly us'd,
Gives more delight than crowds refus'd.'
Will you come? (*Beckons him.*) Won't you? Well, consider of it, and when you
know your own mind, you may change it again. (*Exit.*)

MILLAMOUR: There, now! Everything by turns, and nothing long. Fickle, do they
call me? A man must be fickle, who pursues her through all the whimsies of her
temper. Admire her in one shape, and she takes another in a moment.
'One charm display'd, another strikes our view,
In quick variety for ever new.'

ACT V

SCENE 1.   *A room in* MRS BROMLEY's *house. Enter* MILLAMOUR *and*
DASHWOULD.

MILLAMOUR: Am I to be sacrificed to your humour?

DASHWOULD: Am I to be sacrificed to your absurdity?

MILLAMOUR: When pleasantry is out of all time and place . . .

DASHWOULD: Why, then, I shall be tired of all time and place.

MILLAMOUR: Lookye, Mr Dashwould, it is time to be serious. The wit that wounds
the breast of a friend is the pest of society.

DASHWOULD: The passion, Mr Millamour, that runs headlong without cause and
will not hearken to reason, is a greater pest to society than all the little wit that
has been in the world. What does all this mean, sir? What is it about?

MILLAMOUR: If I lost money at play, was it for you to carry the tale to my father? For
you to subject me to his reproaches?

DASHWOULD: I don't know by what fatality it happens, but that generally comes
last, which ought to be mentioned first. I repeated nothing to Sir John. Who did?
Do you ask that question? Malvil, sir, with his usual duplicity.

MILLAMOUR: Malvil! He has this moment told me how pleasant you were upon the
subject, and at my expense.

DASHWOULD: Yes, when he had revealed the whole, and with false tenderness
lamented your folly.

MILLAMOUR: 'Sdeath! I understand it now. I have been absurd here.

'*By our distress . . .* ': Duke of Buckingham, *To a Coquette Beauty* (1701).

DASHWOULD: I don't dislike you for your absurdity; that serves to divert one. Malvil excites other feelings. You know the character he gave you of Lady Bell?

MILLAMOUR: Yes, and all slander.

DASHWOULD: I left him but now representing you to Lady Bell in the same colours. And here (*Shows a letter.*), here I have him fast. An anonymous libel upon Sir Harry, sent for his own purposes to Miss Neville. All his contrivance, dictated by himself, and written at an attorney's desk. You know old Capias?

MILLAMOUR: Did he pen the letter?

DASHWOULD: One of his clerks was the scribe. The young man is now in the house, at my request, and ready to prove Malvil the author. Here he comes. Things are not ripe as yet, say nothing now.

(*Enter* MALVIL.)

MILLAMOUR: Walk in, you come opportunely.

MALVIL: If I can be of any service . . .

MILLAMOUR: To be of disservice is your province, and when you have done the mischief, you can transfer the blame to others.

MALVIL: I have been rather off my guard today. I am not used to be overtaken in that manner, my head is not quite clear.

MILLAMOUR: Then this business may sober you. What was your whisper to me about that gentleman?

MALVIL: That he treated with wanton pleasantry what I thought a serious matter. I may mistake the means, but the end of my action I can always answer for. Sir John might hear of the affair from another quarter, and so to soften his resentment . . .

MILLAMOUR: You took care to excite it.

MALVIL: I – I – I am apt to carry my heart at my tongue's end.

DASHWOULD: I knew his heart was not in the right place.

MALVIL: I did not address myself to you, sir.

MILLAMOUR: I know you have the grimace of character, Mr Malvil, armed at all points with plausible maxims, but which of your maxims can justify the treachery of betraying the secret of a friend? Who does it is a destroyer of all confidence, and when he attempts to varnish his conduct with the spurious name of friendship, the malignity strikes the deeper, artful, smiling malignity!

MALVIL: I deserve all this. Friendship in excess is a fault. There are bounds and limits even to virtue. It would be well if a man could always hit the exact point. There is, however, something voluptuous in meaning well.

DASHWOULD: Well expressed, Malvil! Ha, ha! You are right.

MILLAMOUR: No more of your musty sentences!

MALVIL: Morals are not capable of mathematical demonstration. And – now I recollect myself – it did not occur at first – it was Madam La Rouge told the affair to Sir John. This gentleman here – I suppose you will take his word – he says she hears everything, tells everything, and he calls her a walking newspaper. Not that she means any harm. I only mean to say . . .

DASHWOULD: Oh fie! Don't be too severe upon her.

MALVIL: She said at the same time – you know her manner – she told Sir John that you are in love with half a dozen, and will deceive them all, and Lady Bell into the bargain.

MILLAMOUR: Distraction! She dare not say it. This is another of your subterfuges. You know, sir, how you traduced Lady Bell, and made that gentleman the author of your own malevolence. At any other time and place, this sword should read you a lecture of morality.

MALVIL: You are too warm, and since I see it is so, to avoid contention, I shall adjourn the debate. (*Exit.*)

MILLAMOUR: Deceived Lady Bell! Whoever has dared to say it – Madam La Rouge lives but a little way off – I'll bring her this moment to confront this arch impostor. (*going*)

DASHWOULD: You'll be sure to return?

MILLAMOUR: This very night shall unmask him. (*Exit.*)

DASHWOULD: I shall depend upon you. Malvil shall answer to Sir Harry; all his artifices shall be fairly laid open.

(*Enter* BYGROVE.)

BYGROVE: Mr Dashwould, we are now good friends. I have reposed a confidence in you. You know everything between me and Mrs Bromley, but you see how she goes on!

DASHWOULD: And I see how you go on. You are the dupe of your own policy.

BYGROVE: How so?

DASHWOULD: The widow's schemes are seconded by your own imprudence. Can't you see that if Millamour were once married out of your way, Mrs Bromley would then be at her last stake and you might have some chance? And yet your son has it in command to defeat my friend Millamour with Lady Bell.

BYGROVE: How! Light breaks in upon me! Gull that I was! My son shall marry Lady Jane directly.

DASHWOULD: To be sure; and the consequence is that Lady Bell declares for Millamour.

BYGROVE: Right. I am forever obliged to you – I'll go and speak to my son this moment. Lady Jane shall be his without delay. (*Exit.*)

DASHWOULD: So much for my friend, the Captain. I have settled his business. So, so, what have we here? Mrs Bromley from the labours of the toilet, new dressed, and the whole artillery of her charms pointed at Millamour. I shall take care to counterplot her. (*Exit.*)

(*Enter* MRS BROMLEY, *richly dressed.*)

MRS BROMLEY: Well, dressing is an intolerable fatigue, but I must make one effort more, or Millamour is lost, and to take up with Mr Bygrove. No, that will never do. (*Enter* TRINKET, *in* MRS BROMLEY's *former dress.*) Upon my word, Trinket, I should hardly know you. That dress becomes you. Go upstairs to Neville, and show her what a present I have made you. Go and torment her to the quick.

TRINKET: I know how to do it, ma'am.

MRS BROMLEY: Humble that proud spirit of hers, and, do you hear, tell her you shall be my favourite for the future. (*Exit.*)

TRINKET: I warrant, I'll tease her. An upstart thing! She is no better than myself, with all her airs. – Law! Here is my Lady Bell and Mr Dashwould. I am quite ashamed to be seen so fine.

(*Enter* LADY BELL *and* DASHWOULD.)

LADY BELL: I can't believe you, Mr Dashwould. (*seeing* TRINKET'*s back to her*) Aunt, what do you think he says?

TRINKET: Dear ma'am, I am in such confusion . . .

LADY BELL: Trinket? I vow I took you for my Aunt Bromley.

DASHWOULD: And here is another will do the same. Let us try the experiment.

LADY BELL: By all means. Here Trinket, here's my fan. Hold it up to your face. Come, Mr Dashwould. (*Goes with him to the top of the stage.*)

TRINKET: I tremble from head to foot.

(*Enter* BYGROVE.)

BYGROVE: Mrs Bromley, at length I have found her alone. Mrs Bromley! She turns away with disdain.

TRINKET: (*aside*) I wish I was far enough, so I do.

BYGROVE: Since the opportunity favours, will you not revive me with one kind look?

TRINKET: (*aside*) I was never in such a quandary in all my born days.

BYGROVE: How have I deserved this cold aversion?

TRINKET: (*aside*) I shall certainly laugh in his face.

BYGROVE: After all the tender promises with which you encouraged my growing passion.

(*Enter* MRS BROMLEY, *listening.*)

MRS BROMLEY: (*aside*) So, so, I have caught you both, have I?

BYGROVE: Then, madam, since it is come to this, give me leave to tell you, that your various artifices are now too plain. You have played all the tricks of your sex, you have flattered me with hope, and at the same time thrown out the lure for others.

MRS BROMLEY: (*aside*) Mighty well, go on.

BYGROVE: It will make a fine story. Dashwould will help it about; his licentious tongue will make you the public jest, the butt and ridicule of the town. With all my heart, you will be handed about in vile poetry, through all the newspapers, the just reward of falsehood and dissimulation.

TRINKET: (*aside*) I can't hold out any longer.

BYGROVE: Not a word yet? Can nothing soften you to compassion? You know, in spite of all that has happened today, that I love you still.

TRINKET: (*laughing*) I know it.

BYGROVE: If a faithful heart is worth your acceptance, thus on my knees I devote myself to you.

MRS BROMLEY: (*coming forward*) Perfidious monster!

BYGROVE: How! Mrs Bromley! To whom have I been talking?

TRINKET: (*curtseying*) Me, sir.

MRS BROMLEY: Now give it a turn, but it is too late. As for you, madam, you are worse than Neville already. You must have a lover here in my very house.

BYGROVE: You wrong the girl, and me too.

MRS BROMLEY: Yes, take her part. – Do you quit my sight, Mrs Convenient. Go this moment, and send Neville to me directly. I shall take her into favour again.

TRINKET: Yes, ma'am. I never was in such a scrape before. (*Exit.*)

BYGROVE: If you will but let me explain . . .

MRS BROMLEY: It is plain enough already, sir.

DASHWOULD: (*coming forward*) Yes, plain enough of all conscience, Mr Bygrove. I admire your taste.

BYGROVE: There, there, you see it was all a plot.

LADY BELL: (*coming forward*) Aunt! The treachery of your lovers is intolerable. Mr Bygrove is worse than Millamour, I think.

MRS BROMLEY: None of your impertinence.

LADY BELL: Ha, ha, ha! Mr Dashwould, what a discovery. (*Exit.*)

DASHWOULD: Mr Bygrove! What's too high for love, or what too low? My licentious tongue will make a story of this. Ha, ha, ha! (*Exit.*)

MRS BROMLEY: There, sir, you have exposed yourself, and me too.

BYGROVE: If you will but hear me, it is all a mistake.

MRS BROMLEY: Did not I hear you? See you?

BYGROVE: By heaven, I took her for you, all the time.

MRS BROMLEY: Took that wretch for me? I have done, sir. I am glad I have found you out. I shall send your favourite about her business. I wish you success in your amour. (*going*)
      (*Enter* TRINKET.)

TRINKET: Miss Neville is not to be found, ma'am.

MRS BROMLEY: Not to be found?

TRINKET: We have searched high and low. She is gone away.

MRS BROMLEY: Gone away! The ingratitude of you all! You shall do the same, I promise you! You shall go too. More vexation! Leave the room, Mrs Malapert. (*Exit* TRINKET.) Where can Miss Neville be gone to? A girl that I was so fond of, and never so much as said an angry word to. Who has put this into her head? How long has Millamour been gone? You know, Mr Bygrove, how tender I have been of that girl. I understand it. This is Millamour's doing.

BYGROVE: I wish it may turn out so.
      (*Enter* LADY BELL, LADY JANE *and* CAPTAIN BYGROVE.)

MRS BROMLEY: There, Lady Bell, there's your lover! Run away with your cousin.

LADY BELL: I can depend upon her, and still venture to answer for her honour.

BYGROVE: She will come back, you need not alarm yourself.

MRS BROMLEY: You have seduced her for anything. I know I am distracted by you all, and will hear no more. (*Exit.*)

BYGROVE: Mrs Bromley, permit me to say a word to you. (*Exit.*)

LADY BELL: I hope there is nothing amiss. I can rely upon Miss Neville's discretion. I think I can. Come, sister, let us go and enquire. (*Going, looks back.*) Hey! You two are staying to say delicate things to each other.

CAPT. BYGROVE: Our difficulties, you know, are at an end. I have my father's orders to follow my inclinations. Had Millamour stayed, I have a plot would have fixed him your ladyship's forever.

LADY JANE: And we shan't see him again this month, perhaps.

LADY BELL: Let him take his own way. I am only uneasy about Miss Neville at present.

LADY JANE: For fear Millamour should be gone off with her. I know you, sister.
      (*Enter* TRINKET.)

TRINKET: Madam, madam. You are wanted, ladies.

LADY BELL: What's the matter? Have they discovered anything?

TRINKET: It's all about her and Mr Millamour. There is a letter come. A letter to Mr Dashwould.

LADY BELL: But what does the letter say? Come let us go and hear it. (*Exit with* CAPTAIN BYGROVE *and* LADY JANE.)

TRINKET: Mrs Bromley is angry, and Mr Dashwould laughs, and they are all in an uproar, and I don't know what to make of it. (*Exit.*)

SCENE 2. *An apartment at* MADAM LA ROUGE's. *Enter* MILLAMOUR *and* LA ROUGE.

MILLAMOUR: Have you sent to Dashwould?

LA ROUGE: Yes, I have sent him letter.

MILLAMOUR: Miss Neville here, you say?

LA ROUGE: She come an hour ago, all in tear.

MILLAMOUR: Then she is safe. You are sure you never said anything to Sir John about the gaming business?

LA ROUGE: Sur mon honneur. What I tell? I know nothing. And I not see Sir John in my house, it is two, tree months.

MILLAMOUR: You shall come and confront Malvil at Mrs Bromley's.

LA ROUGE: Bagatelle! Vat you go dere for? Bo! Dis all put me off – pay your littel bill. Vat is money to you? I so poor, you so rich.

MILLAMOUR: You did not say that I should deceive Lady Bell?

LA ROUGE: Monsieur Malvil, he tell you so?

MILLAMOUR: Yes, and I tremble for the consequence.

LA ROUGE: It is von great villain. I great respect for you – Vous êtes aimable – Monsieur Malvil, he is great fripon, and I ver sorry he be marry to Mademoiselle Neville.

MILLAMOUR: Married to her?

LA ROUGE: You not know it? He is marry to her dis day. He take my apartment tree week ago. He not have it known dat he is marry for five, six day – write letter to me dis afternoon – he must be let in ver private – de servant not to see him – go up de back stairs to her room, and so l'affaire est faite.

MILLAMOUR: And thus he has seduced her from her relations? Let me see the letter. (*Reads aside.*)

LA ROUGE: I not tink him so bad to talk of me, and tell such parcel of story, vid not one word of true.

MILLAMOUR: So, here he is, in black and white. To come privately, is he? If I could detain him here and prevent all means of his escaping . . .

LA ROUGE: Escape? Up back stairs, he must come through dat apartment. (*pointing to a door in the back scene*) I turn de key in de back door: voilà votre prisonnier! He is prisoner.

MILLAMOUR: Exquisite woman! I'll lock this door and secure the key. (*Locks the door in the back scene. A rap at the street door.*) Hush!

LA ROUGE: Le voilà! He come now.

MILLAMJOUR: Fly, let him in! Send once more to Dashwould. I want him this instant. Fly – despatch!

LA ROUGE: I do all vat you bid me. (*Exit.*)

MILLAMOUR: It is honest of her to make this discovery. If this be Malvil – a soft whisper that – (*Listens.*) 'Tis he, I hear his voice. I shall have the merit of defeating villainy and protecting innocence. Don't I hear Miss Neville? (*Goes to a room door.*) Miss Neville!

> (*Enter* MISS NEVILLE.)

MISS NEVILLE: Madam La Rouge! – Oh, sir! What brings you hither?

MILLAMOUR: It is your interest to hear me, your happiness depends upon it.

MISS NEVILLE: Alas! I fear he is too rash.

MILLAMOUR: Command your attention and listen to me. Malvil has planned your ruin.

MISS NEVILLE: Impossible! He has too much honour. Why will you alarm me thus? I am unfortunate and you, sir, need not add to my afflictions.

MILLAMOUR: You have trusted yourself to a villain! He means, at midnight, to gain access to your person, to triumph over your honour and then leave you to remorse, to shame and misery. Read that letter. (*Gives it her and she reads it to herself.*) She's an amiable girl and, I dare say, will make an admirable wife – Hark! I hear him in yonder room. Suppress each wild emotion of surprise and wait the event.

MISS NEVILLE: I can scarce believe what I read. What have I done? (*Weeps.*) You have led me into a maze of doubts and fears, and there I wander distracted – lost, without a clue to guide me.

MILLAMOUR: I will direct you. Rely upon me.

> (*Enter* DASHWOULD, LADY BELL *and* LADY JANE.)

DASHWOULD: La Rouge has told us the whole story.

MILLAMOUR: Hush! No noise.

LADY BELL: My sweet girl, how could you frighten me so?

MISS NEVILLE: I blush for what I have done, but Mrs Bromley's cruelty drove me to despair.

LADY JANE: My dear, all will be well, don't flurry yourself.

LADY BELL: Though my aunt vexed you, why run away from me?

> (*Enter* MRS BROMLEY, BYGROVE, SIR HARRY LIZARD *and* CAPTAIN BYGROVE.)

MRS BROMLEY: Where is this unhappy girl?

MILLAMOUR: A moment's patience. (*Enter* MADAM LA ROUGE.) Is he safe?

LA ROUGE: He is dere in de room, as safe as in Bastille.

MILLAMOUR: Speak to him through the door. Now all be silent.

LA ROUGE: Monsieur Malvil, open de door.

MALVIL: (*within*) Do you open it, you have the key.

LA ROUGE: De key, it is dere. Miss Neville, it is gone to bed, all de house asleep, I in de dark, now is your time.

MILLAMOUR: (*to* LA ROUGE) Hush! Here is the key. (*Takes away the lights.*)

MALVIL: Will you despatch?

LA ROUGE: Attendez. Here is de key. I let you out. (*Unlocks the door.*)

MALVIL: (*entering*) All in darkness! Is she gone to bed?

LA ROUGE: (*leading him*) She wait for you. Vere was you marry?

MALVIL: St James's parish. Say nothing of it yet awhile.

LA ROUGE: No, not a vord. Tenez, I get light for you. (*Exit.*)

MALVIL: So, I have carried my point. The family will be glad to patch up the affair, to avoid the disgrace.

        (*Enter* MADAM LA ROUGE.)

LA ROUGE: Ah! You look en cavalier. Ver good apartment for you, and dere is good picture. It is Tarquin and Lucrete, Tarquin go to ravish de lady in de night. It was villain, was it not?

MALVIL: A terrible fellow!

LA ROUGE: And dis room it velle furnish. Look about you, more picture and all original. (*Turns him to the company.*)

OMNES: Ha, ha, ha! Your servant, Mr Malvil!

MALVIL: Hell and confusion!

MILLAMOUR: (*taking him by the arm*) There are bounds and limits even to virtue.

DASHWOULD: (*at his other arm*) Morals are capable of mathematical demonstration.

LADY BELL: (*to* MISS NEVILLE) Let us withdraw from all this bustle. Sir Harry, step this way; I want you. (*Exit, with* MISS NEVILLE, LADY JANE *and* SIR HARRY.)

DASHWOULD: This is all according to the fitness of things!

MILLAMOUR: Something voluptuous in meaning well!

BYGROVE: Dashwould, your ridicule is now in season to expose such a character. He is fair game, and hunt him down as you please.

LA ROUGE: Ah, Monsieur Tartuffe! (*Exit, laughing.*)

MALVIL: The fiends about me! Mr Bygrove, you are a thinking man, I appeal to you.

MILLAMOUR: I appeal to this letter, sir. (*Reads.*) 'Madam La Rouge, Miss Neville has this day given me her hand in marriage. I would not have it known for some time. Conduct me to her apartment, unknown to your servants. The way up the back stairs will be best. Your secrecy shall be rewarded by MARTIN MALVIL.'

OMNES: Ha, ha, ha!

MALVIL: The letter is forged – let me see it. (*Snatches at it.*)

DASHWOULD: And I appeal to another letter. This anonymous scrawl, written by your direction, and sent to Miss Neville, to give a stab to the character of Sir Harry. Do you deny it, sir? Your secretary is now in the house; I brought him with me. He is ready to prove you the author of this mean, clandestine mischief.

MALVIL: All false, all a forgery. Where is this French impostor? Where is your witness, sir? (*to* DASHWOULD) I'll put them both to the proof, this moment. (*Exit.*)

DASHWOULD: No private parleying. (*Exit.*)

BYGROVE: No, we must all hear. (*Exit.*)

MRS BROMLEY: Yes, all must hear. (*Exit.*)

MILLAMOUR: (*going*) My presence may be necessary.

CAPT. BYGROVE: Millamour, stay and give me joy.

MILLAMOUR: Of what?

CAPT. BYGROVE: The idol of my heart! Tomorrow makes her mine.

MILLAMOUR: Well I give you joy. Who is she?

CAPT. BYGROVE: My Lady Bell, thou dear fellow! Come, let us go and see what they are about.

MILLAMOUR: Let us go and see who shall cut the other's throat.

CAPT. BYGROVE: A pleasant employment?

MILLAMOUR: You shall tear this heart out, before you tear Lady Bell from me.

CAPT. BYGROVE: Very well, have your frolic. (*aside*) This works as I could wish! (*Exit.*)

MILLAMOUR: Despair and frenzy! If she is capable of a treachery like this . . .
> (*Enter* LADY BELL.)

LADY BELL: You have done some good at last, Mr Millamour.

MILLAMOUR: Lady Bell – (*Pauses and looks at her.*) I once thought – but you will break my heart.

LADY BELL: It will bend a little, but never break.

MILLAMOUR: Will you listen to me? There is a tyrant fair and you have interest with her. You can serve me. All the joys of life are centred there.

LADY BELL: (*Smiles aside.*) He is mine against the world. And so you want my interest? That's lucky, for I have a favour to beg of you.

MILLAMOUR: Is there a favour in the power of man, you may not command at my hands?

LADY BELL: You are very good, sir. There is a person, but the levity of his temper . . .

MILLAMOUR: (*aside*) She means me. Your beauty will reclaim him.

LADY BELL: (*Smiles at him.*) May I rely upon you?

MILLAMOUR: (*aside*) What an angel look there was! And do you ask the question?

LADY BELL: When sincere affection . . .

MILLAMOUR: It is generous to own it.

LADY BELL: And since the impression made by . . .

MILLAMOUR: Do not hesitate.

LADY BELL: Made by Captain Bygrove . . .

MILLAMOUR: Made by Captain Bygrove! (*Turns away.*)

LADY BELL: That wounds deep – and if you will assist my fond, fond hopes – it will be generous indeed.

MILLAMOUR: This is a blow I never looked for. Yes, ma'am, it will be generous – and, in return, if you will intercede for me with Lady Bell – po! with a – Lady Jane, I say – I say, if you will intercede for me with Lady Jane . . .

LADY BELL: Oh! By all means. And, as I approve of your choice (*He walks away, she follows him.*), I hope you will approve of mine, and, by mutual acts of friendship, we may promote each other's happiness.
> (*Enter* DASHWOULD.)

DASHWOULD: Malvil is detected.

LADY BELL: And Sir Harry has settled everything with Miss Neville. Go and wish him joy. (*Exit* DASHWOULD.) My sweet friend will be happy at last. (*going*)

MILLAMOUR: (*taking her hand*) But you won't marry the Captain?

LADY BELL: Will you make interest for me?

MILLAMOUR: How can you torment me thus?

LADY BELL: You have done some service, and you may now entertain a degree of hope. (*smiling at him*) But have you another copy of verses for my aunt?

MILLAMOUR: How can you? (*Kisses her hand. Exit* LADY BELL.) She yields and I am blessed indeed!
> (*Enter* BYGROVE, MALVIL *and* CAPTAIN BYGROVE.)

BYGROVE: The fact is too clear, Mr Malvil.

MALVIL: And shall the word of that French impostor . . .

MILLAMOUR: She has acted fairly, sir, and what reparation can you make the lady, whose ruin you have attempted?

MALVIL: Mrs Bromley promised her a fortune, and I have promised her marriage.
(*Enter* DASHWOULD.)

DASHWOULD: And I forbid the banns. Sir Harry has concluded a match with Miss Neville. I should have thought him ridiculous, if he had not.

MALVIL: That you will do, whether he deserves it or not.

MILLAMOUR: You, sir, deserve something worse than ridicule. You are thoroughly understood. Your tenderness for your neighbour is malignant curiosity; your half hints, that hesitate slander, speak the louder, and your silence, that affects to suppress what you know, is a mute that strangles.

MALVIL: The probity of my character, sir . . .

DASHWOULD: Ay, probity is the word. He has had pretty perquisites from his probity; legacies, trust money, and the confidence of families. For aught I see, probity is as good a trade as any agoing.

OMNES: Ha, ha, ha!

MALVIL: The still voice of truth is lost. You are all in a combination.

BYGROVE: And you have forced me to be of the number.
(*Enter* MRS BROMLEY.)

MALVIL: Mrs Bromley! You will judge with candour.

MRS BROMLEY: Oh, sir! It is all too plain.

MALVIL: It is in vain to contend. I shall be cautious what I say of any of you. My heart is with you all. (*Exit.*)

BYGROVE: Farewell, hypocrite!

OMNES: Ha, ha, ha!
(*Enter* LADY BELL, MISS NEVILLE, SIR HARRY LIZARD *and* LADY JANE.)

LADY BELL: Here, Sir Harry, in the presence of this company, I give you, in this friend of mine, truth, good sense and virtue. Take her, sir, and now you have got a treasure.

SIR HARRY: (*to* MISS NEVILLE) It shall be my pride to raise you to that sphere of life, which your merit and your sufferings from . . . (*Looks at* MRS BROMLEY.)

MRS BROMLEY: Why fix on me, sir?

SIR HARRY: They are much mistaken, who can find no way of showing their superior rank, but by letting their weight fall on those, whom fortune has placed beneath them.

DASHWOULD: And that sentiment, however I may rattle, I wish impressed upon all the patrons of poor relations, throughout his majesty's dominions.

MISS NEVILLE: Mrs Bromley, I have much to say to you. My obligations to you I shall never forget. I am not ashamed, even in the presence of Sir Harry, to own the distress in which you found me. If, at any time, I have given offence, if, under your displeasure, I have been impatient, you will allow for an education that raised me much above my circumstances. That education shall teach me to act as becomes Sir Harry's lady, with affection, with duty to him, and to you, madam, with gratitude for that bounty which saved me from calamity and ruin.

MRS BROMLEY: Your words overpower me! I feel that I have done wrong. I now see that to demand in return for favours conferred, an abject spirit and mean compliance, is the worst usury society knows of. I rejoice at your good fortune, your merit deserves it. (*They embrace.*)

DASHWOULD: Why, this is as it should be. – Mr Bygrove, I hope soon to wish you joy.

BYGROVE: Compared to Malvil, thou art an honest fellow, and I thank you.

DASHWOULD: Millamour, is there no recompense for your virtue? In a modern comedy, you would be rewarded with a wife.

MILLAMOUR: Lady Bell has more than poetical justice in her power. I wish Sir John were here, he would now see me reclaimed from every folly by that lady.

MRS BROMLEY: If it is so, I can now congratulate you both.

LADY BELL: It is even so, aunt; the whim of the present moment. Mr Millamour has served my amiable friend, and I have promised him my hand – and so – (*Holds up both hands.*) – which will you have? Puzzle about it, and know your own mind, if you can.

MILLAMOUR: With rapture, thus I snatch it to my heart.

LADY BELL: Sister, what nunnery will you go to? Mr Bygrove, command your son to take her.

CAPT. BYGROVE: That command I have obeyed already.

LADY JANE: Since the truth must out; we made use of a stratagem, to fix my sister and that gentleman.

LADY BELL: To fix yourself, if you please. I knew you would be married before me.

MILLAMOUR: Dashwould, give me your hand. Your wit shall enliven our social hours, and, if ever I deviate into error again, you shall laugh me into the right.

DASHWOULD: You do me honour, sir. And, if Mr Bygrove will, now and then, give and take a joke . . .

BYGROVE: As often as you please, but take my advice and don't lose your friend for your joke.

DASHWOULD: By no means, Mr Bygrove. – Except now and then, when the friend is the worse of the two.

MILLAMOUR: Well, there is some weight in Mr Bygrove's observation – and yet, as Dashwould says, conversation, without a zest of wit, may flatten into a sort of insipidity, and . . .

LADY BELL: Oh, to be sure! Change your mind about it.

MILLAMOUR: There is one subject, Lady Bell, upon which my mind will never change. The varieties of life, till now, distracted my attention.

But when our hearts victorious beauty draws,
We feel its pow'r, and own its sov'reign laws;
To that subservient all our passions move,
And ev'n my constancy shall spring from love.

EPILOGUE

written by Mr Garrick
spoken by Mrs Mattocks

> If after Tragedy 'tis made a rule,
> To jest no more, I'll be no titt'ring fool,
> To jog you with a joke in Tragic doze,
> And shake the dew-drops from the weeping rose.
>   Prudes of each sex affirm, and who denies?
> That in each tear a whimp'ring Cupid lies.
> To such wise, formal folk, my answer's simple;
> A thousand cupids revel in a dimple!
> From their soft nests, with laughter out they rush,
> Perch'd on your heads, like small birds in a bush.
> Beauty resistless in each smile appears;
> Are you for dimples, ladies, or for tears?
> Dare they in Comedy our mirth abridge?
> Let us stand up for giggling privilege;
> Assert our rights, that laughter is no sin,
> From the *screw'd simper* to the *broad-fac'd grin*.
>   So much for self; now turn we to the Poet.
> 'Know Your Own Mind' – Are any here who know it?
> To know one's mind is a hard task indeed,
> And harder still for us, by all agreed.
> Cards, balls,beaux, feathers, round the eddy whirling,
> Change every moment, while the hair is curling.
> The Greeks say – 'Know Thyself' – I'm sure I find,
> I *know myself* that I don't *know my mind*.
>   Know you your minds, wise men? – Come let us try.
> I have a worthy cit there in my eye; (*looking up*)
> Tho' he to sneer at us takes much delight,
> He cannot fix where he shall go tonight:
> His pleasure and his peace are now at strife,
> He loves his bottle, and he fears his wife.
> He'll quit this house, not knowing what to do;
> The Shakespeare's Head first gives a pull or two,
> But with a sidling struggle he gets through,
> Darts across Russell Street; then with new charms,
> The Syren, Luxury, his bosom warms,
> And draws him in the vortex of the Bedford Arms.
> Happy this night! – But when comes wife and sorrow?
> 'Tomorrow, and tomorrow, and tomorrow.'

After Tragedy . . . to jest no more: for *The Grecian Daughter* (1772) Murphy had departed from the customary comic epilogue, and other tragic authors had followed his lead.
laughter is no sin: a common assertion in opposition to the fashionable Sentimental Comedy.

I see some laugh here, pray which of you
Know your own minds? – in all this house but few!
Wits never know their minds: – our *Minor Bards*,
Changing from bad to worse, now spin *Charades*.
O'er *Law* and *Physic* we will draw a curtain;
There nothing but uncertainty is certain:
Grave looks, wigs, coats – the Doctors now relinquish 'em;
They're right – from *Undertakers* to distinguish 'em.
    The *Courtiers*, do 'em justice, never doubt,
Whether 'tis better to be *in* or *out*.
Some *Patriots* too, know their own mind and plan;
They're firmly fixed, to get *in* when they can;
Gamesters don't waver; they all *hazards* run,
For some must cheat, and more must be undone.
Great Statesmen know their minds, but ne'er reveal 'em;
We never know *their* secrets, till we feel 'em.
    Grant me a favour, Critics, don't say nay;
Be of *one mind* with me, and like this Play;
Thence will two wonders rise; Wits will be kind,
Nay more – behold a Woman *Knows her Mind*!

Patriots: the Whigs, who, in 1777, were attacking strongly Tory policies in the American War of Independence.

THE PUBLISHED PLAYS OF SAMUEL FOOTE AND ARTHUR MURPHY

Dates of publication rather than first performance are given here.

Samuel Foote

Taste. London 1752
The Englishman in Paris. London, 1753
The Knights. London, 1754
The Englishman Return'd from Paris. London, 1756
The Author. London, 1757
The Minor. London, 1760
The Orators. London, 1762
The Mayor of Garrett. London, 1763
The Lyar. London, 1764
The Patron. London, 1764
The Commissary. London, 1765
With Isaac Bickerstaff, *Doctor Last in his Chariot*. London, 1769
Wilkes: an Oratorio. London, 1769. A political skit, probably not for perform-
    ance
The Lame Lover. London, 1770
The Maid of Bath. London, 1771
The Bankrupt. London, 1776
The Devil upon Two Sticks. London, 1778
The Nabob. London, 1778
The Cozeners. London, 1778
A Trip to Calais. London, 1778
The Capuchin. London, 1778

Apart from collections assembled from various editions (e.g. 1786; 1799; 1809), the first complete collection is *The Works of Samuel Foote; With Remarks on Each Play, and an Essay on the Life, Genius, and Writings of the Author*. 3 vols. ed. John Bee, Esq. (John Badcock) (London, 1830).

Tate Wilkinson in *The Wandering Patentee* (York, 1795), includes two alternative second acts from *The Diversions of the Morning*, one of which is subtitled 'Tragedy-à-la-Mode'.

Arthur Murphy

The Apprentice. London, 1756
The Spouter: or, The Triple Revenge. London, 1756
The Upholsterer; or, What News? London, 1758
The Orphan of China. London, 1759
The Way To Keep Him, in three acts. London, 1760
The Way To Keep Him, in five acts. London, 1761
The Old Maid. London, 1761
All in the Wrong. London, 1761
The Desert Island. London, 1762
The Citizen. London, 1763
What We Must All Come To. London, 1764
No One's Enemy but His Own. London, 1764
The School for Guardians. London, 1767
Belasarius. London, 1768. Translation of the play by Marmontel
Zenobia. London, 1768
The Grecian Daughter. London, 1772
Alzuma. London, 1773
Three Weeks After Marriage. London, 1776
Know Your Own Mind. London, 1778
The Rival Sisters. London, 1793
Arminius. London, 1798

The Works of Arthur Murphy, Esq. 7 vols. London, 1786

Major literary works:
An Essay on the Life and Genius of Samuel Johnson. London, 1792
The Life of David Garrick, 2 vols. London, 1801
The Works of Cornelius Tacitus, 8 vols. London, 1805
The Works of Sallust. London, 1807

BIBLIOGRAPHY

Sources

See 'Note on the texts' for details of the plays included in this collection, but other plays are available in the following collections and modern editions:

Bee, John (John Badcock). *The Works of Samuel Foote*, 3 vols. London, 1830
Byrnes, J.A. *Four Plays of Samuel Foote*. New York, 1963
Murphy, Arthur. *The Works*, 7 vols. London, 1786
Emery, J.P. *'The Way To Keep Him' and Five Other Plays by Arthur Murphy*. New York, 1956
Bevis, R.W. *Eighteenth Century Afterpieces*. Oxford, 1970

General

Bevis, R.W. *The Laughing Tradition*. London, 1980
Burnim, K. *David Garrick, Director*. Pittsburgh, 1961
Gray, C.H. *Theatre Criticism in London to 1795*. New York, 1931
Hughes, Leo. *A Century of English Farce*. Princeton, 1956
    The Drama's Patrons. Austin, 1971
The London Stage, part 4, 1747–76, ed. G.W. Stone Jr; part 5, 1776–1800, ed. C.B. Hogan. Carbondale, S. Illinois, 1962/68
Nicholson, W. *The Struggle for a Free Stage in London*. New York, 1906
Nicoll, A. *A History of English Drama, Late Eighteenth Century*, 3rd edn. London, 1952
Pedicord, H.W. *The Theatrical Public in the Time of Garrick*. New York, 1954
Price, C. *Theatre in the Age of Garrick*. London, 1973
The Revels History of Drama in English, vol. 5, 1660–1750, ed. J. Loftis; vol. 6, 1750–1880, ed. M. Booth. London, 1975/6
Sherbo, A. *English Sentimental Comedy*. Michigan, 1957
Stone, G.W. Jr (ed.) *The Stage and the Page*. Berkeley, 1981

Samuel Foote

Bee, John (John Badcock). Biographical Introduction to *The Works*. London, 1830
Belden, M.M. *The Dramatic Work of Samuel Foote*. New Haven, 1929
Cooke, W. *Memoirs of Samuel Foote*, 3 vols. London, 1805
Fitzgerald, P. *Foote, a Biography*. London, 1910
Stinko, G. *Foote, the Satirist of Rising Capitalism*. Warsaw, 1950
Trefman, S. *Sam Foote, Comedian*. New York, 1971

Arthur Murphy

Dunbar, H.H. *The Dramatic Career of Arthur Murphy*. New York, 1946

Emery, J.P. *Arthur Murphy, an Eminent English Dramatist of the 18th Century.*
    Philadelphia, 1946
Foot, Jesse. *The Life of Arthur Murphy.* London, 1811
Spector, R.D. *Arthur Murphy.* Boston, 1979